The Unofficial Disneyland 1955 Companion

The Anecdotal Story of the
Birth of the Happiest Place on Earth

Jim Korkis

Foreword by Bill "Sully" Sullivan
Afterword by Bob Gurr

Theme Park Press
www.ThemeParkPress.com

© 2016 Jim Korkis

No part of this publication may be reproduced, distributed, or transmitted in any form or by any means, including photocopying, recording, or other electronic or mechanical methods, without the prior written permission of the publisher, except for brief quotations embodied in critical reviews and certain other noncommercial uses permitted by copyright law.

Although every precaution has been taken to verify the accuracy of the information contained herein, no responsibility is assumed for any errors or omissions, and no liability is assumed for damages that may result from the use of this information.

Theme Park Press is not associated with the Walt Disney Company.

The views expressed in this book are those of the author and do not necessarily reflect the views of Theme Park Press.

Theme Park Press publishes its books in a variety of print and electronic formats. Some content that appears in one format may not appear in another.

Editor: Bob McLain
Layout: Artisanal Text

ISBN 978-1-68390-008-5
Printed in the United States of America

Theme Park Press | www.ThemeParkPress.com
Address queries to bob@themeparkpress.com

To my dad and mom, John and Barbara Korkis, who despite financial challenges always made sure that my two brothers and I went to Disneyland at least twice a year and enjoyed the benefits of their Magic Kingdom Club card.

And to all the original Disneylanders who worked so hard and without recognition to make Walt's dream a reality.

Contents

Foreword v
Introduction ix

1	Inspirations for Disneyland	1
2	The Mickey Mouse Park and Disneyland Prospectus	13
3	Disneyland, Inc.: ABC-TV	25
4	Disneyland, Inc.: Western Publishing	33
5	Anaheim	39
6	Disneyland's Cast of Characters	47
7	The Men Who Landscaped Disneyland: Jack and Bill Evans	57
8	The Woman Who Landscaped Disneyland: Ruth Patricia Shellhorn	63
9	Dateline: Disneyland, July 17, 1955	67
10	Disneyland's First Snow White	85
11	When Did Disneyland Open: July 17 or July 18?	89
12	The Story of the Disneyland Tickets	97
13	Disneyland 1955 Highlights	101
14	These Many Worlds	109
15	Main Street, U.S.A.	115
16	Adventureland	129
17	Frontierland	135
18	Fantasyland	145
19	Tomorrowland	151
20	Mickey Mouse Club Circus	159
21	In Their Own Words: Memories of Disneyland 1955	171
22	In His Own Words: Walt Disney on Disneyland 1955	193
23	Disneyland 1956	197

Afterword 203
Appendix A: The United States in 1955 205
Appendix B: Walt Disney Productions in 1955 213

Selected Bibliography 221
Acknowledgments 223
About the Author 225
More Books from Theme Park Press 227

Foreword

I started working at Disneyland on July 27, 1955, about a week and a half after the park opened.

Watching the opening on television on July 17, just three months after my nineteenth birthday, it looked like a fun place. Living nearby, I thought I would go out there and see if I could get a job. I got one, as a full-time ticket taker on the Jungle Cruise attraction in Adventureland.

I was soon promoted to a Jungle Cruise skipper and eventually a foreman on the ride, spending two and a half years there before going off to other adventures like director of Epcot Center and vice president of the Magic Kingdom. It was never boring, and I would never change a minute of it.

Those early days in 1955 were amazing. The park was brand new and there was a lot of stuff going on. It was fun to walk down Main Street and see all the people already having so much fun. That's one of the things that made Disneyland so exciting: it entertained so many different guests every day.

One of the biggest differences at that time was that Walt was there. He was there just about every weekend and every Wednesday for the Park Operating Committee meeting. He was very hands-on with the running of Disneyland. We all learned about what Disneyland culture was and how to behave through watching and listening to Walt.

He insisted that the people were not customers but guests, just like guests in your house. Take care of your guests and they will take care of you. They are the ones paying your salary.

Walt was actually a quiet, down-to-earth kind of guy. One foggy night at the Jungle Cruise, he was just walking around checking out his park like he often did and came over and sat down with us. We all sat there, smoked, and just talked. He was always receptive to hearing what we thought about the ride and the park and the changes we suggested.

If he was working, he would usually wear his old gray pinstriped pants, a leather jacket that looked like he got it out of the Goodwill, and a straw hat. I remember him in that outfit when he was building Tom Sawyer Island.

But if he was just out there visiting and meeting guests, he'd wear his blue serge suit and his Smoke Tree tie, and the guests would crowd around him if he wasn't careful and we would have to help him slip backstage.

He was popular with everyone and just a nice guy. He loved to talk to the guests and hear what they thought about the park. He loved to talk to the employees. That's one of the things that made Disneyland so different in those early days. The boss was there and you really wanted to please him.

It was a new adventure for all of us. We were the pioneers blazing a new path for something that had never been done before. We learned quickly from our mistakes and went out and made new ones.

Disneyland was out in the middle of nowhere. There were still strawberry patches and orange groves surrounding it. People came to the park dressed up in hats and gloves. Even the kids were dressed up because it was something special, something different than a usual amusement park.

My fondest memory of working at Disneyland in that first year was meeting the most wonderful girl who would become my patient and supportive wife for fifty-seven years. She was the night manager of Waltha Clarke's Hawaiian Shop, a lessee located right across from the Jungle Cruise. They sold bathing suits and Hawaiian shirts and straw hats.

It is hard for me to believe that it has been sixty years since Disneyland first opened. I can still remember it so vividly and all the many friends I worked with at the park. It was a different place back then, and I am so proud that I was a part of it all.

I am happy that Jim Korkis has decided to write about that first year. Jim wasn't there, but through his massive research and interviews with those of us who were, he has been able to share with new generations what it was like when Walt walked the park.

I have always been surprised and impressed by the depth of Jim's knowledge of Disney history and how he can prod so many half-forgotten memories out of me. Diane Disney and others have enjoyed his historical books because they are so accurate and entertaining.

In person, he has always been eager and appreciative to hear my stories. I am glad he wrote all that stuff down.

With so few people still left who were there at Disneyland in 1955, this book is a wonderful trip back in time that preserves the memories, facts, and fun that we all experienced. And, boy, did we have fun!

Bill "Sully" Sullivan
Vice-President, Magic Kingdom (Retired)
Member of Club 55

Introduction

I never intended in my entire life to ever write a book about Disneyland.

I love Disneyland. I grew up in Southern California, so I visited the park frequently as a kid, a teenager, and an adult, and have many fond memories. I eagerly collected information about what the park was like when Walt Disney was alive.

However, there are a ton of books already out there written about Disneyland, and some of them are excellent. Early in 2014, I realized that in another year we would be celebrating the 60th anniversary of Disneyland and knew that over the last three-and-a-half decades I had interviewed many people who had shared with me interesting stories about what the park was like in 1955.

Documentarian Ken Burns once stated that history is actually biography. Not just the biographies of the big famous figures like Walt, but of the average person who was involved in making it all happen on a day-to-day basis.

I figured I could just cull some snippets from those interviews and share them in a book and readers might be entertained. Over two-and-a-half years later, I was still struggling with the manuscript.

As I started to gather the quotes, I realized that I needed to also include some background information so that readers could better understand what these people were discussing.

Nomenclature was much different in the early days of the park. Some things were only there briefly and needed explanation, as did relatively obscure people who had made significant contributions.

What was the parking lot like? Exactly which amusement venues directly inspired Disneyland? What gave Walt the idea for putting live baby alligators at the queue entrance to the Jungle Cruise? Who wrote Walt's opening day speech? Why did managers all wear gray suits and orange ties?

Dozens of similar questions troubled me and the answers didn't exist even in the most excellent of books about the earliest days of the park. Six decades had passed since Disneyland first opened and that information was getting lost every day as people died or their memories became clouded with age.

Documentation was not as easy to confirm as I had first hoped. Early publicity material produced by Disney was often a mixture of fact and wishful thinking. There was disagreement over dates, spelling of names and locations, and more.

People were so busy getting Disneyland built, opened, and maintained that much of the information and changes were never recorded and only some of it could be recovered through the memories of the people who were actually there. Some of those memories were faulty.

Many familiar tales are not repeated in this book, like the building of the railroad or women's high heels sinking into newly laid asphalt on Main Street or horses being spooked by the whistle on the *Mark Twain* riverboat. These stories are readily available in so many other places that it made little sense to include them here when the space could instead be used for previously unrecorded stories.

Even just concentrating on the early months, there was still not enough room to include everything from my files. There is enough left for another book. This is not a definitive narrative, but an entertaining, and informative glimpse into that special time that focuses on the people who were there.

A 1950s Disneyland employee handbook states:

> Disneyland is people. Our assets may show up in financial reports in terms of buildings...land...equipment and facilities...but the most important asset is our people. Disneyland begins with people...the guests who come to find happiness and pay for the continuance of the dream. It continues with people... the individual human beings who create happiness and preserve the dream.

In the movie *Back to the Future* (1985), Marty McFly goes back to Saturday, November 5, 1955, in his time-traveling DeLorean. Disneyland opened at 10am to guests on that day and the temperature in Anaheim was 83 degrees after a summer of record highs. The park had already significantly changed since its opening nearly four months earlier, and was preparing for even greater changes over the next few months.

This book shares what Marty might have seen if he had made a detour from Hill Valley to Anaheim on that fateful day. It is a grab bag of nuggets of information, memories, quotes, fun facts, anecdotes, and strange stories. It is meant to be a companion to other histories of the park, filling in some gaps, correcting some myths, and concentrating on the people.

Walt's Disneyland really was, and still remains, the Happiest Place on Earth. Most people, including those who worked for Walt, felt it would be lucky if the place lasted through its first year or two. It not only survived but thrived and became not just a part of American culture but international culture. This is the story of how it all began, often told by those who were there.

Jim Korkis
Disney Historian
March 2016

CHAPTER ONE

Inspirations for Disneyland

The Canadian Broadcasting Corporation (CBC) introduced *Telescope* in 1963 as a 30-minute television program that would "examine, reflect and project the Canadian image", and for ten years this documentary series covered a wide range of subjects pertinent to Canadians.

Generally, the show featured a personality profile of a Canadian (a national figure, an international celebrity, or sometimes a notable but little-known citizen). Since Walt's father, Elias, was born in Canada, Walt was invited to be interviewed by host Fletcher Markle on September 25, 1963.

At the time, the affable Markle, who was born in Winnipeg, had just finished directing the Disney live-action film *The Incredible Journey* which was filmed in Calgary, Canada.

During the interview, Walt shared the story of the birth of Disneyland:

> Well, it came about when my daughters were very young and Saturday was always Daddy's day with the two daughters. So we'd start out and try to go someplace, you know, different things, and I'd take them to the merry-go-round and I took them different places and as I'd sit while they rode the merry-go-round and did all these things...sit on a bench, you know, eating peanuts. I felt that there should be something built, some kind of an amusement enterprise built, where the parents and the children could have fun together. So that's how Disneyland started. Well, it took many years. It was a period of maybe 15 years developing. I started with many ideas, threw them away, started all over again. And, eventually, it evolved into what you see today at Disneyland. But it all started from a Daddy with two daughters wondering where he could take them where he could have a little fun with them, too.

As a teenager, Walt first announced his interest in building a different kind of amusement park. It was a dream that he kept coming back to several times during his life, even occasionally making tentative planning attempts over the years, before Disneyland became a reality in 1955.

"When we consider a new project," he said, "we really study it—not just the surface idea, but everything about it."

When Walt Disney traveled the United States and Europe, he visited many outdoor attractions, zoos (to see how live animals were displayed and whether they were caged or roamed free), museums, county fairs, state fairs, circuses, arcades, shooting galleries, carnivals, amusement parks, and national parks.

When he did so, he wasn't just enjoying a well-deserved vacation. He was studying the attractions and how they worked and what made them appealing. He talked with people to find out what entertained them and what frustrated them in these venues. He sometimes took notes in a small notebook that fit easily in his coat pocket.

He visited with amusement park owners and with people who made rides and bombarded them with a seemingly endless stream of questions. His curiosity was insatiable. When a Disney studio employee asked how he enjoyed his vacation, Walt snapped back, "I was working!"

Walt assembled a team consisting primarily of Bill Martin, Bill Cottrell, Bruce Bushman, Harper Goff, Ed Schott, and George Whitney, and assigned them to a variety of tasks like measuring the walkways at Knott's Berry Farm, and how the audience flowed from one attraction to another, and what caused that flow to jam up.

Goff recalled that in the summer and fall of 1954:

> Walt sent us all around to every amusement park in the country. We would take pictures and come back and tell Walt all about what they were doing. One of the things we tried to get was their "gate"—how much they charged, how many people came through, and how much they made. Also what kinds of operating problems they had, such as dishonesty.

Goff visited New Orleans during Mardi Gras, Old Sturbridge Village in Massachusetts, the Erie Canal, the Lincoln Museum in Chicago, the Smithsonian Institution in Washington, Colonial Williamsburg, Marineland in Florida, and the Steamboat Museum in St. Louis, among other sites, over a two-year period.

Walt's team visited Fairmont Park in Philadelphia, Palisades Park in New Jersey, Playland Park in Rye, New York, and other amusement venues, including replica historic towns and small museums across the country, and locations like Forest Lawn Cemetery that attracted large numbers of tourists.

They visited amusement venues in New Orleans, Cincinnati, San Francisco, and other cities, and reported back not only on the rides, but on attendance, food, amount of money spent, layout of the area, and other factors.

Some of the best information came from studying the San Diego Zoo, with its year-round attendance of two million visitors. Because it was open all year, unlike some of the other venues, a pattern of month-to-month visits could be plotted, calculating the average attendance of the fifteen highest days as a reasonable yardstick for the size of the park.

All of these reports helped Walt formulate what he wanted and what he did not want in his park.

Walt Disney Productions stockholders did not agree that the company should be getting involved in such a project. When Walt was prepared to buy property in a beautiful valley in Calabasas for the new park, the stockholders filed and won a lawsuit to prevent him from doing so.

In an impassioned and tearful address to the stockholders, Walt stated:

> I don't want this company to stand still. We have prospered before when we have taken chances and tried new things. This is our golden opportunity—a chance to move into an entirely new field.
>
> You say we are not in the amusement park business. No, we're not. But we are in the entertainment business. And amusement parks are entertainment.
>
> I know it is difficult for you to envision Disneyland the way I can. This kind of thing has never been done before. There's nothing like it in the entire world. I know, because I've looked. That's why it can be great, because it will be unique. A new concept in entertainment, and I think...I KNOW...it can be a success!

Even Walt's older brother Roy was not thrilled with the idea, and limited the studio's initial investment to just $10,000.

Walt raised $100,000 by borrowing on his life insurance policy, and then he sold his vacation home in Palm Springs to finance his own design company, WED Enterprises (now Walt Disney Imagineering).

WED Enterprises was a separate business entity from the Disney Studio, but it used some of the same employees, and its primary function was to create Disneyland. All of those employees were paid by Walt, not by the Disney Studio, even though some costs were getting charged to the studio.

In 1952, Walt established Walt Disney Incorporated with himself as president. Roy was concerned that stockholders would be upset about the use of Walt's name in a different company, so in 1953 the name was changed to WED (standing for **W**alter **E**lias **D**isney). For years, people assumed the company must have something to do with weddings.

In 1965, Walt Disney Productions purchased WED and its assets, rechristening it as Walt Disney Imagineering in 1987.

Despite all the research and initial planning, it was not until the ABC television network signed on as an investor that Walt got the cash and line of credit he needed to actually build Disneyland.

Some visits made to certain locations may have been more influential than others in the final version of Disneyland, and here is a quick glimpse at those venues.

Electric Park

In 1911, Walt's parents moved the family to Kansas City, Missouri, which had its own amusement park, Electric Park. A previous version, with the same name, had burned down, and its replacement built in May 1907.

The new park was located about fifteen blocks north of the Disney home. Walt often walked there and looked through the fence. Not having the money for admission, nine-year-old Walt and a friend of his sometimes snuck under the fence to get in, to the horror of Walt's younger sister. In 1911, the park attracted one million people, averaging 8,000 paying customers per day.

The park was inspired by the 1893 Columbian Exposition World's Fair where Walt's father had worked as a carpenter. Electric Park was illuminated at night by 100,000 lights. A train ringed the park and there were daily fireworks at closing time. There was a wide variety of entertainment, including concerts, an alligator farm, a penny arcade, a scenic railway, boats, a circle swing, a shooting gallery, a carousel, and fortune telling booths. Advertisements proclaimed it "Kansas City's Coney Island". This park also burned to the ground, in 1925.

Coney Island

New York's Coney Island was home to multiple amusement parks over the decades, and from 1880 to just after World War II, it was the largest amusement venue in the United States, attracting millions of visitors each year. Unfortunately, in the late 1940s and early 1950s it fell into a decline from which it never fully recovered, due to fires, neglect, street gangs, and portions of its audience choosing safer, cleaner entertainments.

After a day visiting Coney Island in the early 1950s with his wife, Lillian, Walt was downhearted. He told her:

> I'm almost ready to give up the idea of an amusement park after seeing Coney Island. The whole place is so run-down and ugly. The people who run it are so unpleasant. The whole thing is almost enough to destroy your faith in human nature.

In August 1953, Walt made a trip to Coney Island in New York with the specific intention of gathering information to apply to Disneyland. He was accompanied by actor Richard Todd who was in the city as part of a promotional tour for his role in the Disney live-action film, *The Sword and the Rose* (1953).

In an interview with animation historian and author Michael Barrier, Todd said:

> [Walt] rang me up one day and said, "Come to Coney Island with me." I could feel my face falling. It wasn't my ideal place, but, anyhow, I said, "Yes, yes,

thank you." We had a hell of a good day, actually. That was the beginning of Disneyland. He was going to see what the things were that people liked doing. We did everything—the switchbacks [roller coasters], the horses, everything. We ate the fluffy stuff [cotton candy]. We had a lovely day, thoroughly enjoyed ourselves.

Griffith Park

Griffith Park is a large municipal park in the Los Feliz neighborhood of Los Angeles where Walt lived for most of his life. In December 1896, Colonel Griffith donated five square acres of his Rancho Los Feliz estate to Los Angeles to be used as "a place of recreation" for "the plain people".

During Walt's lifetime, there were several attractions located on the park grounds, including an observatory, a zoo, a theater, pony rides, and a special section dedicated in December 1952 called Travel Town, an outdoor museum to preserve and celebrate Southern California railroads with actual vehicles that people could explore.

More important, there was the Griffith Park Merry-Go-Round. Built by Spillman Engineering Company and brought to Griffith Park in 1937, the merry-go-round has 68 horses that were finely carved with jewel-encrusted bridles and detailed draped blankets, and decorated with sunflowers and lion's heads. A Stinson 165 Military Band Organ, reputed to be the largest band organ accompanying a carousel on the West Coast, played over 1500 selections of marches and waltz music.

On weekends, Walt would take his two young daughters to ride the merry-go-round. Supposedly, while sitting on a nearby bench, he decided to build a place where parents and children could have fun together.

Henry Ford Museum and Greenfield Village

The Henry Ford Museum and Greenfield Village began as a personal collection of American historical objects obtained by entrepeneur Henry Ford. Greenfield Village was founded in Dearborn, Michigan, on October 21, 1929, as an educational and historic landmark, maintaining the buildings and stories of America's past for future generations.

Greenfield Village houses nearly one hundred historic buildings in a village setting, including the Wright brothers' bicycle shop, Thomas Edison's Menlo Park laboratory, and Noah Webster's Connecticut home. In addition, there was a 1913 Dentzel merry-go-round and an operating stern-wheeler riverboat.

Walt first visited Greenfield Village on April 12, 1940, and spent the day enjoying himself. He visited a second time on August 23, 1948, with Disney animator Ward Kimball during a trip they took to the Chicago Railroad Fair. Walt had tintype pictures of himself taken both times as a souvenir.

Disney wrote a memo dated August 31, 1948, about his plans for an amusement venue which included ideas inspired by Greenfield. He described a main village with a railroad station, an opera house, a movie theater, a horse car, a magic shop, a kids' clothing store, and other structures he had seen there.

Beverly Park Amusement Center

David Bradley, whose wife, Bernice, worked in story research at the Disney Studio, opened Beverly Park, a small theme park on less than an acre of land on the corner of Beverly and La Cienega Boulevards in Beverly Hills in 1946.

The park was so successful that Bradley recouped his investment in the first two years. His philosophy was that the park should be spotless and that customers should feel safe and comfortable on all the rides. He often spent hours in his little machinist shop on the property repairing and inventing rides.

Walt would often take his two young daughters to visit there on weekends. Bernice Bradley remembered:

> Our park was very tiny. There was a carousel, a little train ride, and another little boat ride for children. ... Walt was out there almost every day, sitting on the end of the bench, watching how children enjoyed the rides.
>
> He also talked to a lot of the children, which is what he enjoyed the most. He challenged them. "How was that horse you were riding? What color was it painted? Did you like it?"

Beverly Park had a 1916 C.W. Parker carousel, tiny motorcycles on the minibike race course, a kid-sized roller coaster, a ferris wheel, and a boat ride. Through a remote microphone, Bradley projected his voice as the blue hippopotamus that talked to children outside the Haunted Castle. Inside the castle, two giant freak faces rolled their eyes and a bat flapped up and down in front of visitors. Young children sometimes came out sobbing.

Bradley's primary business was building amusement rides and Beverly Park was to some extent a demonstration area for prospective customers.

There were usually about twelve kid-sized rides running at any one time, as well as live animals, hot dogs, and cotton candy. Parents sat on benches watching their children ride the carousel, and birthday parties were celebrated at picnic tables. Because of its location, many celebrity families visited as well, and it became a haven for divorced dads who only had their children on weekends.

Bernice introduced her husband to Walt Disney, who hired him to consult for the Disneyland project. Walt sent Bradley to Europe to photograph rides, and it was Bradley who convinced Walt to build Main Street at a reduced scale and introduce themed photo opportunities to the park. They remained good friends even after Bradley returned to full time operation of his own park after Disneyland opened.

After the Beverly Park closed in 1974, Bradley continued to be an innovator in building modern amusement park rides. Higher rent, expanded oil drilling on the surrounding property, and the accumulated fatigue of running his park for nearly three decades convinced him it was time to close.

Next door to Bradley Park was Ponyland, operated by Leo "Pat" Murphy and his wife. Ponyland consisted of dusty old wooden stalls with a three-track riding ring for young children. People often visited both venues on the same day.

Tivoli Gardens

Tivoli Gardens is the second oldest amusement park in the world. It opened on August 15, 1843, in Copenhagen, Denmark. Founder Georg Carstensen said in 1844, "Tivoli will never be finished," alluding to the concept that it would continue to grow over the decades with new attractions and events.

Located in the heart of the city, the venue is an actual garden dotted with Chinese pagodas, Japanese water streams, brilliant flowers, and many rides designed to blend with the architecture and the landscaping. It is home to one of the oldest wooden roller coasters in the world.

Tivoli Gardens drew Walt's attention in 1951 when he visited with his good friend and TV personality Art Linkletter. Linkletter recalled Walt scribbling notes about everything from the benches, the layout of the gardens, the type and operation of rides, food, and other details. Linkletter said:

> As we walked through it, I had my first experience of Walt Disney's childlike delight in the enjoyment of seeing families and in the cleanliness and the orderliness of everything. He was making notes all the time about the lights, the chairs, the seats, and the food.

Linkletter asked Walt what he was doing and Walt replied:

> I'm just making notes about something that I've always dreamed of, a great, great playground for the children and the families of America.

The park featured twinkle "popcorn" lights and a variety of outdoor entertainment areas, typical of Disneyland's Main Street. The Danish amusement park was known to be clean and orderly, and it banned alcohol.

Tivoli Gardens is completely gated in, and has three entrances. There's a small admission fee to enter the park, and the rides are pay-as-you-go. The park is open from mid-April to mid-September, after which it re-opens to celebrate Halloween for two weeks in October and then opens again for the Christmas season in mid-November and stays open through December. More than 120,000 incandescent light bulbs illuminate Tivoli at night.

Children's Fairyland

On April 17, 1954, Walt flew to San Francisco on some unspecified company business and toured Children's Fairyland, a park located in Oakland since 1948. He invited its executive director Dorothy Manes to visit his park if she found herself in Southern California. In January 1955, she did come down to visit and was hired as the head of Disneyland's youth activities, a position she held until 1972.

Guests enter the park through the Old Mother Goose Shoe. There is a train, an attraction inspired by Alice in Wonderland, a scaled-down enclosed ferris wheel, and a pirate ship where kids could play, among other attractions for young children.

According to legend, Walt asked to contribute a cartoon to a wall in Children's Fairyland. When given permission, he drew Mickey Mouse.

Madurodam

Madurodam opened in The Hague district of the Netherlands in 1952 with a collection of miniatures depicting famous Dutch castles and other quaint buildings, including an airport, a shipping port, and windmills. Every object in Madurodam had been built at a scale of 1:25.

The park showcased a scaled-down sample of familiar locations of the Netherlands. Everything, even flora and street decorations, were modeled to a miniature scale. The miniature figures surrounding the buildings had their attire changed according to the seasons.

Walt visited in July 1952 with his brother-in-law Bill Cottrell. He studied the miniatures closely and sent Ken Anderson to study the park as well. What he saw influenced him to include realistic miniatures in Disneyland, such as Fantasyland's Storybook Land Canal Boats, and influenced his early plans for a Lilliputian Land at Disneyland.

Bud Hurlbut's unnamed kiddie park in El Monte

Skilled at woodworking, Wendell "Bud" Hurlbut began building miniature trains. By 1943, he had sold several trains to amusement parks. Around the same time, he opened his own small amusement park in El Monte, California, in the parking lot of Crawford's Market located at Five Points. The market had been there since 1937.

The small amusement area featured one of Hurlbut's trains and had a tiny car ride, a boat ride for children, pony rides, a carousel, a ferris wheel, and other attractions. It was to be a showcase for potential buyers of his rides.

In a conversation with author Christopher Merritt, Hurlbut recalled:

> I saw this man on my property. When he was there the second or third time I thought he didn't look like a customer. So I spoke with him and told

him it looked like he was interested in the amusement park business. He was a really nice fellow so I sat down with him and he asked about rides.

The man, of course, was Walt Disney, who visited several times and brought over some of his Disneyland staff to Hurlbut's shop.

Hurlbut started working for Walter Knott around 1955, operating a Dentzel Menagerie carousel at Knott's Berry Farm that he had kept in storage. Hurlbut went on to create memorable rides for Knott's Berry Farm, including the Calico Mine Train and Timber Mountain Log Ride.

Hurlbut also owned Castle Park in Riverside, which opened after the Knott family sold their park. It featured a miniature golf course and arcade, with amusement park rides added in 1985. Hurlbut sold the park in 1999.

Playland at the Beach

Playland at the Beach was a ten-acre seaside amusement park in the San Francisco area. In 1926, George Whitney became the general manager, and over the succeeding years, he and his brother purchased all the attractions and the land. In 1952, Whitney bought out his brother and continued to operate the park until his death in 1958.

Whitney was one of the amusement park owners who pointed out all the potential flaws in Disneyland to Walt and his staff.

George Whitney's son, George K. Whitney, would become director of Ride Operations at Disneyland (and the park's seventh employee) after being personally recruited by Walt. He was directly involved in projects like the Mickey Mouse Club Circus and the Frontierland Indian canoes. He left Disney to take over the operation of Playland at the Beach. The park closed in 1972.

Knott's Berry Farm

This famous theme park grew out of a berry farm in 1920 where Walter Knott and his wife, Cordelia, sold boysenberries and later homemade chicken dinners. In 1940, a replica Wild West Ghost Town with actual buildings from Old West ghost towns was built to entertain guests who were waiting to eat. It was officially named Knott's Berry Farm in 1947 and proved so popular that it continued to expand, with attractions and themed areas.

Walter Knott and Walt Disney had a friendly relationship. Walt had been invited to the inaugural run of the Ghost Town and Calico Railway in 1952. In 1953, Walt and his staff, including Harper Goff, visited and studied the design and operation of Knott's Berry Farm, although Knott was not forthcoming with some proprietary information.

"We'd measure the width of the walkways, the traffic flow and study how people moved about," recalled Imagineer Richard Irvine.

Walt invited Walter and Cordelia Knott to the grand opening of Disneyland. He also gave them a Gold Pass to the park.

Forest Lawn Memorial Park

Hubert Eaton took over the management of Forest Lawn cemetery in 1917. He envisioned it not as a cemetery, but a memorial park "devoid of misshapen monuments and other signs of earthly death, but filled with towering trees, sweeping lawns, splashing fountains, beautiful statuary, and ... memorial architecture". The grounds are adorned with 1,500 statues, some of which are replicas of famous works of art.

Forest Lawn is a popular tourist attraction, with nearly one million visitors each year, because of its beauty and serenity, as well as the many celebrities interred there. Prior to the opening of Disneyland, Forest Lawn was the most popular tourist attraction in Los Angeles.

Walt's mother and father loved spending a day just walking the grounds. Forest Lawn also presented various religious shows. It was later discovered that visitor patterns paralleled, on a smaller scale, those of Disneyland.

Chicago Railroad Fair

The Chicago Railroad Fair was an event organized to celebrate and commemorate one hundred years of railroad history west of Chicago. It was held in Chicago, Illinois (the birthplace of Walt Disney), in 1948 on fifty acres of land, with Lake Michigan as a backdrop.

It is often referred to as "the last great railroad fair" with 39 railroad companies participating. In addition to being the last great assembly of some classic original (and replica) railroad equipment and technology by participating railroad companies, the Fair hosted other activities and events.

Trains circled the perimeter of the fairgrounds with stops that mimicked the tourist attractions that guests might visit on an actual train trip, such as New Orleans, Yellowstone Park (with a working replica of Old Faithful), and an Indian village. And, of course, there were nightly fireworks.

Carolwood Pacific

When Walt and his family moved into their new home at 355 N. Carolwood Drive, he built a 1:8 scale live-steam miniature railroad dubbed the Carolwood Pacific in the backyard. He was inspired by the backyard railroads of two of his top animators, Ward Kimball and Ollie Johnston.

There was 2,615 feet of track that circled through the backyard and looped back and forth, including a trip over a trestle and through a tunnel. It first started operation on May 15, 1950.

One weekend there was an accident in which the engine turned over on its side and released a jet of steam that slightly burned a curious five-year-old girl who had run over to see what had happened.

The next morning, Imagineer Roger Broggie drove to Walt's home, stored the freight cars in the tunnel, put the caboose in Walt's barn, and took the engine back to the studio, where for several years it was stored under Imagineer Bob Gurr's drafting table.

Disneylandia

In 1950, Walt developed a concept called Disneylandia that involved a series of small animated dioramas reflecting Americana with moving miniature figures that would be exhibited in a series of train cars traveling from town to town. Walt described it as "visual juke boxes with the record-playing mechanism being replaced by miniature stage setting".

Imagineer Harper Goff recalled:

> Walt envisioned a big, long train which would go all over America. In each city, people would come and go through the railroad cars. They would start at the back of the train, and all the cars would have these little animated things you could watch.
>
> Walt didn't want poor people to have to come clear across the country and stay in a hotel. He wanted to have something here [in Burbank, California] permanently, but he also wanted to put a show on the road.

Walt built the first exhibit, Granny Kincaid's Cabin, himself, and work had started on the second exhibit, referred to as Project Little Man, where a vaudevillian dancer figure would perform on a miniature stage. Before a third exhibit featuring a barbershop quartet could get started, Walt came down and told Imagineer Roger Broggie to stop all work because, "We're going to do this thing for real!"

Of course, Walt took inspiration from many other places, like Lincoln Park, a major family gathering spot in Los Angeles, owned by Ross Davis. Davis was passionate about the importance of carousels in city parks. He was responsible for the one in Griffith Park as well as those in San Diego (Balboa Park), San Francisco (Golden Gate Park), and Berkeley, California (Tilden Park). Davis later helped Walt obtain a carousel for Disneyland.

There were many things that made Disneyland different than an amusement park, but what made it successful was the "stay time", the amount of time a customer would stay at the location. When Disneyland was built, the average amusement park stay time was less than two hours. With Disneyland, however, the average rose to almost seven hours. During that increased time, customers spent more on food, souvenirs, and ride tickets. People were not going for a particular attraction because Disneyland itself was the attraction. It was refreshing, clean, friendly, and pleasant.

It was also well planned. Where most amusement parks had been built and expanded in a haphazard fashion, Walt set the patterns where guests would walk before building anything. The park was planned from the perspective of the guest.

More important, it was a *theme* park, meaning there was a coherent story. Rather than being designed for the benefit of the operators, Disneyland was designed for the guests. It was a movie set with the guests becoming participants in their own movie, not just passive spectators watching a screen.

Walt felt that most amusement parks were a potpourri of visual contradictions where the sound and color of the individual rides and games competed for attention. Even worse, these parks were a nightmare of design, with twisted, criss-crossing pathways that disoriented and exhausted people.

While Disneyland is generally considered the first theme park, there is another contender for that honor, Santa Claus Land.

In the late 1840s, a group of German settlers formed a small community in Spence County in southern Indiana. On a December night in 1852, with the entire city gathered at the local church to determine a name for the town, the doors flew open and they saw snowflakes and heard sleigh bells.

Since everyone was in the church, including the children, and there was no one else who lived anywhere nearby, they reasoned that it must have been Santa Claus outside, and so the town was so named Santa Claus, Indiana. Letters addressed to the merry old elf from children were answered each year by volunteers at the post office.

In 1935, attorney Milton Harris worked out an arrangment with the Curtiss Candy Company to build Santa's Candy Castle for selling candy to visitors. He also built a factory where Santa Claus' sleighs pulled by reindeer were built. A few toy companies built small plants to build and display toys in an area called Toy Village. In 1935, a twenty-two-foot tall statue of Santa Claus was built on the highest hill by Carl Barrett, who had plans for a never-realized Santa Claus Park.

After World War II, retired Evansville industrialist Louis J. Koch (the father of nine children) decided that there needed to be a more prominent presence for Santa Claus with a place where children could see that this was the mythical elf's home and where they could become participants, not just voyeurs.

On August 3, 1946, Koch opened Santa Claus Land, arguably the first theme park in the world since everything was connected to the themes of Santa Claus and Christmas. The park included the Mother Goose Train with its one-fourth size locomotive taking visitors through Mother Goose Land, a toy factory with elves at work, a place to visit Santa Claus, and a food and souvenir shop.

In 1984, the park expanded to include celebrations of Halloween and the Fourth of July, and was renamed Holiday World.

CHAPTER TWO

The Mickey Mouse Park and Disneyland Prospectus

After World War II, Walt's idea for an outdoor amusement area was once again sparked, and he felt he would do something connected with his animation studio.

In the late 1940s, tourism to California began increasing, with studies showing that the top three things tourists wanted to do were put a foot in the Pacific Ocean, pick an orange, and visit a movie studio.

Walt told animator Ward Kimball:

> You know, it's a shame people come to Hollywood and find there's nothing to see. Even the people who come to the [Disney] Studio. What do they see? A bunch of guys bending over drawings. Wouldn't it be nice if people could come to Hollywood and see something?

Walt aggressively visited various outdoor entertainment venues to get ideas for what he might be able to do in a limited space.

In a memo dated August 31, 1948, to Disney Studio production designer Dick Kelsey, Walt explained his concept for a "Mickey Mouse Park" to be built across the street from the studio on Riverside Drive:

> The Main Village, which includes the Railroad Station, is built around a village green or informal park. In the park will be benches, a bandstand, drinking fountain, trees and shrubs. It will be a place for people to sit and rest...mothers and grandmothers can watch over small children at play. I want it to be very relaxing, cool and inviting.
>
> Around the park will be built the town. At one end will be the Railroad Station...at the other end...the Town Hall. The Hall will be built to represent a Town Hall, but actually we will use it as our administration building. It will be the headquarters of the entire project. Adjoining the Town Hall will

be the Fire and Police Stations. The Fire Station will contain practical fire apparatus...scaled down.

The Police Station will be put to practical use. Here the visitors will report all violations...lost articles...lost kids, etc. In it we could have a little jail where the kids could look in. We might even have some characters in it.

That memorandum also listed these additional attractions: a drugstore with a soda fountain; an opera house and movie theater; toy, book, hobby, doll, and children's clothing shops; a doll hospital and toy repair shop; a candy factory and, next to it, a store selling old-fashioned candy; a magic shop; a store selling dollhouse furniture; ice cream and hot dog stands; a restaurant featuring rooms for birthday parties; a functioning post office; a horse-drawn streetcar; a general store; a pony ring; a donkey pack train; a stage coach; a singing waterfall; and statues of Mickey Mouse, Donald Duck, and other famous Disney characters.

The "magical little park" was going to be built on a sixteen-acre site across the street from the Disney Studio in Burbank. It would have been approximately where the sorcerer hat-shaped Disney Feature Animation Building and ABC Studios building are today.

Imagineer John Hench recalled:

> It was back in the late 1940s. I lived on Riverside Drive in Burbank, quite near the studio. I remember several Sundays seeing Walt across the street in a weed-filled lot, standing, visualizing, all by himself. He was stepping off something, measuring the space. He had a paper in his hand and I thought that was where he was going to put his park.
>
> We had heard rumors about a park at the studio and I thought, *Well, that's where it is going to be.* I think he really thought he could get it all in there, but when you knew Walt you knew the idea wouldn't stay that small. The longer Walt thought about the park, the more ideas he got, and suddenly the weed-filled lot wasn't big enough.

On March 27, 1952, a front-page headline in the *Burbank Daily Review* newspaper revealed for the first time: "Walt Disney Make-Believe Land Project Planned Here".

Imagineer Harper Goff had done up several color aerial designs of the park layout. Architect John Cowles had done some architectural drawings based on Goff's ideas and storyman Don DaGradi had also made some sketches for the project which for a while was called Mickey Mouse Village.

The article mentioned that the park would have "various scenes of Americana, rides in a Space Ship and submarine, a zoo of miniature animals and exhibit halls", and would cost one-and-a-half million dollars to build. The article went on:

> Designed primarily for children, Disneyland is not intended as a commercial venture, park board members [Burbank City Board of Parks and Recreations]

have been assured. The facilities are to be "instantly available" for youth groups, Parent-Teacher Associations and other organizations devoted to civic and social welfare.

In September 1952, the Burbank City Council rejected the proposal because they feared it would just be another noisy carnival attracting the wrong type of people and behavior. At the time, kiddie parks were small and crude and larger amusement parks like Coney Island had been neglected during the war and had become seedy spots inhabited by vagrants, prostitutes, and drug dealers.

Walt was not disappointed because, as Hench had surmised, his dreams had gotten larger. In December 1952, Walt set up a business entity that would eventually become Walt Disney Imagineering with the sole purpose of creating Disneyland. He hired several people in the spring of 1953 and set them up in a building on the studio backlot that was referred to as the Zorro building since it was to be used as a set for the planned television series.

For this first hire, Walt chose Richard Irvine, an art director at 20th Century Fox who had worked for Walt on some live-action portions of Disney films in the 1940s. Among his other responsibilities, Irvine was to be Walt's liaison with the architectural firm of William Pereira and Charles Luckman which Walt had engaged to build the park in Burbank.

Irvine brought on two other movie art directors, Bill Martin and Marvin Davis. They joined Walt's brother-in-law, Bill Cottrell (who was working on the Zorro project), and a promoter named Nat Winecoff.

The Zorro building was "a ramshackle, wallboard thing, very temporary, hot in the summer and cold in the winter", according to Imagineer Marvin Davis who worked there to come up with the initial layout of Disneyland. Walt had built it for a Zorro project (either a television series or feature film) that would help finance the park. The wooden furniture in the building had been purchased by Walt himself to be used as set props for the show.

The actual *Zorro* television series was finally developed in 1957 after the park opened. The building was used as part of the hacienda of Don Diego de la Vega in the series.

Working with some of the initial plans for the Mickey Mouse Park that had been developed by Harper Goff (who had been moved over to assist on the feature film *20,000 Leagues Under the Sea*), Marvin Davis developed the first diagrammatic plan for Disneyland.

Walt referred to Davis, Irvine, Bill Martin, Sam McKim, Harper Goff, and art directors who worked on the early Disneyland as "brick-and-mortar men", which irritated Davis because it seemed to suggest they weren't creative.

In fact, their background in film helped them to design an environment meant for activity, not just a stationary tableau. On the other hand, they were accustomed to designing sets that were just temporary and easily dismantled, so Walt needed people who had expertise on building structures to survive the ravages of weather, aging, and usage by millions of visitors.

On the morning of August 8, 1953, Walt reviewed the site map that Davis was currently working on and picked up a No. 1 carbon pencil and drew a triangle around the plot of land to indicate where he wanted his railroad to run.

"I just want it to look like nothing else in the world," said Walt. "And it should be surrounded by a train."

That historic drawing still exists today.

For two years, Davis worked on more than a hundred different versions of the master plan for Disneyland. He remembered in an interview:

> I was working in what they call the Zorro building as the project designer for master planning of the park at the time. This was before they even knew where the park was going.
>
> Before they bought the property—I guess I must have done, well, I know I did at least 129 different schemes for the solution of the thing because we had no idea where the park was eventually going to be or anything else about it...different entryways...until finally it developed into the scheme that it is now with the single entrance and the walk for the avenue, which is Main Street, up to the center of the Hub. Walt's idea was to have the whole thing as radials from that hub.

He told another interviewer, "Walt wanted to see every idea that you could possibly have before he settled on something." For example, the iconic castle went through multiple changes. "The one thing Walt had the most vivid picture of in his mind was Fantasyland with the entrance through a castle. The castle was all his idea," emphasized Davis.

At first, the iconic castle was set far in the back of, not the front of, Fantasyland, and resembled Herb Ryman's design for the cathedral-like shape with lofty towers of the castle in the 20th Century Fox film that he had art directed called *The Black Rose* (1950).

In the original prospectus, it was simply referred to as the Medieval Castle. On early artwork and promotional material, it was sometimes just called the Fantasyland Castle. On at least one item, it was called the Fairy Castle.

Walt briefly considered naming the castle Robin Hood Castle in reference to his live-action feature film *The Story of Robin Hood and His Merrie Men* (1952), which may explain why costumed live-action performers impersonating Robin and his Merry Men were often found by guests wandering in front of the castle in the early days of the park.

At one time, the castle was to resemble Cinderella's palace from the 1950 animated feature film. For a brief while, there was no actual castle at all but what was referred to as a "Disney Fantasy" building that suggested a castle, as well as another brief version where it was toward the front of the park and the railroad station.

On his weekly television program, and in publicity material sent to local newspapers in December 1954, Walt even sometimes referred to the castle as Snow White's Castle and no one corrected him because the plans had been so fluid that his staff assumed Walt now intended the structure to be called by that name.

By the time the castle was seen on television, it had its familiar shape of being shorter and balanced between horizontal fortification walls and vertical turrets with the primary emphasis on the drawbridge and the portal entrance. Herb Ryman had visited the famous Neuschwanstein castle in Germany that influenced the final design.

In a bold marketing move, Walt finally christened it Sleeping Beauty Castle to publicize his in-production animated feature *Sleeping Beauty* that was not released until 1959. In fact, work on the park had slowed work on the production of the film that otherwise might have been released years earlier.

However, Walt was forced, before he was truly ready, to formalize some of his many ideas.

In order to get investors interested in the project, Walt developed a "pitch kit" for his older brother Roy that contained an eight-page, single-spaced document filled with ideas for different rides and themed areas entitled the Disneyland Prospectus.

Selling dreams is more difficult than selling something more tangible, and since Walt would not be accompanying his older brother Roy to New York to try to get funding, Walt wanted a strong package to convey his dream. So the Disneyland Prospectus included everything Walt could possibly imagine wanting. Bill Walsh is credited with writing the document based on Walt's ideas. At the time, Walsh was also writing the *Mickey Mouse* comic strip, among other things.

The document revealed that at Disneyland guests would be able to order and purchase anything they saw at the park, like a real, live pony by mail, and there would be a section of the park called Lilliputian Land (inspired by *Gulliver's Travels* and Walt's love of miniatures).

Walt was not necessarily being final in some of the concepts, but rather trying to evoke an image of what the park might be like. Here are some excerpts:

> Walt Disney sometime—in 1955—will present for the people of the world—and to children of all ages—a new experience in entertainment. In these pages is proffered a glimpse into this great adventure...a preview of what the visitor will find in...Disneyland.

Like Alice stepping through the Looking Glass, to step through the portals of Disneyland will be like entering another world. Within a few steps the visitor will find himself in a small mid-Western town at the turn of the century.

Main Street has the nostalgic quality that makes it everybody's hometown. On the corner is the great Disneyland Emporium where you can buy almost anything and everything unusual. Or you can get the big mail-order catalogue and purchase by mail. If you want a real pony and cart or a miniature donkey thirty inches high, you'll find it in the catalogue. Or if you want the latest Disney book or toy, you can order by mail and the gift will arrive wrapped in a special Disneyland paper bearing the postmark: "Disneyland, California"—direct from the Disneyland U.S. Post Office.

The Hub is the crossroads of the world of Disneyland. Straight ahead lies Fantasy Land, to your left is Frontier Country, the world of yesterday. And to your right is The World of Tomorrow. But between these central spokes of the wheel are other exciting avenues of adventure.

True-Life Adventureland is entered through a beautiful botanical garden of tropical flora and fauna. Here you can see magnificently plumed birds and fantastic fish from all over the world, and which may be purchased and shipped anywhere in the U.S. if you so desire.

If you wish refreshments that are in keeping with your surroundings, there are fresh pineapple sticks, crisp coconut meats, and exotic fruit punches made from fresh tropical fruits.

A river borders the edge of True-Life Adventureland where you embark in a colorful Explorer's Boat with a native guide for a cruise down the River of Romance. As you glide through the Everglades, past birds and animals living in their natural habitat...alligators lurk along the banks, and otters and turtles play in the water about you. Monkeys chatter in the orchid-flowered trees.

The World of Tomorrow. A moving sidewalk carries you effortlessly into the World of Tomorrow where the fascinating exhibits of the miracles of science and industry are displayed. The theme for the World of Tomorrow is the factual and scientific exposition of Things to Come.

Among the exhibits, that will change from time to time, are The Mechanical Brain...a Diving Bell...Monorail Train...The Little Parkway system where children drive scale-model motor cars over a modern freeway...Models of an atomic submarine, a Flying Saucer...The Magic House of Tomorrow, with mechanical features that obey the command of your voice like a Genie. You say "Please" and the door opens, a polite "Thank you" will close it.

And if you are hungry, conveyor belts will carry your food through the electronic cooking device of Tomorrow where you will see it cooked instantly to your liking.

Lilliputian Land. A land of Little Things...a miniature Americana village inhabited by mechanical people nine inches high who sing and dance and talk to you as you peek through the windows of their tiny shops and homes. In Lilliputian Land, there is an Erie Canal barge that takes you through the famous canals of the world, where you visit the scenic wonders of the world in miniature.

Here a little diamond-stack locomotive engine 17-inches high steams into the tiny railroad station. You sit on top of the Pullman coaches like Gulliver, and the little 9-inch engineer pulls back the throttle taking you on the biggest little-ride in the land.

And for the little people who have little appetites—you can get miniature ice cream cones, or the world's smallest hot dog on a tiny bun.

Frontier Country. Along Frontier Street are a harness shop and a blacksmith shop, livery stable, assayer's office, sheriff's office, and the jail. There is a shooting gallery, the Wells Fargo Express office, and an old-fashioned saloon with the longest little bar in the world serving root beer Western style.

Ride shotgun on the stagecoaches...past Granny's Farm, a practical working farm operated with real live miniature horses, cows, oxen, and donkeys. Carry the mail on the Pony Express Ride around the little track.

Treasure Island. Mickey Mouse, the best-known personality in the world has his Mickey Mouse Club headquarters at Disneyland located on Treasure Island in the middle of the river, a fantastic hollow tree and treehouse serves as the Club meeting place. The hollow tree is several stories high, with interesting rooms and lookout spots for club members. There is a Pirate cove and buried treasure on the island...and direct from this location the Club presents the Mickey Mouse Club Television Show.

Holidayland is a showplace of Special Attractions that change with the seasons. Its theme is as current as the calendar. Its decorations, entertainment, or exhibits follow the flowers in spring with its Flower Festival... the Mardi Gras and special Easter activities. Mother's Day...St. Valentine's Day...Boy Scout week.

Summer brings the Fourth of July...and Circus Time...with a circus parade down Main Street...and under the big top, a one-ring circus with special acts from all over the world.

Fall ushers in the Harvest Festival..Halloween...Girl Scout week.. Thanksgiving.

And winter with its ice skating rink, sleigh rides, and Bobsled Hill with real snow...and Christmas Tree Lane that leads to Santa's home at the North Pole.

Disneyland will be the essence of America as we know it...the nostalgia of the past, the exciting glimpses into the future. It will give meaning to the pleasure of the children—and pleasure to the experience of adults. It will focus a new interest upon Southern California through the mediums of television and other exploitation. It will be a place for California to be at home, to bring its guests, to demonstrate its faith in the future...

And mostly as stated at the beginning—it will be a place for people to find happiness and knowledge.

Some of those items were never realized, like the little Carolwood Pacific railroad pulled out of storage to traverse Lilliputian Land or the full-sized Granny Kincaid working farm inspired by Walt's first model for the Disneylandia project.

Walt's descriptions of Disneyland included everything but the kitchen sink to attract investors. However, Walt was convinced that it was still not enough. Being an artist, he responded to visuals, not to words, and felt that others did as well.

Artist Herbert Ryman started working at the Disney Studio in 1938. In his role as art director, he made significant contributions to such films as *Dumbo*, *Fantasia*, and *Saludos Amigos*. He left to work on the 20th Century Fox movie *Anna and the King of Siam* (1946) and years later toured with the Ringling Brothers Circus making famous paintings of that popular entertainment.

Ryman was well versed in how to present faraway places, having taken a two-year around-the-world trek beginning in 1935. His work in the MGM studio art department for several years gave him experience in painting fantasy scenes that had to seem real.

On Saturday morning, September 26, 1953, at 10 a.m., Ryman was working on a circus painting when he received an unexpected phone call at home. It was from his friend, art director Richard Irvine, who was working at the Disney Studio.

Suddenly, Walt Disney was on the phone asking Herb how long it would take him to get to the studio.

"You're at the studio working on a Saturday?" asked Herb.

"Yes, I can work on a Saturday or a Sunday or whenever. It's *my* studio," replied a surprised Walt.

"Well," said Herb, "if I don't change, I can get there in fifteen minutes, but if I shave and shower and change clothes, it will be about a half hour."

"Don't change," said Walt. "Get here as quick as you can and I will meet you at the studio gate."

Herb arrived and Walt escorted him to the Zorro building where Irvine, Marvin Davis, and Bill Cottrell were waiting in a room filled with concept sketches and elevation diagrams.

Walt excitedly told Herb about his plans for a unique amusement enterprise. He said, "My brother Roy is going to New York on Monday to arrange for financing. You know bankers. They have no imagination. They just can't visualize it when you tell them, so I am going to show them a big sketch of the park."

An excited Herb asked, "I would love to see it. Where is it?"

Without a pause, Walt answered, "You're going to do it."

Herb declined. He felt in such a short amount of time that he would only embarrass himself and Walt with any attempt he made on this massive and personal project.

Walt asked the others to leave the room.

"Walt paced around the room with his arms folded," Herb would later remember. "He stood and looked out a window with his back to me. He said quietly, 'Herbie, this is my dream. I've wanted this for years and I need your help.' He looked at me over his left shoulder with a little kind of sheepish grin like a little boy. He had a tear in his eye. 'Will you do it if I stay here with you?'"

Moved by Walt's sincerity, Herb relented. For the next forty-two hours, the pair remained in the building. Walt sent out for tuna salad sandwiches and malted milks for lunch to help sustain them.

They went over some of the preliminary work done by others and Walt's vivid verbal descriptions enhanced how the final vision should look. Marvin Davis' elevation diagram was added to the lower right hand of the final drawing for reference to understand the layout.

Early Monday morning, Imagineers Marvin Davis and Dick Irvine walked into the room and found a bedraggled Walt and Herb slumped near a vellum 43″ by 70″ illustration featuring a bird's eye view of the proposed park.

In the lower left corner, a scroll proclaimed: "Disneyland—schematic aerial view—approximately 45 acres within railroad tracks—designed by WED Enterprises."

Walt produced several copies of a booklet that featured the written prospectus along with a copy of the Ryman illustration done with mechanical reproduction using brownline or photostat in the days before Xerox. Davis and Irvine colored each copy of the famous illustration by hand.

"It was just a carbon pencil drawing with a little color on top of it, but Roy got the money so I guess it turned out all right," said Herb.

Later, in 1953 and 1954, similar booklets were produced along with large presentation portfolios of artwork on stiff paper backing for use on an easel during meetings with nervous investors and sponsors of concessions or attractions. These later booklets included photographs of little model buildings, painted and lighted to look remarkably real.

All of this was done to help people comprehend Walt's vision that Disneyland was not an average amusement park or carnival but something very different.

While the Disneyland that finally opened in 1955 is recognizable in the drawing, there were many significant differences. There was no large hot air balloon floating high over the Hub, and Ryman later admitted he had put it in there because it easily covered a large block of acreage that hadn't been defined.

Ryman always advised later Disney designers to be "specifically vague", meaning that it didn't need to be accurate or definite, but it did need to suggest something that people immediately recognized.

The elegant, detailed Ryman drawing not only captured the spirit of Disneyland, but at times anticipated additions that would later be made.

In 1953, artist Peter Ellenshaw, who had done matte paintings for Disney's live action films made in England, showed up at the Disney Studio in California thinking that Walt had a job for him.

Walt didn't, but recognizing Ellenshaw's great talent, he found some work for the artist until Ellenshaw was assigned to the live action film *20,000 Leagues Under the Sea* (1954).

One of those first assignments was to draw a more elaborate and accurate map of the proposed Disneyland.

As Ellenshaw told me in a lengthy interview in 1997:

> Walt came in and said, "I want you to paint a picture. We've got the plans of Disneyland. If you could do a perspective, aerial drawing of it, that's what I need." I got a storyboard. We had big storyboards there about four feet by eight feet and I thought I'd paint on that.
>
> We didn't have the facilities that they have now. I set this thing up in a room at the studio and started painting it using the references I had been given and Walt's directions.
>
> I also used some luminescent paint so that under fluorescent light it would show what the park would look like at night with all the lights and blurs. Walt did do that trick on one of the television shows going from day to night in seconds by changing the lighting on the picture and it was very effective.
>
> He used that same image not only on the very first Disneyland television show but also on a postcard. He sold thousands and thousands of postcards and I never got a penny of that! [laughs] It was used on the cover of a souvenir book. All over the place. They later found it in a shed at the Disney Studio somewhere decades later and it was restored and exhibited at the Disney Gallery at Disneyland.

The painting first appeared in print as a two-page, full-color spread in the November 2, 1954, issue of *LOOK* magazine.

Ellenshaw continued:

> I've known people who say they designed Disneyland. But I know. I was there. It was Walt. People say how much they did on it.... But they were just the tools of Walt. He did it all.

Retlaw—"Walter" spelled backward—was incorporated on April 6, 1953. The company would give Walt a way to generate income to fund the development of Disneyland as well as provide financial protection for his family if he lost all his money. He owned one-third of the company, and his daughters owned the other two-thirds.

He negotiated the following deal: in return for licensing his name to Walt Disney Productions, he would receive either a five-percent royalty from every merchandising transaction, or he would take a share of up to fifteen percent in every Disney project. Since the Walt Disney name appeared on virtually everything, the agreement was especially lucrative over the years. In addition, the company could continue to use Walt's name after his death. Walt said, in justification of Retlaw:

> I borrowed on the insurance I'd been paying on for thirty years, and sold my house in Palm Springs to get Disneyland to a point where I could show people what it would be. My wife complained that if anything happened to me, I would have spent all the family money.

The first year that Disneyland opened, Retlaw owned the old-fashioned steam railroad that encircled Disneyland, the Frontierland Shooting Gallery, and the Tomorrowland Art Corner. The railroad paid twenty percent of its gross revenues to Walt Disney Productions for the right-of-way. Employees of Retlaw did not work for the Disney Studio or Disneyland. They worked directly for Walt and their paychecks came from Retlaw.

Roy O. Disney and his family did not benefit from this new company and the use of the Disney name and that became a sore point between the brothers.

Retlaw was ultimately purchased by Walt Disney Productions on July 8, 1981, for $46.2 million worth of stock.

Walt was able to find one early investor for Disneyland, the Bank of America, which had supported his many risks including *Snow White and the Seven Dwarfs* (1937). One day Roy Disney was in his office when he got a call from a banker friend who said, "Walt was in my office today."

"Oh?" said Roy.

"It's about the park. We went over the plans he showed me. You know, Roy, that park is a wonderful idea," the banker said.

Roy asked, "Did Walt try to borrow from you?"

"Yes, he did. And you know what? I loaned it to him."

Walt even had Hazel George, the studio nurse and Walt's confidante, canvas the studio for additional investors. They called that group of early believers the Disneyland Backers and Boosters. Roy finally realized his brother was deadly serious about making this dream come true.

CHAPTER THREE

Disneyland, Inc.: ABC-TV

Disneyland, Inc. was incorporated in California on December 16, 1952. At that time, Walt was considering building the park in Burbank, but its city council would not approve the project for a variety of reasons.

By 1954, Disneyland, Inc. was a jointly owned venture of Walt Disney Productions, Western Publishing, ABC, and Walt Disney himself to build and manage the Disneyland theme park in Anaheim. The investment pool consisted of 34.485% by ABC (at a cost of $500,000 and guaranteeing up to $4.5 million in bank loans), 34.48% by Walt Disney Productions ($500,000), 13.8% by Western Printing and Lithography Company ($200,000), and 17.5% by Walt Disney ($250,000).

As a provision for the joint ownership, Walt Disney Productions had the option to repurchase the shares of the other investors within seven years. With the initial success of Disneyland, the company was able to buy back early the shares held both by Walt Disney and by Western Publishing in 1957.

By 1958, Walt Disney Productions reported a profit of $2.9 million, attributable primarily to its (by then) 65% interest in Disneyland, Inc. Additionally, Walt Disney Productions stock had grown to around $60 per share, thanks to the profitability of the park.

The next hurdle was to buy back the outstanding shares held by ABC.

The American Broadcasting Company television network made its debut on April 19, 1948, as a natural extension of the ABC Radio Network that was still enjoying popular success.

Yet, by 1949, ABC was on the verge of bankruptcy.

Also in 1949, United Paramount Theaters (UPT), which operated a chain of movie theaters, was forced by the U.S. Supreme Court to become an independent company, separate from Paramount Pictures. The government had mandated a split of the movie exhibition business from the five major Hollywood studios that also controlled production and distribution.

In the process, UPT had to sell some of its assets and found itself with an influx of cash to invest. UPT president Leonard Goldenson sought to diversify the company by purchasing ABC. On February 9, 1953, after determining there was no conflict of interest, the FTC approved UPT's purchase of ABC for $25 million in shares.

In 1950, Robert Kintner had been made ABC's president, but left in 1955 as Goldenson took more and more direct control. It was Kintner who worked with Walt Disney at the start of Disney's weekly television show. Kinter would go to NBC where he would later help broker a deal in 1961 between Disney and NBC.

With the merger, Goldenson aggressively networked with his personal contacts at movie studios for them to supply television series for ABC.

Eventually, Warner Brothers provided television shows, including several Westerns like *Maverick, Sugarfoot,* and *Cheyenne* that were so popular they helped spark a plethora of similar Western television shows in the late 1950s. Goldenson later did the same with such Warner Brothers detective shows as *77 Sunset Strip, Hawaiian Eye,* and *Surfside 6.*

However, it was the Walt Disney anthology series *Disneyland* that made the ABC network more than what industry wags referred to as the "Almost Broadcasting Company" because of its lack of affiliates.

Comedian Milton Berle used to joke, "If the Russians ever drop a bomb, let's all run over to ABC because they've never had a hit."

Disneyland was the first ABC television show to ever make it into the top ten most-watched programs. In fact, before *Disneyland*, ABC had not even been able to get into the top twenty-five shows.

Walt Disney said on July 17, 1965, at a gathering of Disneyland employees at the Disneyland Hotel in celebration of Disneyland's 10th anniversary:

> I remember that we were dealing with all three networks...they wanted our television show. And I kept insisting I wanted this amusement park.
>
> And everybody said, "What the hell's he want that damn amusement park for?"
>
> And I couldn't think of a good reason except...I don't know...I wanted it.
>
> I remember we had a session with NBC. They wanted this Disney television show and we were stubbornly insisting we wanted to start an amusement park with it. David Sarnoff was sitting in on this thing and he said, "I want your television show, but why the hell do we have to take that damned amusement park?"
>
> Same thing went with CBS. Yeah, they wanted the television show, but the insistence on the backing of this amusement park....

ABC needed the television show so damned bad [loud laughter from the audience] that they bought the amusement park.

Walt had always had an interest in television, but as he told an interviewer:

I saw that if I was ever going to have my park, here at last was a way to tell millions of people about it...with TV. TV was the start of Disneyland.

CBS wanted a show from Disney to promote their new color system which was inferior to the one developed by RCA, the parent company of NBC. They had no interest in the theme park, with William Paley, the president of CBS, referring to it as "just another Coney Island".

Negotiations promptly stopped when Paley failed to show up for an important meeting with Disney, claiming another urgent commitment, and offending the Disney brothers.

Walt and Roy spent months negotiating with NBC and word was sent that David Sarnoff, the head of RCA, was finally ready to sign the deal. However, when Roy O. Disney showed up, he discovered that they had decided they still needed more time. Roy was so incensed that, according to him, he stormed out of the office, picked up the first phone he saw, and phoned Goldenson to see if ABC was still interested.

Goldenson responded, "Roy, where are you? I'll be right over."

While ABC was eager to make the deal even if they had to invest in what they referred to as "Walt's fairground", it still took many long meetings to hammer out the agreement.

The first rumors of the deal came in March 1954 with an official announcement on April 2, 1954, when the papers had been signed by both sides.

President of ABC Robert Kintner stated:

Walt Disney is undoubtedly the greatest creative force in the entertainment field today. His entrance into TV marks a major and historical step forward for the industry. ABC is very proud of the privilege of working with the Disney organization, which will bring a new conception to television.

However, Walt still faced three major challenges. First, he hadn't settled on a format for the series. Second, most of Walt's creative talent was focused on creating Disneyland the park. Third, Walt had to allay the fears of other movie studios and theater owners that he was still aggressively committed to producing new films and hadn't surrendered to "the idiot box" television that was stealing audiences from theaters.

Within a month, Walt and his team had come up with the concept of an anthology series so that different teams could be working on different segments at the same time. The show would be split each week into segments that aligned with the themed lands of Disneyland so that Disneyland the park and *Disneyland* the show would be the same.

Besides offering the highest values in entertainment, the show would promote Disneyland and Disney films being released to theaters. Kintner accepted the proposal with no changes.

For a $500,000 investment in Disneyland, plus guaranteeing up to $4.5 million in potential bank loans and receiving all profits for ten years from the park's food concessions, ABC owned 34.485% of Disneyland, had a commitment for a weekly television show produced by Disney, and first refusal on all future Disney television projects.

The network's interest in running the food concessions reflected UPT's experience in American cinemas, where most of the profit came from retailing drinks, popcorn, candy, and other items, rather than from ticket sales.

Frank Stabile managed all the UPT concessions. He was sometimes mistaken for Walt Disney because they looked similar, with Stabile having the same type of mustache as Walt. He was often asked for his autograph when he was spotted in the park.

Stabile knew all his employees at Disneyland by name and sight and would constantly be walking through the park even though he had underlings taking care of the grunt work. He was remembered as a nice guy and a brilliant manager who had a "sixth sense" about trouble and was pro-active in resolving it quickly. While he did report to higher-ups, he was fairly autonomous in the day-to-day operations.

The *Disneyland* television show attracted nearly half of ABC's advertising billings during 1954, the final year that the network operated at a loss.

The three-year contract (with an option for four additional years) called for only twenty-one original episodes each season (and later up to twenty-six episodes in the second and third seasons), with each one repeated once, and twelve broadcast a third time during the summer hiatus.

ABC would pay Walt Disney Productions $50,000 per show the first year, $60,000 the second, and $70,000 the third. In addition, they would pay $25,000 per repeat the first year, $30,000 the second, and $35,000 the third.

Walt, of course, exceeded the cost of the shows out of his own pocket by filming them in color and insisting on high production values. Walt had estimated that each program would cost his studio about $65,000 per episode, which was one of the reasons for the use of so much recycled material like animated shorts to significantly reduce the cost of some shows to cover the overruns on others.

The three hour-long episodes of the *Davy Crockett* series cost nearly $750,000 in total, more than three times the industry standard for a similar production. However, during just that first year alone, the cost was spread over two separate network broadcasts and a theatrical release. In addition, the show sparked a merchandizing bonanza of over $300 million of Davy

Crockett items being sold during 1955 that more than covered the extra cost of producing the show.

On October 27, 1954, ABC aired the first *Disneyland* TV show, on Wednesday night, from 7:30 to 8:30pm. The first episode, "The Disneyland Story", explained what to expect on the new television show as well as what to expect of the new theme park. Approximately 30.8 million Americans watched the show, which received critical acclaim the next day.

Walt got a weekly platform to build anticipation for his new theme park and tempt audiences into wanting to come visit it, since they saw the behind-the-scenes construction and felt they were included in the process. In addition, the show was able to define the new entertainment enterprise as a national attraction rather than a local one.

Walt became an established and recognized avuncular television personality and was able to re-introduce audiences to the Disney Studio and its impressive library of films.

While the show used material from the Disney film library, Walt Disney Productions still owned every film while other movie studios had sold their films directly and completely to television.

Nearly a third of each episode of *Disneyland* was devoted directly to studio promotion. All costs not covered by the network's payments were often charged to the studio's promotion budget.

The contract with ABC also resulted in the network doing the largest live remote television broadcast up to that time on July 17, 1955, when it aired the show *Dateline: Disneyland* featuring the celebrity-studded opening of the theme park.

ABC also took advantage of airing two other series produced by Walt Disney Productions. October 3, 1955, saw the debut of the original *Mickey Mouse Club* series, consisting of five one-hour shows per week with Jimmie Dodd and the Mouseketeers. October 10, 1957, saw the debut of the popular half-hour television series *Zorro* featuring actor Guy Williams as the black-garbed hero of Old California.

In 1955, Donn Tatum, the head of ABC's West Coast operation, moved to Walt Disney Productions because the Disney brothers had been impressed with his work and wanted someone with experience in television. He eventually became an executive vice-president in the company.

The *Disneyland* television series changed its name in 1958 to *Walt Disney Presents* as it was no longer necessary to so aggressively promote the park. Three years later, in 1961, the company's contract with ABC was due to expire.

NBC (which was aggressively promoting RCA color television sets and needed a flagship show to help increase sales) approached Walt with the offer to finance color broadcasts of his show.

Walt had always filmed the show in color, at his own expense, and jumped at the opportunity for it to be seen in color by audiences and have someone else pick up the tab. ABC did not have the technical or financial resources to broadcast in color, and so could not counter NBC's offer.

In addition, there had been a growing tension between ABC and Disney. Walt and Roy had become increasingly unhappy with the deal that had been made with the network. Not only did the deal benefit ABC far more than it did Disney, but ABC was meddling with the product. It was insisting that Walt produce more Westerns for his anthology series, and Walt hated being told what to do.

Also, ABC was adding more and more commercials to *The Mickey Mouse Club*, prompting complaints from viewers that were directed at Walt who had no control over that aspect of the show. In addition, ABC canceled the popular *Zorro* television series for the upcoming 1959 fall season and then tried to prevent Walt from offering it to another network.

On July 2, 1959, Disney filed a lawsuit against ABC, asking the court to invalidate the contract between the two companies under provisions of the federal antitrust laws. Roy felt strongly that it was a "breach of faith" for ABC to claim ownership of the two Disney shows aired on its network. He stated:

> Several weeks ago, the ABC network advised us and announced publicly that they would not televise *Zorro* or *The Mickey Mouse Club* over their network next season, and at the same time they told us we could not offer these programs to any other television outlet.
>
> Subsequently, they have interfered with our attempts to offer these programs to any other networks or independent television stations. Although we do not dispute ABC's right to discontinue these, or any other, programs on their own network, we will certainly fight ABC's maneuvers to suppress these programs from public exhibition over other television stations.

The legal wrangling continued for roughly a year which surprised Roy, who had written to Walt that:

> In all common sense and business reasoning, I can't believe they will let this go to a big court fight. They have too many things they would rather have kept quiet and not brought out in court.

Finally, the matter was settled out of court, with one of the provisions being Disney buying back the ABC shares in Disneyland for $7.5 million.

The amount was not arrived at by any complicated mathematical process. It was pulled out of the air by Roy himself who felt that all the publicity about the financial success of Disneyland had created an inflated idea of the value of the shares. He also hoped it would be attractive enough that ABC, in need of money for expansion, would not argue. Roy was vocal in wanting to be rid of the deal even if it were financially unattractive for Walt Disney Productions.

Disney had to borrow from Prudential to secure the cash to pay off ABC, about which Roy later said: "They [ABC] were not likeable, workable people."

The deal was completed in June 1960, giving Walt Disney Productions complete ownership. In May 1961, Disneyland, Inc. was merged into the parent company of Walt Disney Productions.

Walt said, in 1965:

> My brother figured we better buy those guys out. They had a third interest. They only had a half-million dollars invested in the park.
>
> But my brother figured, "If we don't buy 'em out now, we're going to be payin' a lot more later." And it was a smart move that he did it then.

Despite the settlement, Walt felt that too much time had passed to revive either *The Mickey Mouse Club* or the *Zorro* television series, and so he decided to move on to other projects.

ABC felt no sorrow at the loss of Disney. It had become so strong because of its counter-programming and its targeting a young audience that it no longer needed the cachet of its association with Disney. In September 1960, ABC had started broadcasting one of the first prime-time animated cartoon series, *The Flintstones*, and so was able to retain part of the same demographic.

In his 1991 autobiography *Beating the Odds*, Leonard Goldenson wrote:

> The Disneys turned out to be terrible business partners. Disneyland had become enormously successful, but Disney kept plowing his profits back into park expansion. I feared that it would be a very long time before we started seeing any return on our original investment.
>
> ABC needed cash to finance its own growth. We made a $7.5 million deal to sell back our share of Disneyland and we parted company. We took $7.5 million in cash and Disneyland's concession profits for five more years. I felt they would bring in about $2.5 million a year, and I wasn't far wrong.

The Disney company purchased Captial Cities/ABC in 1996 for $19 billion as part of the "circle of life" philosophy. Goldenson had been one of the mentors of former Disney CEO Michael Eisner, who said when Goldenson died in 1999 at the age of 94:

> I met Leonard Goldenson on the first day of my employment at ABC. He was as nice to me then as he was the day the Walt Disney Company acquired ABC thirty years later. He showed me it was acceptable to ask an insatiable amount of questions, to support the creative process.

CHAPTER FOUR

Disneyland, Inc.: Western Publishing

Western Printing and Lithographing is often just referred to as Western Publishing and was based in Racine, Wisconsin. Western had a successful, long-standing relationship with Walt Disney Productions.

In 1933, Disney's legendary merchandising executive Kay Kamen signed the initial contract granting Western exclusive book rights to all the Walt Disney characters for a series of children's publications.

In 1937, Kamen negotiated for Western to take over the production and publication of the *Mickey Mouse Magazine,* a popular periodical. That magazine evolved into the comic book *Walt Disney's Comics and Stories* in October 1940. Western produced the material (writing and artwork) for the comic book as well as other Disney comic books, but since that division of the company was financed and distributed by Dell Publishing, the comic books are referred to as Dell comics.

Besides Disney, Western licensed other animated cartoon character properties from companies like Warner Brothers, Metro-Goldwyn-Mayer, and Walter Lantz. In addition, Western had a line of comic books with Wild West themes such as Roy Rogers, Gene Autry, the Lone Ranger, and adaptations of movie and television shows.

Walt Disney's Comics and Stories was the highest selling comic book of its time, with a circulation of over three million copies per month in 1953. Western paid Disney one quarter of one cent for every issue printed, not sold.

In a special June 1954 ceremony celebrating the company's 25th anniversary, Walt Disney himself purchased the two-and-a-half-billionth Dell comic for ten cents. The 1955 output of Dell comics represented more than 50% of all comic books printed that year.

However, in 1954, a book entitled *Seduction of the Innocent* by Dr. Fredric Wertham was released condemning comic books. A few weeks later, a United States Senate subcommittee opened a hearing in New York (homebase for most comic book publishers) on the reported connections between juvenile delinquency and comic books.

The result was several comic book publishers going out of business and the surviving publishers forming the Comics Magazine Association of America that administered the Comics Code Authority which reviewed all comic books for objectionable material before publication.

Dell was one of three publishers that refused to be part of this organization. The other two publishers were EC and Gilbertson (Classics Illustrated). Dell created its own, even higher standards that it said would "eliminate entirely rather than regulate objectionable material". The slogan "Dell Comics Are Good Comics" appeared in each Dell comic book.

Because of its long association with Disney, Western Publishing didn't hesitate to invest $200,000 (a considerable figure in the mid-1950s) in Disneyland, Inc., giving them 13.8% of Walt's new theme park.

Western considered it an outstanding partnership because it gave them the rights to unlimited merchandising of the Disneyland name for its own products. In turn, Disneyland was able to use Western's printing presses and expertise to produce high quality press kits, guide maps, brochures, menus, premiums, and other publications for Walt's new park, with the added benefit of refreshing some of that material on a frequent basis.

Western produced many promotional publications for the park. A small color folder entitled *Disneyland: A Dream Come True* which opened to a map of the park was designed so that sponsors, lessees, exhibitors, and travel agents could imprint their names in a small space on the item. Three million copies were distributed before Disneyland opened.

A special brochure for Bank of America called *Your Guide to Disneyland* had over 250,000 copies distributed free during the early months of the park. A special giveaway menu for the Carnation Ice Cream Parlor on Main Street was also created by Western.

The *Adventure in Disneyland* comic book made for Richfield Oil was available at gas stations across the country and the initial order of 750,000 copies were given out within just a few days of release. Eventually, 1,260,450 copies were distributed.

Adventure in Disneyland is a sixteen page full-color story written by Carl Fallberg and illustrated by Al Hubbard of an outer space family (who are human but attired in futuristic clothing) low on gas so they land their spacemobile in Disneyland. Junior has adventures in Adventureland (where he uses his disintegrator pistol to evaporate a mechanical crocodile), Sis in Fantasyland (where she goes on the Snow White and Peter Pan Flight attractions), Mom in Frontierland (where she ends up being the engineer on the train), and Pop in Tomorrowland (where he drives a car on Autopia). Afterward, the family fills up their spacemobile with Richfield ethyl gasoline: "The ol' bus never had this much soup before! Must be that Richfield!"

In the park, Western ran the Story Book Shop, sometimes referred to as the Arcade Bookstore, on Main Street. It provided a "billboard" to remind guests that Dell comics were tied directly to the wholesome world of Disney at a time when comic books were coming under heavy scrutiny and suffering from reduced sales.

The shop was a small space (only eighteen feet by twenty-three feet) with bookshelves from floor to ceiling along three walls located in the Crystal Arcade just behind the Upjohn Pharmacy. There was an entry through the Emporium and also from West Center Street across from the Carnation Ice Cream Parlor and the Flower Mart. It was separated from the rest of the Emporium by an interior wall of dark wood and glass so that guests could easily look inside to see the books.

The store had a huge assortment of Western-produced publications, and when it came to comic books, it was not unusual to see the current Dell issue of *Tarzan* or *Gene Autry* next to a copy of an adaptation of *Lady and the Tramp*.

Today, that location is considered an extension of the Emporium and is just another area with the usual Disney merchandise. In the early years, Disney comic books were also sold at the newsstand out by the ticket kiosks entrance.

As the opening of Disneyland drew near, Western Publishing's editors and artists readied items for release that July to be available not only in the park, but in newsstands, drug stores, and book shops across the country.

Western sent two dozen of its executives (with their spouses) from their offices in Racine, Poughkeepsie, and St. Louis to Anaheim in July 1955. They attended the Hollywood Bowl testimonial to Walt Disney on July 15 and then were part of the invitational preview of the park on July 17.

Accompanying the group to California to participate in the opening ceremonies and also confer with Disney officials on future publishing projects were George Delacorte, the president of Dell Publishing in New York City; Robert Bernstein, the sales manager for Little Golden Books; and Mrs. Jo Jasper Turner of Simon and Schuster. Their arrangements were made by R.S. Callender, the vice president of Whitman Publishing in Beverly Hills and his assistant, Al Stoffel.

The regular newsstand Dell comic books showcased a "Win a Trip to Disneyland" contest for several months not only to promote the park but to get demographic information from its young readers.

Between 1955 and 1960, Dell produced ten giant-sized Disneyland comic books containing hundreds of pages of new, original content. By

1960, the Disney company had reacquired Western's shares in the park, so it was no longer a priority to aggressively promote Disneyland and to pull writers and artists from regular titles to do Disneyland-specific titles.

Through its Whitman line, Western continued to create coloring, story, and activity books and puzzles featuring Disneyland.

The first Dell Giant at ninety-six pages and costing twenty-five cents (when most comic books sold for a dime) was entitled *Donald Duck in Disneyland* (primary artwork by Tony Strobl and Al Hubbard) and was available for sale at the park on opening day, even though its official on-sale date was July 19, two days later.

Of course, since the book had to be produced at least three months before July, the artists only had concept sketches and maps to use as references to the park, so several things that were depicted in the comic book were not altogether accurate.

The cover painting showed Donald Duck riding on a magic carpet photographing Disneyland from overhead. The backcover showed a painting of Mickey, Goofy, Huey, Dewey, and Louie riding on Dumbo (holding a "D" flag with his trunk) high over Disneyland where they can see the castle, the TWA Moonliner, Autopia, the Jungle Cruise, and part of the *Mark Twain* steamboat.

Inside the front cover was a "Welcome to Disneyland" with Donald pointing to a map featuring Tinker Bell and the layout of Disneyland, and at the bottom: "Let Donald point out some of the wonderful things to see and do at Disneyland, kids. He's numbered each one so you'll know just where to look."

The story begins with Donald and Daisy Duck, Huey, Dewey, and Louie, Mickey and Minnie Mouse, Pluto, Goofy, Grandma Duck, and Uncle Scrooge arriving at Disneyland to meet a special blue-suited and capped guide wearing a black tie and looking like a bus driver tour guide who tells them that: "[Walt Disney] thought you should have a special preview of the park before it officially opens. You've got the whole place to yourselves."

Mickey decides that since they all want to see something different, they should break up into separate groups, see what they want to see, and then regroup at the end of the day.

Donald and Daisy board the "Congo Queen" Jungle Cruise boat and Donald recounts an African adventure he had in the Belgian Congo with Uncle Scrooge and his nephews. However, Daisy is so entranced by all the sights to see on the attraction that a disappointed Donald discovers as they end the ride that she was not paying any attention to his tale.

Grandma Duck and Huey, Dewey, and Louie visit Frontierland where they find a picture of Davy Crockett hanging in the Golden Horseshoe Saloon. Grandma tells the boys about how Davy Crockett fought Big Foot Mason and his two cronies who were stealing land from the Indians. As she starts to tell the story, the artwork becomes more realistic and is done by Jesse Marsh, a former Disney animation concept artist, who was doing the Crockett stories in the other Dell comic books and newspaper strip.

Goofy, Minnie Mouse, and Pluto go to Fantasyland and ride the Mad Tea Party, Dumbo, Mr. Toad's Wild Ride, and Peter Pan's Flight, and then hook up with Jiminy Cricket who takes them on the Snow White attraction. Unfortunately, Goofy and Pluto get lost on the ride and end up in Wonderland where they anger both the Red Queen and the Old Witch from Snow White, but thanks to help from Peter Pan and Tinker Bell, Goofy, Pluto, and Jiminy safely rejoin Minnie on the ride by the end of the story.

While on Peter Pan's Flight, Minnie assures Pluto: "Just remember... in Disneyland no matter how exciting and thrilling everything is...it's always perfectly safe!"

Mickey Mouse and his nephews Morty and Ferdy go to Tomorrowland and board the Rocket to the Moon. The nephews got up so early because they were anxious to go to Disneyland that they are very tired. They drift off for a short nap and dream that they and Mickey, accompanied by inventor Gyro Gearloose, rocket to the moon for real and upset a dastardly scheme hatched by Pegleg Pete.

Uncle Scrooge is missing all day because he was searching for a dime he lost in the Hub, but he still had a good time because he not only found the dime but also a nickel and two pennies.

At the end of the comic book, the characters have only one question for the guide who is still back at the train station: "What time does it open tomorrow morning?"

The comic also contained nine pages devoted to puzzles, activities, and games in the back of the book, a common practice in the Dell Giants.

The park was in constant flux right up until opening day, so many of collectibles released in 1955 reflected misinterpretations of early concept art, some of which was obviously done by outside artists for the vendors who used their experiences at circuses, fairs, and other events as inspiration. Incorrect names, inaccurate depictions of areas, and things that never got built abound on these items.

The Disneyland Game from Transogram lists The Land of Tomorrow, and a Frontierland tray puzzle from Jaymar lists a land as being Frontier County, to cite just two examples.

Stationery produced to be sold at Disneyland shows the Main Street Station listed as The Railroad Station with the train going in the wrong direction, and the floral Mickey head in a sideways profile view facing left. The castle is identified as The Fairy Castle with a picture of Snow Mountain towering behind it.

The Disneyland Electric Tours (Jacmar) indicates that Frontierland is devoted to just Davy Crockett and has a full-sized Alamo, while in Fantasyland it shows Peter Pan and the Three Little Pigs enjoying attractions such as Crocodile Creek and a Dumbo ride where the elephants could fly upside down. Tomorrowland has flying saucers, space stations, missile launchers, and a monorail with egg-shaped vehicles dangling beneath its tracks.

Western also released in 1955 a Little Golden Book titled *Donald Duck in Disneyland* about Donald taking his three over-eager nephews to tour the park. The story was by Annie North Bedford, with illustrations by Campbell Grant.

In addition to Disney comic books, Disneyland sold a variety of other Dell comic books featuring characters that were the property of Disneyland Hotel owner Jack Wrather, such as the Lone Ranger, Lassie, and Sergeant Preston of the Yukon. All of these characters were currently in television series and made public appearances at Disneyland as well.

Other comic books that were at the Disneyland bookstore in 1955 included issues featuring I Love Lucy, Rex Allen, Gene Autry, Roy Rogers, Annie Oakley, Rin Tin Tin, Tarzan, Little Lulu, and cartoon characters from Warner Brothers, Metro-Goldwyn-Mayer, and Walter Lantz, as well as a host of Wild West-related titles.

The Dell Comics Distinguished Achievement Award for 1956 was presented to Walt Disney on January 15, 1957, "in appreciation of his continuous and significant contributions in combining so successfully the fields of entertainment and education for American youth". Among those Disney comic books that specifically combined entertainment and education were *Man in Space* and *The Nature of Things*.

As mentioned, the cessation of Dell Disneyland comic books in 1961 was probably related to the fact that Walt Disney Productions had bought out Western Publishing's share of the park.

Western used the significant profits from that sale to break off from Dell Publishing and start their own imprint, Gold Key. While Gold Key still published Disney-related comic books, they were not Disneyland-related except for one comic featuring earlier reprint material. That book celebrated Disneyland's Tencennial anniversary in 1965.

In the August 1955 issue of its in-house magazine, *The Westerner*, the company touted:

> Dell Comics are Good Comics. Comics based on Disney characters and materials have helped to establish the truth of the slogan. The fact that Walt Disney Comics have been the all-time best seller among all comic magazines for many years testifies to the good taste inherent in at least the majority of children and their parents. Like all Disney creations, and like all Dell Comics, they offer nothing but clean and wholesome entertainment at all times.

CHAPTER FIVE

Anaheim

Anaheim was not the first choice for Walt's Disneyland. Nor was it the second choice or really even in the original top ten. Over forty different parcels in Orange County alone were considered. Other possibilities included a pistol range in Chatsworth, a coastal spot in Palos Verdes, a huge 440-acre plot in La Cañada, a rural parcel in Calabasas, the Golden Oak Ranch that Disney used for movies, a stretch of property on Knott Avenue in Buena Vista that proved too small, a site that turned out to be the location for a labor camp of Mexican nationals, and even areas in Riverside and San Diego counties.

In the end, however, Walt chose Anaheim, a city in Orange County, California, that is considered part of the Los Angeles metropolitan area.

The word Anaheim is a combination of "Ana" after the nearby Santa Ana River and "heim", a Germany word meaning "home", so it was a "home by the river". Anaheim was founded in September 1857 by fifty German-Americans who had all originally come from San Francisco. The city was incorporated in 1878.

The new owners intended to use the land to make wine as the Anaheim Vineyard Company. During the period of 1860 to 1885, Anaheim wineries produced more than 1.25 million gallons of wine annually.

In 1885 a strange disease attacked the vines and within five years the two million vines that made up the huge vineyard were dead. In their place, citrus trees were planted and proved more successful thanks to the local hills which protected the fruit against the cold winds coming down from the mountains.

Processors and growers included Anaheim Orchid, Anaheim Supreme, Balboa, Blue Vase, Pride of Anaheim, Siren, and Hi-Class. The Southern California Fruit Growers Exchange, which was later renamed Sunkist, was organized in 1893.

Rudolph Boysen, Anaheim's first park superintendent from 1921 to 1950, created a hybrid berry that Walter Knott later named the "boysenberry" in Boysen's honor and was sold and served at Knott's Berry Farm in its famous pies.

The city marked its centennial in 1957 with a year's worth of activities, culminating in a week-long Centennial Celebration which featured a beard contest, an old-fashioned fashion show, a giant square dance, a time capsule burial in City Park (the capsule was dug up and opened in 2013), and a grand ball with the coronation of a centennial queen. A highlight of the festival was the nightly performance of Centurama, an elaborately staged pageant of Anaheim history with a cast of 1200 residents.

It was a final hometown celebration before the city was radically transformed by the popularity and success of Disneyland into a more modern metropolis.

In the mid-1950s, Anaheim was a small, quiet, rural community, where agriculture was the primary industry. The city jail had only two cells and the 42 police officers had to supply their own cars when on duty. A brochure from before Disneyland was built described the city as:

> No better place to Live. Anaheim. The City of Beautiful Parks. In the Heart of the Southland.

In 1955, the city had a population of about 15,000 people. Today, the population is nearly 340,000.

In the early 1950s, the city was four square miles. Today, it is approximately forty-two square miles. In 1955, the year Disneyland opened, 3,300 more acres were included within the city limits. By the end of that year, Anaheim was four times the size it was in 1953 when Walt first started looking at the area.

When Disneyland opened in 1955, Anaheim had only five small hotels and two motels, with a total of 87 rooms. There were 34 restaurants in the city. Today, there are thousands of rooms and hundreds of restaurants.

Anaheim had twenty-seven independent industries employing 1,400 workers. A decade after Disneyland opened, there were 460 industries employing 48,500 workers.

With the immediate success of Disneyland, the streets surrounding the park became a chaotic and tawdry hodgepodge of motels, hotels, restaurants, liquor stores, bowling alleys, cheap souvenir shops, and other tourist traps.

Many of these places tried to align themselves with Disneyland by creating superficial design elements, primarily on their signs, to suggest the theme of Hawaii, outer space, and the Old West, among others. At the time, Anaheim had no restrictions on signs, zoning laws, or a master plan for expansion. By 1959, twenty-five motels were pressed together in the perimeter around the park aggressively promoting themselves as within "walking distance of Disneyland".

Walt referred to this "Glitter Gulch" area as a "second-rate Las Vegas" and made him want land where he could control the space around his park, resulting in him going to Florida a decade later.

As Anaheim's city manager from 1950 to 1976, Keith Murdoch remembered that the city was as interested in having Disney just as much as, if not more than, Disney was interested in locating its theme park in Anaheim. The city wanted to raise its profile and attract some major businesses. He said:

> We were looking to improve the economic status of the city by attracting new industries. We looked at Disney as another industrial opportunity.

On August 19, 1966, the Disney company received from the First American Title Insurance & Trust Company the "chain of title" tracing Disneyland from the original land grant to the present.

Disneyland was located on parcels of land in the Rancho San Juan Cajon de Santa Ana, which had been under the jurisdiction of the King of Spain in 1769. After becoming part of Mexico, the area was given to Juan Pacifico Ontiveras in 1837.

After California became part of the United States, the government officially confirmed that the land belonged to Ontiveras. He later sold 1165 acres at $2 an acre to the founders of Anaheim in 1857. Nearly a century later, that same land would cost Walt over $4,000 an acre.

In June 1953, Walt hired the Stanford Research Institute to make two surveys. One would find the ideal location for Disneyland. The other would determine the economic feasibility of building Disneyland. Disney paid $23,000 for the site study and a four-month feasibility study.

Charles Luckman, one of the architects that Walt had hired to construct the never-built Mickey Mouse Park in Burbank, recommended Harrison "Buzz" Price, head of the Los Angeles office of SRI. The project manager was C.V. Wood Jr., but it was Price who was the "numbers" guy.

By late August, Price had narrowed down the potential areas, but also concluded that Los Angeles was becoming increasingly decentralized and land too expensive for any area there to be viable.

In addition, Walt had immediately ruled out any location near the beach, since he felt that he'd lose as much as half his potential audience to the free fun of the Pacific Ocean. Walt also feared that dripping wet swimsuit-clad guests might then stop off at his park, causing maintenance issues.

Price identified Orange County as having the best climate as well as being where the center of population seemed to be moving, especially with the new Santa Ana Freeway then under construction that would supposedly be finished late in 1954.

Price also had to take into account a good location for television transmission because Walt intended to broadcast from the park. One of the caveats was that obstructions such as power lines couldn't be in a direct line from the park to the antennas atop Mount Wilson in the San Gabriel Mountains.

Anaheim City Manager Keith Murdoch, working with Earne Moeller, the manager of the Anaheim Chamber of Commerce, outlined two possible sites. Both were mainly orange groves with few buildings.

One Saturday, on the way to the first site, Walt passed a Catholic cemetery that had fallen into disrepair and was unkempt. He immediately rejected the site, not wanting Disneyland visitors to drive by it, despite assurances that it would be cleaned up. He liked the second site and decided to put down a deposit on some of the land there.

Afterward, on their way back to Burbank, Walt and his team stopped at Knott's Berry Farm, one of the few places Walt knew in the area, for lunch, and had an enthusiastic discussion about the possibilities of that site. At a nearby table was a realtor from Garden Grove who listened intently to the conversation and then on Sunday obtained options on some of the key parcels in hopes of making a fortune.

That killed the deal on Monday morning, and Walt forfeited his deposit. Murdoch searched and found two other locations, but both of those failed to materialize.

Finally, a clever Murdoch found a block of land held by only seventeen owners who were thinking of selling it to a housing subdivision. The only problem was that Cerritos Avenue, which went from Harbor Boulevard all the way to the Pacific Ocean, ran right through the middle of it.

With willing property owners, the street could be closed and abandoned, and the area was very close to one of the pins that SRI had put on a map of potential sites.

"If you can close that street, we've got a deal," Walt told Murdoch.

The street was closed. The orange-growing business was going through hard times and the owners welcomed this opportunity to get out. For the most part, they knew it was Disney that was buying the land and they felt they were getting a good deal.

The price would be relatively inexpensive, at an average of $4500 per acre. The total cost for just the land was $879,000. Its purchase by Disney would not be announced officially until May 1954.

Walt liked the cooperative nature of the Anaheim city government and the growth possibilities of the area. He felt that it would be a good home for his park, and he was right.

Unfortunately, the scheduled public ground-breaking ceremony had to be canceled because of the threat of a protest demonstration by a handful of local residents led by two Garden Grove businessmen who wanted to stall the annexation of the Disneyland site.

Despite these issues, construction on Disneyland began July 21, 1954, when the first trees were removed, leaving approximately 257 working days to build the park.

Earlier, on January 5, 1955, the Disneyland plot of land officially became part of the city of Anaheim and was granted access to all of the necessary infrastructure, from sewage to garbage collection

When Disneyland opened in 1955, county officials predicted that by 1970 Orange County's population would be 720,000. Thanks to Walt's Magic Kingdom, the county hit that number in 1961, nine years ahead of schedule.

Ron Dominguez started working at Disneyland in 1955 when he was nineteen years old and later became the vice president of the park. In 1985, during Disneyland's 30th anniversary celebration, I interviewed him about his unique connection to Anaheim and Disneyland. He was born and lived on the property that became part of the original Frontierland and Adventureland. He told me:

> In the late 1890s, my maternal grandfather came here from Perry, Iowa, and purchased thirty acres of Orange County land. His name was Wyran Knowlton and at first, he planted a walnut grove, then in 1910 changed the walnuts for oranges.
>
> In 1920, Knowlton's daughter, my mother, Laura, married Paul Dominguez, who was part of the family that had the Bernardo Yorba enormous land grants in Southern California. My folks built a house there in 1925.
>
> I was born in that house in 1935. After I had spent years of weeding and tromping through my family's orange grove, I was surprised to hear my parents talk about selling the property to a man who had driven by in a convertible a couple of times. That man was Walt Disney. People had made offers for our land since 1951 or so, but my mother was never interested.
>
> Selling those ten acres was real emotional for my mom who had struggled to hang on to our house and land and make the groves pay after her dad died. She definitely did not envision that it would ever become part of a magical kingdom.
>
> The two real estate men who put the deal together were personal friends of the family. Ed Wagner and Frank Miller. They assured her that she was selling to a quality organization.
>
> Walt invited us all up to the studio to see a presentation so we could see it wasn't going to be a typical dirty amusement park. He was very convincing. She finally agreed to sign the necessary papers and we were the last of the original seventeen families to move out.
>
> There was a man who was caretaker for one of the orange groves and Walt hired him for about a year to keep the trees watered until they decided what they needed to keep. The man lived in one of the houses that had been

moved. Most of the land was cleared by August and some of the trees on our property ended up in the Jungle Cruise jungle.

I can remember the bulldozers uprooting the nearby orchards starting in July 1954 and we didn't pack up until August because our new house wasn't ready yet. When we left, we were stepping around ditches and holes because work was already being done.

They took our house and a house from the Callens estate and put the two together for the Administration building. Another Callens house was used as the personnel office on West Street for the first three years or so.

Before we moved out, we met Earl Shelton who was the Disney coordinator of construction, and I later contacted him to set up an interview for a job. He had been always gently pushing us to get out of the house so his construction crew could start some work there.

I had graduated from Anaheim High School and was at the University of Arizona and my parents kept telling me about all these lines of people along West Street where the personnel office was located looking for work at Disneyland. I think they began interviewing in January 1955.

I told my parents to get in touch with Earl to see if he could get me an interview when I came home in early May. I got a job as a ticket taker at the front gate. I was 19 years old.

The original plan on opening day was to stagger the arrival of guests so there would be a smooth and orderly flow. The tickets all had a specific time so we could spread out all the arrivals.

I was told a crowd management firm had been hired to help, but everyone all showed up early. Everyone wanted to come early to see the movie stars and to see what Walt had done after seeing it being built on all those television shows. It was exciting to see celebrities come in through the front gate, to have them come to my hometown.

On that first day, several rides broke down and only a few restrooms were working. Walt himself was seen running rolls of toilet paper to some of them. But despite all the snafus, the magic feel of the place rubbed off on people at the very beginning. It was a really hot day and it was a madhouse.

I was a ticket receptionist at the main gate for only two weeks, then I was transferred to the trains. After the summer, my boss Doc Lemmon said to me, "You ought to stick around. This place is here to stay. You should get in on the ground floor."

I am glad I took the risk. I spent the first winter working on the Mule Packs and the stagecoach in Frontierland. Within that first year of joining Disney, I was trained on every attraction and was named temporary supervisor of Main Street, U.S.A.

Somebody thought I looked a little like actor Fess Parker and I ended up playing Davy Crockett on the Mike Fink Keel Boats for a while. We had real jousting contests, trying to knock the other guy into the water. I took my share of dunkings.

Our house was located near to where the entrance to Pirates of the Caribbean is today. It was a large Spanish-style two-story house. We had a two-car garage behind the house and a workshop.

They made so many changes to the main house like putting a wall down the middle of my old bedroom upstairs to create two offices that it didn't seem like my house anymore. It was a strange experience going in there for me. They had moved it backstage and it had to be torn down in 1958 because of the building of the Grand Canyon Diorama back there.

They gave me a big sledge hammer and took some publicity shots of me pounding away on my old house. It was very solidly built and took a lot of effort by a construction crew to get it finally down.

A house on the Disneyland Hotel site was moved behind the park for use by the landscapers. The only house from the original property still standing is the one that the Popes lived in when they were handling all the horses at Disneyland for the Pony Farm.

I'm glad my parents decided to sell. Business was always slow at the fruit stand anyway.

There's something from my old orange grove, from that original property, that is still at Disneyland, a palm tree (over by the Indiana Jones Fast Pass, the fat tall tree that punches through the boathouse). For a long time, it was in the queue for the Jungle Cruise.

Walt agreed to save it as part of the deal for buying our property. He was a sentimental guy like my mom and he saw how important it was to her. Besides, he needed all the trees he could get.

It is a Canary Island Date Palm and it was planted in 1896 as a wedding gift to my grandparents from the area's first horticulturist, Tim Carroll. Life is funny. My daughter married the great-grandson of the guy who gave my grandparents the palm tree. Today at Disneyland, it is called the Dominguez Tree.

CHAPTER SIX

Disneyland's Cast of Characters

When Disneyland first opened, Walt Disney famously said:
> You can design and create, and build the most wonderful place in the world. But it takes people to make the dream a reality.

At the time, he was referring to the guests who would be the "actors" that populated the "sets" of his new entertainment venue and made it come alive rather than just being an empty stage.

Over the years, beginning in the Traditions training handbook in 1967, the Disney company has co-opted that statement to use it to refer to the cast members who work so hard to make the magic. Certainly, Walt's innovative dream of a place where families could have a little fun together would not have materialized without the contributions of the following people who are unknown to the general public, much like the behind-the-scenes "technical" casts of most movies.

Karl Bacon and Ed Morgan

In 1946, Arrow Development was started in Mountain View, California, by Bill Hardiman, Angus Anderson, Karl Bacon, and Ed Morgan. The company was involved with several projects, including crop dusting equipment and supplying rides for amusement parks.

By 1954, the company had been given the contract to build six rides for Disneyland: Mad Tea Party, Snow White's Adventures, Mr. Toad's Wild Ride, King Arthur Carrousel, Casey Jr. Circus Train, and Dumbo Flying Elephants.

In an article, "Mountain View Firm Aids Disney", for the *San Jose News*, Keith Kaldenbach wrote:

> At conferences held at Disney's Studios in Burbank, Ed Morgan and his associates were told the important thing to remember was that the rides must be constructed so that they would look exactly like the originals in

the various cartoons. Recently, Disney and some of his movie cameramen visited the Arrow plant to inspect the progress being made.

Over the decades, Bacon and Morgan created entirely new categories of rides like the Matterhorn Bobsleds which is considered the first modern roller coaster, and were inducted into the Hall of Fame and Living Legends by the International Association of Amusement Parks and Attractions (IAAPA) in 1998.

Arrow had a contract with the city of Oakland, California, to put rides in a park at Lake Merritt, so they constructed a small-scale paddlewheel boat ride named Lil' Belle. Unfortunately, a big crop-dusting customer had recently gone bankrupt at the same time and put Arrow in financial jeopardy.

Morgan had read in a newspaper about Disneyland, but it was all very sketchy so he took a chance and wrote to the Disney Studio about the Lil' Belle and Walt and his crew came up to take a look.

Walt wasn't interested in the boat, especially since he had larger plans with the *Mark Twain* paddlewheeler, but he did notice some of the little vehicles that Arrow was building for other amusement parks and liked what he saw.

Morgan was given an original concept sketch by Imagineer Bruce Bushman of the Mr. Toad car with no mechanical specifications. Using aircraft sheet metal shears, he eventually slapped together a prototype that Disney loved after a few minimal changes. It was the beginning of the relationship between Disney and Arrow.

All of the attractions (except the carousel) that Arrow worked on for the opening of Disneyland were systems that largely had never before been attempted which, of course, was the reason for so many re-adjustments in the early years. These rides had to be quiet, take tight turns, be reliable and simple to repair, and be able to operate fourteen hours a day every day.

Imagineer Bob Gurr remembered:

> During these redesign sessions I got a chance to work with Karl Bacon and Ed Morgan of Arrow Development. They built a lot of the Disney ride machines over the years. They were never upset that Roger Broggie had me redesigning their products like the Tea Cup Ride. We were both interested in getting it right for Walt. And I learned so much from their designers and fabricators as to their very clever ways to design and build neat stuff.

Ed Morgan said:

> Disney's people made the actual elephants [for the Dumbo attraction] and they were a lot heavier than the specifications they had given us to begin with. But we were able to pull it off. We were in charge of making the elephants go up and down and making sure their ears flapped. But it started to become erratic, so the elephants would hesitate, then come on strong, then hesitate again.

Karl Bacon added

> Dumbo didn't work right. They were flying but not satisfactorily. The hydraulic system was spewing out this foam. The nitrogen was mixing with the oil and creating this "shaving cream" that was throwing the whole thing out of stability.

Morgan continued:

> So we left Paul Harvey there on opening day when they were operating the ride to drain the fluid and put new fluid back in between time of load and unload. We rushed to military surplus stores to buy hydraulic pumps all day until ten at night.

Dana Morgan, Ed's son, was used as the test subject for the prototype for the Mad Tea Party attraction. He said:

> They had only one tea cup on it. I rode it a lot then. I think I was almost certainly the first kid to ride it. I was the guinea pig, used to see if a kid was strong enough to turn it, and could stand it without throwing up after riding it. All of those early Disneyland rides were done on very, very tight schedules, and very, very tight budgets.

On Casey Jr. Circus Train, Karl Bacon said:

> Movie star Jerry Colonna was supposed to drive the locomotive as an opening day stunt, but when he saw a steep hill the ride had to climb, he chickened out. So Wardrobe got me into Colonna's clothes and everything went smoothly.

On King Arthur Carrousel, Ed Morgan said:

> It was actually from Sunnyside Park in Toronto, Canada. I supervised the dismantling piece by piece. We rebuilt much of the ride, using sturdier materials. We had to replace some of the wild animals on the ride so that they were all horses to fit with the King Arthur theme. It was originally a three row, 72-animal menagerie Dentzel from 1922. Two other carousels gave up their horses so that the Dentzel became a four row, 85-horse machine.

On Snow White's Adventures, Morgan said

> Disney had used regular door hinges and the air cylinders that were supposed to open them were so powerful they blew them right off and they fell onto the tracks. The operators would stand on the rear bumpers as the car came into the station, jerking the front ends off the track and blowing the fuses. Some of those guys weighed something like 175 pounds and they'd lift the guide unit off the track and that would blow the fuses.

Morgan recalled about Walt:

> When Disneyland was being built, Walt would sometimes come to the shop and we used to go to lunch with him. Walt never brought any money with him. He'd look at Vic Greene or Bruce Bushman and ask if they had any money. He knew they did.

Not that Walt was stingy. When Disneyland opened, Walt asked Bacon and Morgan how they came out on all the rides. Morgan explained that since it had been a fixed bid of the rides, they had lost money on every one they did for Disneyland. The contract with Disney for the Fantasyland rides was fixed at $250,000. Walt told them, "I don't want you boys to lose money on my work. I'll cover your costs." And he did.

Cornelius Vanderbilt Wood Jr

Usually just referred to as C.V. Wood or "Woody", Wood was a controversial and important part of the development of Disneyland. This extroverted salesman was the vice-president and general manager of Disneyland and was responsible for bringing in corporate lessees like Swift and TWA to sponsor things at the park. Wood and his team managed park hours, employment, policies, and other daily logistics.

Under circumstances still somewhat unclear, but which included charges of money mismanagement and kickbacks from some of the smaller lessees, Wood was asked to resign in January 1956.

Most people assumed Wood's departure was because he took too much public credit for the creation of Disneyland. Wood billed himself as the "Master Planner (or Builder) of Disneyland" until a lawsuit by Disney in May 1960 for misrepresentation stopped him from doing so. In particular, the lawsuit was filed to prevent Wood and his company from representing themselves as having "conceived the idea for Disneyland or designed, engineered or constructed" the park.

In the May 23, 1960, issue of the trade newspaper *Billboard*, Disneyland executive vice-president Donn Tatum said that in filing the suit Disney was not asking for monetary relief. The purpose of the action, Tatum said, was to set the record straight that Disneyland "was designed and built by the Walt Disney organization and that no connection exists between it and the Wood projects".

Tatum contended that Wood's position was that of an operations manager and did not include decisions in creative concepts, design, or construction of the park. The suit was settled out of court.

While he claimed Walt considered him as a son, Wood also constantly butted heads with Walt, especially about the Mickey Mouse Club Circus, and developed his own team that was loyal just to him. He was also known for his off-color jokes, something that Walt had never cared for at his studio.

"There was room for only one showman," Harrison "Buzz" Price wrote in his memoir *Walt's Revolution! By the Numbers*. "Their clash of egos was oil and water and Walt was the boss." Wood was Price's boss at the Stanford Research Institute and Price was the person who found the location for Disneyland.

It was Wood who also brought in the legendary Van Arsdale France to create the training for Disneyland, as well as Admiral Joe Fowler, who managed the actual construction of the park.

"In one week, Wood was holding his regular meetings as usual, with an office crowded every minute of the day," France was quoted as saying in Randy Bright's *The Disneyland Story*. "Just about overnight, he was out." According to Dick Irvine, Walt had his brother Roy fire Wood after a heated argument.

Wood's name was expunged from Disneyland history. Some who worked with him at Disneyland like Bob Gurr considered him a devious con man or just simply refused to talk about him after his departure.

Walt wanted managers to be clearly visible to both guests and employees, and wanted them constantly in the park rather than hiding backstage. In the earliest days of Disneyland, managers wore gray suits and orange ties on their white shirts.

Early cast member Bill "Sully" Sullivan recalled:

> I wore a white shirt and orange tie when I got promoted to manager. That was how people could identify a manager in the park. They wore orange ties. It was something C.V. Wood and his Texans brought in with them because it was their school's colors [University of Texas at Austin], orange and white. In fact, they called that burnt orange color "Texas Orange".

After leaving Disney, Wood formed Marco Engineering, providing market research, design, engineering, and construction to the leisure industry. To aggravate the situation, he took along some of the people he had worked with at Disneyland.

He was later responsible for amusement parks like Denver's Magic Mountain (1957), Massachusetts' Pleasure Island (1959), and New York's Freedomland (1960) which had many similarities to Disneyland. He was also responsible for the initial work on Six Flags Over Texas (1961).

Richard "Dick" Irvine

Irvine organized and led the team of Imagineers who created Disneyland. In 1952, Walt Disney hired Irvine away from 20th Century Fox, where he was an art director, to act as liaison between Walt Disney Productions and an architectural firm, Pereira & Luckman, that was being considered for designing Disneyland.

Walt felt the architects were using "aircraft thinking" (concentrating on "bricks and mortar") rather than "show thinking", and needed someone to communicate his vision in their language.

Imagineer John Hench recalled:

> Because Dick had worked with movie set designs, creating structures and settings, he understood our needs more than standard architects.

After a few preliminary meetings with the architects, however, Irvine concluded that the people who could best design the Magic Kingdom were members of Walt's own staff. This was a recommendation that was supported by Walt's friend and neighbor, architect Welton Beckett, who Walt had asked to help design the park.

Irvine helped establish and lead the new team of artists, architects, designers, and engineers, known as Imagineers. One of the reasons he was so perfect for the job was that he had previously worked at the Disney Studio as an art director on *Victory Through Airpower* (1943) and *The Three Caballeros* (1944) so he knew how Walt worked and the Disney culture. Irvine eventually became the president of Imagineering.

He was later deeply involved with the design and building of the Magic Kingdom in Florida as well, and that was the reason the steamboat for the Rivers of America in Frontierland was christened the *Richard F. Irvine*. His daughter, Maggie Elliott, and his daughter-in-law, Kim Irvine, made some significant Imagineering contributions to Disneyland over the years. Not only does Irvine have a window on Main Street at Disneyland, but there is also a window for "Alexander Irvine, M.D.", Dick's opthamologist father and Walt's eye doctor.

Marvin Davis

Irvine needed someone to work on the elevation drawings for Disneyland and so he brought in Marvin Davis in 1953. Davis was also an art director at 20th Century Fox where he had worked on *Gentlemen Prefer Blondes* (1953) and *Asphalt Jungle* (1950).

Davis was reportedly as stubborn as Walt and had married Walt's niece Marjorie Sewell. He was the one who scaled the park to match the acreage.

Imagineer John Hench recalled:

> Because Marvin had a rich background in live-action motion picture design, he had a strong sense and understanding of theater and how to give life or meaning to structures, which, typically, most formally trained architects aren't interested in. He knew how to create architectural form that had a message for people. For instance, his structures on Main Street, U.S.A. are irrepressibly optimistic.

Herb Ryman's iconic artistic renderings of Disneyland were based on the layout and elevations done by Davis. Davis once said that he remembered there were roughly 120 artists, designers, and sculptors involved in the creation of Disneyland.

Owen Pope

Pope and his wife, Dolly, made their living exhibiting horses when, in 1950, Walt caught one of their shows at the Pan Pacific Auditorium in Los Angeles. Pope was well known for the excellent horse trailers he built while living in Fort Worth, Texas. In March 1951, Walt Disney asked the Popes if they would be interested in beginning training horses for Disneyland.

They accepted, and a week after Thanksgiving, Pope moved his trailer onto the Disney Studio lot, where ten stalls had been built for horses. The Popes stayed at the studio for about two and half years, the only people to ever live there, with Walt visiting them everyday.

Once the horses were moved to Disneyland, Pope set up loud speakers that had crowd noise, loud music, and the sound of gunshots (because of the shooting galleries) cranked up to the highest volume as he trained the horses to accept the high levels of noise at the park.

In addition, Pope supervised the building of Frontierland vehicles like the stagecoach and Conestoga wagon. He was also a harness maker, and a decade and a half later made the first harnesses for Walt Disney World while working at Disneyland, which is why the Car Barn at Walt Disney World has a window stating: Owen Pope. Harness Maker.

As work was beginning on the construction of Disneyland, one of the houses on the land was moved to a 10-acre location behind Fantasyland dubbed the Pony Farm (and known as the Circle D Corral since 1980). The house had belonged to the Witherills, who were walnut growers on Harbor Boulevard.

The Popes moved into the house three days before the opening of Disneyland. At one time, the stray dog that was the live-action reference model for Tramp from *Lady and the Tramp* (1955) lived with them as well. There were approximately 200 horses at the Pony Farm on Disneyland's opening day.

With the opening of Walt Disney World in 1971, the Popes were relocated to Florida and assisted in the development of Fort Wilderness' Tri-Circle-D Ranch.

Bruce Bushman

Bushman was an artist who started at Disney in the late 1930s and later was the art director for just about all the artwork for the original *Mickey Mouse Club* television show.

He was the Imagineer in charge of the hand-carved German horses of the carousel and took many of the non-horse pieces that were a part of Disneyland's carousel and put them to use on the Casey Jr. Circus Train. He also helped with the design of the Mickey Mouse Club Circus and designed the Phantom Boats as well as concept artwork for several Fantasyland attractions.

Bushman was a large, pear-shaped man who performed as Santa Claus at a local orphanage for over twenty years as well as at Disneyland. Walt decided that his proportions would be used as a guide for the seating on vehicle attractions like Mr. Toad's Wild Ride. If Bruce could get into a Fantasyland ride vehicle, Walt assumed that a regular adult with a child would fit comfortably in that same seat. Bushman was the son of silent screen star Francis X. Bushman.

He left Disney in 1959 to work as art director on television shows including *Sea Hunt, Bat Masterson,* and *Gentle Ben,* and as layout artist for Hanna-Barbera animated cartoon series like *The Flintstones, The Jetsons,* and *Jonny Quest.* Bushman was also involved as the designer for several proposed theme parks like Bible Storyland and Hanna-Barbera Land.

Bob Gurr

Gurr was director of the Special Vehicle Development during the early years of Disneyland. He joined the Disney company in 1954 and worked on just about anything with wheels at the park, including all the Main Street vehicles. It was Gurr's innovative design work on Disneyland's Autopia that made it such an immediate popular attraction.

Gurr officially retired in 1981, although he occasionally came back to consult. He also worked on projects for other companies, such as Universal Studios California's original King Kong attraction.

During his nearly three-decade employment with Walt Disney Imagineering, Gurr worked on more than one hundred designs for attractions that included the Disneyland and Walt Disney World monorails, the Matterhorn Bobsleds, the Tomorrowland Flying Saucers, and attractions for the 1964–65 New York World's Fair.

Joe Fowler

Fowler was a retired rear admiral of the United States Navy with an impressive thirty-five year naval career spanning two World Wars as well as being called out of retirement briefly by President Truman during the Korean War.

He referred to his "29 children in the Navy" as he fondly called the warships he was in charge of designing and building that included the two biggest aircraft carriers of World War II, the *Lexington* and the *Saratoga*.

Originally, Walt Disney brought Fowler in to consult on the building of the *Mark Twain* steamboat, but eventually hired him as the construction boss for Disneyland. He continued to supervise operations and building projects at the park for the next decade before moving on to build Walt Disney World.

As Fowler recalled in an interview in early 1993 before his death:

> Walt said to me a couple of days after I was hired, "Now look, I will try to have the ideas, and you make the engineering realities of them."

He had the nickname "Can Do" for his famous reply to Walt whenever he was asked to do something. Even when he had no idea of how to do it, his optimistic expression meant he would find a way to get it done.

Bob Mathieson, former executive vice-president of Disneyland, said about his old friend Fowler: "He had that great 'can-do' spirit, and he lived it. He was truly, in every sense of the word, an officer and a gentleman. Dick Nunis, former chairman of Disney Attractions, concurred: "Joe built Disneyland in a year. He had a wonderful way of cutting through red tape and getting the job done."

Fred Joerger

Joerger joined the studio in 1953 to work on the models for the film *20,000 Leagues Under the Sea* (1954). He was moved over to WED in 1954 and contributed to the *Mark Twain* steamboat, Sleeping Beauty Castle, and Main Street, U.S.A. Joerger said:

> If you don't get it into three-dimensions first, you may have a disaster. Well, my job was to create the model to avert disaster, which was fun, but a challenge.

Joerger's partner in the Model Shop, Harriet Burns, remembered:

> Most anything at Disneyland, Fred created as a model first. He constructed several versions of Sleeping Beauty Castle, for instance, changing each design, moving the turrets around, changing colors. Walt liked the model with the blue roof because he thought it would blend in with the sky, making the castle look taller.

Jack Olsen

Olsen had managed artists' supply stores and art galleries in the Los Angeles area, and supplied art material to the Disney Studio. He was an artist himself and was hired at the studio in 1955 as a background artist on *Sleeping Beauty* (1959) so Walt could have him on staff. Walt personally pleaded with him to manage Tomorrowland's Art Corner and to handle the souvenirs in the park.

At the time, all licensed Disney merchandise was handled through the New York office. Olsen argued that he needed flexibility to supply lower-cost souvenir merchandise and to be able to deal with competing suppliers to get the best price rather than just with the existing licensees. He wanted to handle all operations from Southern California.

Olsen is probably best known for rescuing cels from the dumpsters of the Disney Studio, putting them in a cardboard frame, and selling them for $1.47 at Disneyland. In the first decade over a hundred thousand cels were sold.

Tommy Walker

Walker, the star place-kicker for the University of Southern California football team, came to Walt Disney's attention during the halftime show for the 1955 Rose Bowl. Walt was in attendance because Disneyland had a float in the parade that year. Walker was also the drum major. He wrote the familiar six-note fanfare for the trumpet section: "Da da da DUT da DUH!" Trojan rooters then screamed in reply, "Charge!"

Walt had him stage the park's grand opening six months later, and Walker stayed on for the next twelve years. Anything entertainment-related at Disneyland from 1955 to his resignation in 1966 involved Walker, from the pigeon release at the opening ceremonies to introducing balloon releases and fireworks into the park. "When the opening was done," he said, "I decided I liked the place, so I stayed."

He was in charge of Entertainment and Customer Relations and was responsible for starting the guided tour program and creating the Dapper Dans singing group. He discovered the Osmond Brothers, who were singing one day with the Dapper Dans on Main Street, and put them on television.

Walker left Disney in 1966 and went on to a spectacular career that included producing pageants for the 1980 and 1984 Olympic Games, the 1986 Statue of Liberty celebration, and Ronald Reagan's 1981 inauguration. He produced extravaganzas for three Super Bowls, eleven Pro Bowls, and World's Fairs in four cities.

In 1986, during his third open-heart surgery in ten years, Walker died. He was 63. At the time of his death, he was executive producer for events at the famous Radio City Music Hall and had just sold his production company to Radio City Music Hall Productions for a seven-figure payoff.

Walker also hired his father, Vesey Walker, to lead the Disneyland Band. It was a two-week contract that lasted nearly fifteen years.

These are just a few of the many other people who contributed significantly in creating early Disneyland, but whose names and accomplishments often go unrecognized.

CHAPTER SEVEN

The Men Who Landscaped Disneyland: Jack and Bill Evans

One of the most significant and distinctive things about early Disneyland was the landscaping, which set it apart from the typical amusement park and contributed in creating the appropriate theming for the different areas.

Morgan "Bill" Evans' first experience with gardening came from his father's three-acre garden filled with exotic plants.

In 1928, Bill joined the Merchant Marine. While he traveled the world aboard the S.S. *President Harrison*, he gathered exotic seeds for his father's garden from such distant lands as the West Indies, South Africa, and Australia.

Bill studied at Pasadena City College, followed by Stanford, where he majored in geology. In 1931, he helped transform his father's garden into a business by wholesaling some of the rare and exotic plants to other nurseries. In 1936, Bill and his older brother, Jack, joined with Jack Reeves to open Evans and Reeves Landscaping, which lasted until 1958.

Their inventory of rare and exotic plants soon caught the attention of Hollywood's elite. Among their celebrity clientele were Greta Garbo, Clark Gable, Elizabeth Taylor, and ultimately, Walt Disney.

In 1952, Bill and his brother, Jack, were called to landscape the grounds of Walt Disney's Holmby Hills home, including the gardens that surrounded Walt's backyard railroad, the Carolwood Pacific. Walt was pleased with their work and asked them in 1954 to landscape the new theme park he was building.

Unfortunately, Jack wasn't able to completely enjoy the accolades for their work on Disneyland. He suffered a massive heart attack two weeks after the opening of Disneyland and was confined to desk work, never able to return to Disneyland after having spent more than a year doing intensive field work there. Jack Evans passed away in 1958.

After Disneyland opened in July 1955, Bill stayed on as a consultant, drawing landscape plans, installing materials, and supervising maintenance of the park. Later, he was hired by the Disney company and was named director of Landscape Design, working on Disneyland additions and the master plan for Walt Disney World.

In a career spanning nearly 50 years with the company, Evans also headed the landscape design effort for Walt Disney World in 1970. A decade later, he and former partner, Joe Linesch, created the landscape design for Epcot.

Although he retired in 1975, Bill consulted with Imagineering on the landscaping for every other Walt Disney World theme park, including Disney's Animal Kingdom, Disney-MGM Studios, and Typhoon Lagoon, as well as Tokyo Disneyland, Disneyland Paris, Disney's California Adventure, Tokyo DisneySea, Hong Kong Disneyland, and Walt Disney Studios Park.

In 1992, Bill was named a Disney Legend, and in 1996, he was honored by the Landscape Architecture Foundation with a Special Tribute award.

Not only did Bill Evans teach several generations of Disney landscapers how to do their jobs, his methods of plant propagation, plant relocation, and recycling are widely used everywhere. He could tell the history of every plant in the park. Bill Evans died August 10, 2002, at the Santa Monica Hospital, at the age of 92.

The following is excerpted from my interview with Bill in spring 1985 about landscaping Disneyland:

> The way Disneyland went together, the whole thing was a teamwork effort. A teamwork project. I wouldn't be there in the first place if it wasn't for my brother, Jack, who struck up a great friendship with Walt through a mutual friend. Of course, we were involved in landscaping Walt's home. We had a little preview of what Walt had in mind on a much larger scale, without knowing it at the time, not having the vaguest notion that we would be invited years later to do all this on a full-scale basis at Disneyland.
>
> Walt had that little scale railroad that he used to tour the neighbor kids on. One kid to a car. He wrapped it around his home two or three times. In late 1951, we were planning railroad berms and trestles and railroad tunnels.
>
> Disneyland existed in Walt's mind for a great many years before the first shovel of earth was turned. Walt's idea of a park was to build an outdoor entertainment facility where the adults would have every bit as good a time as the children. I think today they outnumber the kids substantially. Fortunately for us, he wanted a lot of green plant stuff.

That was one of the elements Walt felt would separate his park from the Coney Island format. This was to be a park that would be clean and beautiful and colorful and a very pleasant place to be. We kept this in mind when we set about to put a green frame around all those adventures and rides and all the great imagination that Walt brought in to being with the help of those people on his team.

My brother and I hiked the area with Walt. The early days when we arrived, the site was still producing a commercial crop of oranges. Every square foot was planted with either oranges or a little patch of walnuts or a little patch of avocados. We were in charge of "greening it up", from a jungle to a Victorian scene to a Missouri River bank to something as contrived as the Storybook Land landscape.

We landscaped all of Disneyland in less than a year with a maximum of arm-waving and a minimum of drawings.

We superimposed a drawing on an aerial photograph of Disneyland over the trees on the land and endeavored to salvage whenever possible the existing orange trees. We did this because they represented to us the equivalent of about five hundred dollars a tree which was a lot of money in 1954. Wherever the grade remained at the original elevation, we could keep the trees.

If we raised or lowered the grade, we lost some trees. We opened the show with a whole lot of the original trees in place. We started with an orange grove and did selective removal. There was a grove of windbreak eucalyptus. We preserved those. You still see those when you take the Jungle Ride. Those eucalyptus trees are what separate you from Main Street.

For the old stagecoach ride, we used some of the trees there. The illusion of pounding through stagecoach country was not enhanced by a crop of oranges. So we had to spend a lot of time picking all the fruit off of those trees. We did the same thing in the Jungle Ride, picking oranges off the trees to avoid the smart cracks of the ride operators who would have loved to see an orange tree when they came round the bend. We festooned those trees with all kinds of tropical vines that grew vigorously to the ultimate dismay of the orange tree hosts. All those orange trees ultimately died under the blanket of those tropical vines.

Some of the walnut trees were subjected to the indignity of being truncated and inverted because Walt had another role in mind for them. We selected some because Harper Goff who was art directing the jungle had the inspiration of turning them upside down to get a kind of a mangrove effect onto which we grafted the top half of the orange tree truncated also to get branches. It gave a pretty good illusion. I believe there are one or two left. They were cast into the concrete lining of the river.

The freeways which were penetrating the suburbs around the Los Angeles area made possible the salvage of a lot of trees that we could not otherwise have found. We literally snatched them from the jaws of the bulldozer the day before they were to be demolished. We'd box 'em out and haul 'em down to Disneyland. When I'm at Disneyland, I can tell you tree after tree. This one was from the Santa Monica freeway and that one was from the Pomona freeway and so on.

The jungle has a horticultural mix from all around the world. That two-acre man-made jungle is the best damn jungle this side of Costa Rica. What we were attempting in this jungle was to try to bring forth the illusion of a jungle. Perhaps what the armchair traveler might have in mind. Turns out when you really plod through an authentic jungle you are apt to travel for a day or two and the scenery doesn't change much. Maybe one or two species without interruption.

We were trying to capture this armchair traveler thing and get all kinds of textures and all kinds of effects. The palms. The tree ferns. The philodendrons. You get a kind of "man-eating" atmosphere. The giant bamboo was not actually a jungle denizen, but it fills a role conveniently. You might discover a rather pedestrian castor bean plant, but the effect is good and it adds to the textures.

We picked material from Brazil, material from Africa, material from India and Asia and Malaysia. We pushed it all together. It's all quite compatible in the sense that it all has that lush, vigorous growth. Really strong growth. What we attempted to do in planting the jungle was to make it look as though we had nothing to do with it. We were working on a pretty tight budget.

In the jungle, a lot of those trees are native to tropical Africa, India, South America, but they are interspersed with things not truly tropical but they have a tropical aspect like that bamboo we use from China that grows 40–50 feet high. You are not aware it isn't tropical. You see it as part of the jungle texture. We take a bit of the real stuff and we interlace it with something else.

The soil at the site was sand. It was almost ball-bearing sand. You could have used this stuff for a good grade of concrete. It wasn't contaminated with any soil. It was just sand. That isn't the best prescription for horticulture, but we made due. We got satisfactory results by pouring a lot of liquid fertilizer on this stuff. Not that many years later with a lot of water and a lot of fertilizer and this Southern California climate, it didn't take a long time to get a lot of growth. The sand was totally lacking in any nutrients.

The purpose of the berm that wraps around the park was to exclude the sight of the freeways and the neon signs and the 20th century through which you travel in order to arrive at Disneyland. Walt didn't want that intruding on his illusions inside. So the solution was to build this berm of sand which was anywhere from ten to twenty feet high and then garnish it with all the vegetation we could lay our hands on to complete the screening and shut out the Edison transmission towers, freeway interchanges, and high rise hotels. That back berm had some very young pine on top of it that within the first ten years grew thirty to forty feet high.

We improvised what I called a tree-planting extender to fill out the berm. That's just a plain, ordinary, garden variety, front-loading tractor, but it wouldn't reach where we had to go, so we took a couple of pieces of water pipe and a chain and put a handle on the front of the tractor so we could put the trees up on the berm. In those days, we didn't have hydraulic cranes that are so convenient today.

Walt liked to have the scene complete when the curtains were drawn open. He wanted that landscaping to being as close to full scale and mature as possible. He didn't want to wait five or ten years for young trees to grow up and produce shape. We scampered around the country to try to find all the mature trees we could and it didn't take long to exhaust the budget. The park was built on a very modest budget.

That story that Walt told at the tencennial dinner in 1965 was absolutely true and I was so proud to be singled out. During the landscaping of Disneyland, I had to tell Walt by the time I got around to the back berm that we had run out of money and plant material and were scraping the bottom of the barrel.

Walt said, "I notice you have some head high weeds out there. Why don't you put some jaw-breaking Latin names on them?" So we did as he suggested. The weeds were growing almost as high as trees, so we put some fancy names on them. Walt got such a kick out of it that he mentioned it at the employee celebration at the Disneyland Hotel in July 1965 for the tenth anniversary of Disneyland.

Walt believed people would know the difference between good landscaping and bad landscaping, and Disneyland was the best.

CHAPTER EIGHT:

The Woman Who Landscaped Disneyland: Ruth Patricia Shellhorn

In 1955, Ruth Shellhorn was a landscape architect working in South Pasadena when just three months before the opening of Disneyland, Walt Disney personally asked her to contribute her talents to his new theme park. She was responsible initially for Town Square, Main Street, and the Plaza Hub, and eventually was involved in the other lands as well.

Shellhorn studied landscape architecture at Oregon State University and then Cornell. She was hired by Bullock's department store chain in 1945 as consulting landscape architect for its Pasadena store, which had been designed by prominent Los Angeles architect Welton Becket.

Bullock's was so pleased with her work that the company hired her to design the landscaping at most of its future stores and manage the maintenance of the chain's landscaping, which she did through 1978.

Welton Becket was a good friend of Walt Disney. In fact, Walt sought Becket's input about the design of Disneyland. Becket, who worked with Shellhorn on several projects, recommended her to Walt, only a few months before Disneyland was to open in Anaheim.

Walt was looking for a liaison between chief landscape architects Jack and Bill Evans and the other designers.

Walt had five different art directors, and he was concerned that the five "lands" wouldn't blend together. Disney wanted Shellhorn to help integrate those disparate parts into a cohesive whole.

Shellhorn recalled:

I was sort of thinking it was going to be some honky-tonk like Venice [California] or something, and I wasn't too sure I wanted to do it.

But the famous Walt charm soon had her working non-stop on what was supposed to be a part-time consulting job in order to make the deadline for the park opening.

The art directors quickly approved her landscaping plan for Main Street, so she continued sketching landscaping designs for the Town Square just inside the main gate, the Plaza Hub at the center of the park, and finally the pedestrian traffic plan.

By using screens and plants compatible with differing styles of architecture, Shellhorn was able to ease the transition from the Victorian look of the Plaza to Western-themed Frontierland, as one example.

The engineering firm of J.S. Hamel was engaged by WED Enterprises to work with the Disneyland designers in solving the many engineering problems of Disneyland. They worked closely with Jack and Bill Evans.

This phase included the making of planting schedules and the development of the planting from designs, sketches, and models made at WED. It also included the design and supervision of the installation of the sprinkler system for the park.

The Evans brothers brought in Ray Miller and consultants Jesse D. Skoss, an agronomist, and Eric Armstrong, another landscape architect.

No steel framing was started at Disneyland until December 1954 and no facade work until January 1955, so it was difficult to introduce landscaping in the midst of the ever-changing construction.

In the April 1956 issue of *Landscape Architecture* magazine, Ruth Shellhorn told the rest of the story of her involvement:

> Even at the time of my introduction to the project in March 1955, there were no buildings started in Tomorrowland, just one in Frontierland, and only parts of the Main Street section and the castle were in evidence. After the master plan was finally set, the tempo of the project was increased. The pressure of work at the site and the selection of plant material left little time for Jack Evans to spend in conferences with the art directors at the studio.
>
> WED designers were tackling the problems of developing site plans for the various areas involving circulation, organization, tree placement, and planting. The plaza especially was presenting many problems, as from it radiated all five sections of the park. Many schemes had been advanced, but none had been selected, and time was growing short.
>
> It was at this stage of progress that I was engaged by WED to work with the art directors as consulting landscape architect until the opening of the park, and to act as liaison officer between the studio and the Evans organization at the site. I was asked to restudy and design the plaza area.

From this, the site planning of one section led to another until every part of the five lands involving pedestrian traffic was studied-as to circulation, paved and planted areas, tree placement, and in some cases as in the plaza, the outline of the water courses.

In some instances, as pressure increased, grades were even "eyeballed" in, on the ground. Changes were being made, even up until opening day, as new ideas were formed or new equipment for the park acquired. The ideas of Walt Disney himself continually bubbled as he spent more and more time at the site, and one had to be ready at a moment's notice to adjust, change, add or subtract some element. I doubt if this procedure could have been followed successfully on any other project on earth, but this was Disneyland and Walt's belief that the impossible was a simple order of the day so instilled this spirit in everyone that they never stopped to think that it couldn't be done—they just did it, and with amazing speed.

Walt Disney wanted a "green" park, everything evergreen, for he recalled the cold winters of his childhood when he used to look up at the bare branches of the trees and shiver. Disneyland must be eternal spring. He also wanted size in trees, the larger the better, so that the park would look cool and inviting. This was no small order, for there are relatively few evergreen trees of size which can be boxed successfully.

After talks with him about the necessity for some deciduous or partially deciduous materials for color and contrasts in foliage texture, we were permitted to introduce a few such trees as flowering peaches, crapemyrtles, jacarandas, and coral trees into the areas where they were most needed, providing they were "backed up" properly.

A change in Frontierland was necessitated when the acquisition of some wonderful old Conestoga wagons made the loading area more important. Shade from an overhead pole trellis and trees was desired in order to make watching more inviting. As this change occurred during the last weeks before opening, and since it involved utilities, paving, construction, and planting, there was no time to waste.

Plans had to be drawn almost overnight. The trees had to go in first, for among other things the overhead trellis was to be built around one of them. Finding tired, twisted, old frontier-type trees on a moment's notice wasn't easy, but Morgan Evans found them, and they were planted by working far into the night so as not to interfere with the other work that had to be done.

As the last days approached, and some 2500 workmen were working in ten-hour shifts, there were the camera and television towers to work around. In one case, a tree could not be planted for months due to the constant "progress shots" being taken of the castle.

There were the orientation classes for some 950 employees of Disneyland and the other 950 employees of the lessees. The shady areas of the plaza, planting operations notwithstanding, were wonderful places to hold them.

It was all a bit disconcerting. But again, this was Disneyland; and as Disneyland, such things seemed perfectly in order. Disneyland will never be finished as long as there is a Walt Disney to dream up new ideas. Even though the park will undergo many changes as the years go on and new ideas are developed, Disneyland will always be a place where the whole family will find a wealth of enjoyment.

It was unusual for a woman to have the responsibilities Shellhorn did in that era. She said, in 2001:

> If you go at it as a person, you're not a woman or a man. It doesn't make any difference. You have a problem to solve. So you cooperate and you work on that problem.

Because landscapes naturally change with time and developers alter plans, few of her many other designs for areas in Southern California remain intact today.

CHAPTER NINE

Dateline: Disneyland, July 17, 1955

On Friday July 15, 1955, the Los Angeles City Council in a colorful certificate proclaimed that day as "Disneyland Day" in honor of Walt's past achievements and to congratulate him on the creation of a "new era" of family entertainment with the opening of Disneyland. Unfortunately, the debut two days later was memorable for all the wrong reasons.

July 17, 1955, was forever known as "Black Sunday" in Disney history because of the disastrous press preview that day when the park opened without being fully operational. Van Arsdale France, founder of Disneyland University and author of the extensive cast member training program, noted:

> They planned for 11,000 people. Our official records indicate that there were 28,154 guests in the park that day, and I'm not one to tamper with somebody's estimates.

An accurate count of the number of people in the park was challenging since the turnstile clickers had not been turned on and some people climbed over a back fence to get inside. One reason for the sizeable increase was that a large number of tickets had been counterfeited and those who were invited brought more guests than expected.

Dateline: Disneyland was the largest live remote broadcast ever attempted up to that time. The press preview and dedication of Disneyland was aired on ABC-TV and over ninety of its affiliates starting at 4:30pm, Pacific Standard Time.

The ninety-minute special was hosted by Art Linkletter, Bob Cummings, and Ronald Reagan. On the East Coast, the show aired opposite *Private Secretary* (a sitcom starring Ann Sothern), *Studio 57* (an anthology show), and *Toast of the Town* (a variety show with musical star Ethel Merman substituting as host for a vacationing Ed Sullivan). In an interview conducted in 2000, Linkletter recalled:

I was a very close personal friend of Walt Disney, and he came to me and he said, "Art, this is a difficult moment for me, because I would like to ask you to be the master of ceremonies of the opening, and work with me, but I don't know how to approach you!"

I said, "What do you mean?" He said, "Well, you don't have an agent! Why don't you have an agent like everybody else I talk to?" And I said, "Well, Walt, you know me—I'm my own business man, I've always done it, never had an agent, and I make my own deals."

"Well," he said, "let me begin by telling you, as you know, we've had cost overruns, I've had to borrow money against my studio—I can't really afford to pay you what you're worth." And I said, "Walt, how about scale?" [Scale is the minimum payment established by the Screen Actors Guild for an actor to receive for certain work. In those days, for this assignment, it was roughly two hundred dollars.]

He said "Scale? A couple hundred bucks?" I said, "Yeah! This is a big community event—it's a national event—in fact it's a world event. And I'd like to be a part of it. And we're good friends."

And I said, "But on the other hand, I'm a businessman, and there's something you can do for me. I'd like to have the photographic concessions for ten years. All film and all cameras sold at Disneyland, and I'll pay your regular concession fee that you would get from anybody who has it." He said, "It's a deal!" And that's how I got the job.

Then he said "Art, suggest a couple more people. We need three or four of us to cover the whole grounds, jumping back and forth from one venue to the other." And so picked two of my very good friends that I thought were very good talkers and ad-libbers, and one of them was Bob Cummings, a wonderful comedian but also a marvelous speaker—and Ronald Reagan.

The four of us showed up with no rehearsal of course, we had kind of a rough working script—and it was all live. And I was perched in various places overlooking various parts of the park, and they were around and we'd hop and jump over.

On one occasion, Walt was going from one place to another, and he was going up an alley shortcut, and there was a guard there. He said, "You can't go through here." And Walt said to him, "Do you know who I am?" And the guard said "Yes, Mr. Disney, I do, but I have my orders—nobody can go through here." And Walt said, "Well, I'M going to go through here. If you get in the way, you know what's going to happen to you!" And he walked right by.

It was exciting. I had been doing the opening of World's Fairs for many years before that and a lot of special live events.

I was an ad-libber, so—chaos is made for me. Rehearsals are NOT made for me. There were times, of course, when there were a few little "boo-boos" made when somebody didn't show up someplace, and we had to do something else, but we covered it pretty well. I remember one time standing at the big steamboat with Irene Dunne and she called me "Walt"!

ABC had a lot of cameras! And since we didn't have any chance to rehearse, and we didn't have time to move cameras around because the park was so big, we just had to have that many.

They had arranged a monitor for me to look at, so I would know what the cameras were looking at, because they were somewhere else covering the parade from another angle. But by the time that the show was on in the late afternoon, the sun was shinning right into the monitor—so I couldn't see what the camera was covering!

So I'd say something like "now here comes Mickey Mouse", and they'd be on a band! And the director of course realized pretty soon that I couldn't follow the cameras, so the cameras had better follow me! So as I would talk about something, they would search it out.

And afterwards, we had a party and celebrated. That broadcast or parts of it have been shown so many times over the last several decades and it is always fun to watch. It was really a highlight of my career in broadcasting.

The three hosts were well known to television audiences and well liked.

Art Linkletter was host of the popular TV shows *Art Linkletter's House Party* with a feature devoted to "Kids Say the Darndest Things" and *People Are Funny* that used audience participation and contests. Linkletter's 43rd birthday was on July 17, 1955.

Bob Cummings was the star of *The Bob Cummings Show*, also known as *Love That Bob*, about a girl-chasing photographer, which is why there is the bit at the introduction in front of the Golden Horseshoe saloon of him kissing one of the pretty female dancers since the persona of his television character was that of a flirtatious playboy.

Ronald Reagan was host of *General Electric Theater* (an anthology series) and was starring in Western films like *Cattle Queen of Montana* (1954) and *Tennessee's Partner* (1955), which is why he introduced Frontierland.

Previously, the largest live remote broadcast had been telecast June 2, 1953, for the coronation of Queen Elizabeth II. Roughly twenty million people watched during the three-hour ceremony. The program used five cameras in the abbey, and 21 cameras deployed across 21 sites along the procession route. It was a smaller area with less activity to cover than the Disneyland event.

Despite its complexity, the coronation was a more informal broadcast relying on the principle that all that had to be done was point a camera at the event from the processional parade to the interior of the abbey. There were huge gaps of activity with no commentary, and close-ups of the queen were avoided by request.

The production of *Dateline: Disneyland* was more challenging, with more cameras, more locations, and more chaos, and over ninety million viewers.

Plans for filming the July 17 event began about two months earlier with an engineering survey to determine the necessary equipment needed for such an undertaking. As a result five separate control rooms were created with enough equipment for twelve TV stations, 85,000 feet of cable, and forty monitors. Equipment was borrowed from Chicago, New York, San Francisco, San Diego, Seattle, and other cities.

Twenty-nine cameras were used. ABC did not have enough, so four were borrowed from NBC, two from CBS, two from KTTV, and two from KCOP, among other stations including the local KABC outlet. Twelve Zoomar lenses were used, allowing the cameraman to go from a wide shot to a close-up and vice-versa with relative ease.

Thirteen hydraulic fork lifts were equipped with special camera platforms in the front so that filming could take place over the heads of the crowds and other obstacles, as well as making the cameras more mobile. Some of the fork lifts sunk into the freshly laid asphalt.

Because Anaheim was experiencing a heat wave, the cameras would overheat and lose picture. This problem was solved by holding a basket of dry ice under the blower of each camera.

For the Disneyland broadcast, the cameras were massive, and not always reliable or manageable. Camera operators were attired in red-and-white candy-striped shirts so that they would be instantly recognizable in the serpentine mess of heavy cables.

A sixty-foot tall tower was built in the Hub. A metal cage welded on a platform to hold a camera was hoisted into the air on a one-hundred-and-ten-foot tall crane to get shots of Tomorrowland.

The production included seven directors (including John Rich and Stuart Phelps), five assistant directors, and twelve stage managers. ABC hired eighty crowd control people to keep guests away from the cameras and other equipment. The coordinating producer, Sherman Marks, was resented by the other directors because he did not respect their authority or share information with them.

Musical Director Walter Schumann was in charge of eighty-two music cues. During the final days of rehearsal in the park, he suffered a heart attack and was not replaced. He watched the show on TV from his hospital bed.

The interest in the opening was so great that by the end of March, ABC had sold all the advertising slots, which is one of the reasons that Walt was locked into the July 17 date.

Every Sunday, beginning on May 12, ABC crews rehearsed. However, rehearsals were constantly interrupted by workmen, material, and trucks passing through in a rush to complete the park.

Adjustments had to be made. After one rehearsal to establish where the camera would be placed for a shot, the following day saw a fence and part of a building erected in the space that had been allocated for it. Another time, a mature tree had sprung up in a previously assigned camera spot.

ABC had taken out $40,000 worth of full-page newspaper advertisements to publicize the live telecast.

When looking at publicity photos from July 17, the ones where Walt Disney was not wearing a tie are from rehearsals. The photographs of Walt wearing a tie are from the actual broadcast.

Earlier in the week, Walt had asked his wife, Lillian, and his two daughters to stay home. He told them that he "didn't want any of you women out there. It's going to be a mess and I don't want to have to worry about you, too!"

Fresh asphalt trucked up from San Diego was laid on Main Street just after dawn and was still so soft that women's high heels sunk into it and they had to step out of their shoes.

The Opening

The live television coverage began with local television personality Hank Weaver seated behind a manual typewriter supposedly in the Disneyland "press office which is equipped to serve over one thousand members of the working press", but looked suspiciously like a small, hastily furnished set posing as the press office. He said to the camera:

> For the past year, this signature (music of "When You Wish Upon a Star") has announced the opening of Disneyland, the show. Now, it announces the opening of Disneyland, the place.
>
> The people and eyes around the world are focused on these one-hundred-and-sixty acres here in Anaheim, California. This afternoon, Disneyland, the world's most fabulous kingdom, will be unveiled before an invitation world premiere, and you our guests. Art Linkletter will be your host, and with ABC crews and cameras, he will guide you through this truly magic land.

On July 11, 1955, just six days before the park opened, Joe Fowler sent a memo to Jack Evans: "When are you going to plant Mickey Mouse at the entrance? Looks to me like the time is getting pretty late." The image then cut away to the floral Mickey Mouse head at the front of the park. This would become the most photographed location at Disneyland. Bill Evans told me:

> It was Walt's idea. Just like the face [on the title card] before every [theatrical] Mickey Mouse cartoon and audiences would start cheering.

The camera then moved to Art Linkletter standing on the Main Street railroad platform awaiting the arrival of Walt Disney who was steaming the *E.P. Ripley* passenger locomotive to the Main Street station.

The *Ripley* was named after Edward Payson Ripley (1845–1920), the first president of the Atchison, Topeka & Santa Fe Railway in 1895. E.P. Ripley's son, grandson, and great grandson were part of the opening day ceremony. The *C.K. Holliday*, named after Cyrus Kurtz Holliday (1826–1900) who founded the Atchison & Topeka Railroad in 1859, pulled freight cars disembarking from only the Frontierland station. The Santa Fe & Disneyland Railroad provided an uninterrupted ride around the entire park to help familiarize guests with its layout. The trains ran on parallel tracks.

Accompanying Walt in the cabin were Goodwin Knight, governor of California; Fred Gurley, president of the Santa Fe Railroad; and a large stuffed Mickey Mouse doll hanging out the front window garbed as a train engineer that Walt manipulated from behind so it looked like Mickey was waving. Also on the train, as Linkletter informed the audience, were "the little boys and girls dressed in the foreign costumes of their countries because they are the children of the foreign consuls located here in Los Angeles".

Linkletter continued:

> This job for the next hour-and-a-half will be a delight. I feel like Santa Claus with a $17 million bundle of gifts all wrapped in whimsy and sent your way over television with the help of 29 cameras, dozens of crews and literally miles and miles of cable. Now of course this is not so much a show as it is a special event.
>
> The rehearsal went about the way you would expect a rehearsal to go if you were covering three volcanoes all erupting at the same time and you didn't expect any of them! So from time to time if I say we take you now by camera to the snapping crocodiles in Adventureland and instead someone pushes the wrong button and we catch [movie actress] Irene Dunne adjusting her bustle, don't be too surprised.

After quickly introducing his two co-hosts before sending them off to their locations in the park, Linkletter briefly mentioned the helicopter port. Its pad was located just outside of Tomorrowland.

Walt, Goodwin Knight, and Fred Gurley barreled into the station just in time for a commercial break so they could relocate to the Main Street Town Square.

The Dedication

Reading from notes, Ronald Reagan said:

> All activity on Main Street has ceased. And now Walt Disney will step forward to read the dedication of Disneyland.

There were cheers and applause as a smiling Walt stepped up to the microphone:

> To all who come to this happy place: welcome. Disneyland is your land. Here, age relives fond memories of the past, and here youth may savor the challenge and promise of the future. Disneyland is dedicated to the ideals, the dreams, and the hard facts that have created America, with the hope that it will be a source of joy and inspiration to all the world. Thank you.

That short dedication speech had been written by Winston Hibler who at the time was best known for writing and narrating the *True-Life Adventures* film series, although he made many other varied contributions to Walt Disney Productions.

Reverend Glenn Darrel Puder then stepped up to the microphone to give the invocation. Puder was born November 10, 1911, and died over a hundred years later, on December 19, 2011. He held an honorary doctorate in divinity from Occidental College where he met his future wife, Dorothy, who was Walt Disney's niece. She was the only daughter of Walt's older brother Herbert.

They married on June 10, 1937, and were together for seventy years. The young pastor and his wife served at Immanuel Presbyterian Church in Los Angeles and moved in 1953 to Bakersfield where he ministered at the First Presbyterian Church of Bakersfield. He was also the chaplain for the police department and the memorial hospital.

There had been some concern because he was due to fly in early on July 17 and then be driven to Anaheim. In his book *Window on Main Street* (Theme Park Press, 2015), Van France recalled:

> We worried that he would get tied up in traffic, and not make it in time for the ceremonies. The captain of the Anaheim Police Department was an enthusiastic participant in the preparation and was undaunted by this possible problem. "Don't you worry," he told me. "I'll get him there if I have to bring him on my motorcycle." That extreme measure wasn't necessary, however, because he arrived by car with time to spare.

Puder stood alongside chaplains of the three major American religions at that time: Cardinal James McIntyre (Catholic), Rabbi Edgar Magnin (Jewish), Bishop Francis Eric Bloy (Episcopalian), Bishop Gerald Kennedy (Methodist), and Dr. Carroll Shuster (Presbyterian).

In addition, Walt had invitations sent to editors from eight different religious newspapers (Catholic, Jewish, and Protestant) as well as to nearby churches, including ten Baptist, nine Methodist, eight Catholic, eight Lutheran, seven Christian, six Church of Christ, six Episcopalian, six Presbyterian, five Free Methodist, two Congregational, one Nazarene, and one Jewish synagogue.

Puder stated:

> I have known Walt Disney for many years, and have long been aware of the spiritual motivation in the heart of this man who has dreamed Disneyland

into being. Let us join with him then in dedicating these wonder-filled acres to those things dear to his heart and ours...to understanding and good will among men, laughter for children, memories for the mature and aspiration for young people everywhere.

And beyond the creeds that would divide us, let us unite in a silent prayer that this, and every worthy endeavor, may prosper at God's hand. Let us bow in prayer. [silence] Amen.

Next, Goodwin Knight, the 31st governor of California (1953–1959), and a good Republican, strode to the microphone:

Mr. and Mrs. Disney, reverend clergy, and my fellow Americans. Today is a wonderful day and all America is proud as we open Disneyland. This is a wondrous community with all the charm of the old world and all of the progress and ingenuity of the new world.

Yes, this is a wonderful place for children and grown-ups alike. There are replicas of every town and city in America...stores, libraries, schools, just like your hometown, all built by American labor and American capital under the belief that this is a God-fearing and a God-loving country.

And as we dedicate the flag now, we do it with the knowledge that we are the fortunate ones to be Americans and that we extend to everyone everywhere the great ideals of Americanism, brotherhood, and peace on earth, goodwill towards all men.

The flag was raised by members from the four branches of the U.S. armed services while the Disneyland Band under the direction of Vesey Walker played the "Star Spangled Banner", followed by a flyover by the 146th Fighter Inceptor Wing of the Air National Guard as a tribute to Governor Knight.

Also in attendance was Republican James B. Utt of California who had read into the Congressional Record on June 27, 1955, the announcement of the opening of Disneyland during the first session of the 84th House of Representatives. It was entitled "Disneyland Readied by Mr. Magic".

Other politicians besides California Governor Goodwin J. Knight enjoying that day were California Lieutenant Governor Harold J. Powers, Secretary of State Frank M. Jordan, Anaheim Mayor Charles Pearson (as well as the mayors and councilmen of all Orange County cities), Mayor Norris Poulson of Los Angeles, Mayor George Vermilion of Long Beach, and California Senator Thomas Kuchel. Members of the Chambers of Commerce of Los Angeles, Long Beach, and Anaheim were present as well.

The Parade

A color guard with servicemen from the four branches led the United States Marine Band down Main Street. Walt hopped into an old-fashioned 1903 Pierce automobile with Governor Knight and Knight's wife, Virginia, as the grand marshals.

From atop the second floor of the Kodak Camera Shop, Linkletter announced the parade, but the afternoon glare on his monitor prevented him from accurately matching his commentary with what the camera was showing. As he eloquently described Cinderella in her coach followed by Prince Charming on horseback carrying the glass slipper, the image the audience saw at home was Fess Parker and Buddy Ebsen attired as their Davy Crockett characters riding on horses down the street.

Behind the marching band and Walt's car, the parade was divided into sections representing the lands of the park. The first group represented Fantasyland. Linkletter said:

> Dumbo, Pluto, and Donald Duck and all the other characters are from the Walt Disney costumes created for John Harris' Ice Capades, which is on tour with *Peter Pan* right now around the United States.

Actually, *Peter Pan* was scheduled to premiere for the 1956 season, and the Ice Capades did not feature any Disney number in its 1955 show, which may be why the costumes were available for Walt Disney to borrow them for the broadcast.

In 1949, the Ice Capades, a touring ice-skating show produced by John H. Harris, partnered with the Disney Studio to feature a lengthy segment in each year's show with Disney characters. The first show featured Snow White and the Seven Dwarfs, who appeared on the back of the program book. The partnership lasted through 1966.

The Disney character costumes were designed to provide flexibility for the skater and so they followed the contours of the person's body and not necessarily the proportions of the animated character. In the business, these are known as "pajama" costumes since they are reminiscent of footie pajamas for children.

In addition, the costumes had to be designed to allow the greatest visibility, which explains the horrid teeth on Mickey Mouse since the mesh between his spiky chompers was necessary for peripheral vision, and a face peering out of the mesh on Donald Duck's neck was more than disconcerting.

These costumes were meant, like most theatrical costumes, to be viewed briefly at a distance under proper lighting in an arena setting, not inspected up close by a Disneyland guest. However, Disney guests loved the walkaround characters and their imagination must have clouded their actual visual appearance.

Linkletter seemed a bit confused about the Mouseketeers walking down Main Street, as was the audience at home, since *The Mickey Mouse Club* would not debut on ABC until October 3, 1955. With some help from his son Jack, Linkletter described them as "the performing children who are going to be on the Disneyland Mickey Mouse Club".

This appearance is considered their official television debut. They also appeared on local television shows and events from July through the end of September.

The next group was Frontierland with Parker and Ebsen dressed as their characters Davy Crockett and Georgie Russel from the popular Disneyland television show, riding horses and waving at the crowd.

Tennessee Governor Frank Clement was riding in a Conestoga wagon because the real Davy Crockett was born and raised in that state. A group of square dancers performed on another horse-drawn wagon.

Also riding on a horse was actress Gail Davis in her persona as Annie Oakley. Davis starred in a TV show of the same name that ran from January 1954 through February 1957 and was produced by Gene Autry. Carnation, which operated a shop on Main Street, was a major sponsor for the television show, and Davis did live commercials for that company.

Some of the Indian dancers were coordinated by the Orange Empire Council of the Boy Scouts of America. Comedian Danny Thomas and his family rode in a buckboard.

Included in the Frontierland contingent were several Revolutionary War soldiers described as America's Minute Men, but attired in British uniforms rented from Western Costume.

Adventureland was represented by a half-dozen drummers wearing feathered head dresses, and the Tomorrowland group was led by a costumed spaceman followed by the fleet of Autopia cars.

In my interview with retired Disney Imagineer Bob Gurr in 1990, he recalled:

> Walt had a beautiful, famous redheaded movie star [Gale Storm, who then was appearing in the popular TV series *My Little Margie*] and her young boys [Peter and Paul] with him as the parade was about to start. Since she wanted to tag along with Walt, he told her Bob Gurr would be delighted to babysit the boys for her!
>
> We had a large number of untried Autopia cars in the parade which constantly stopped with fuel vapor lock. They were restarted by hard stomps on a kick starter, and my legs were becoming cramped in the 100-degree heat. All I needed was some little kids to watch. They loved the parade view from inside the cars as their mommy waved back.
>
> Later, her sons had to ride with me in one of the two police cars that were supposed to pace guests in the regular Autopia cars. Their idea of pacing was to get me to chase their mother's show biz friends with red light and siren. "Git him!" they hollered as we pursued a short man wearing an eye patch. We hit him and he went over the curb onto the grass, giving us a startled look. The next morning's paper had photos of the famous guests, and sure enough—it was Sammy Davis Jr.

I didn't see her until very late after dark when she finally came back to Autopia to collect her kids. If she only knew what a wild day we had!

The final group, the Firehouse Five Plus Two band, had been hanging out in front of the firehouse in Town Square. Disney animator (and band member) Frank Thomas remembers leaning back in a chair outside the building reading a copy of the *Policeman's Gazette* and when it was time to get up the asphalt had hardened and the chair was frozen in a tilt. The leader of the band, Disney animator, Ward Kimball, had supplied his collection of vintage architecture books to be used in the design of Main Street buildings.

At the Hub, the groups divided to go to their separate lands as Bob Cummings addressed the audience about how proud he was to be at the opening of Disneyland.

Frontierland

Walt read the dedication plaque for Frontierland followed by Ronald Reagan describing the stockade entrance and the frontier village behind the gates "that could have been carved out of the wilderness a hundred years ago" as the parade group entered the land.

The camera shifted to Art Linkletter and his family just beyond the sheriff's office awaiting the arrival of Davy Crockett who would come from the direction of the Painted Desert.

Imagineer Randy Bright recalled:

> At the sound of an ill-timed gunshot, Davy Crockett [played by Fess Parker] rode his horse through Bill Evans' newly planted pine forests. A television director gave a wrong cue to a gardener, who turned on the sprinklers just as Parker and his sidekick, Buddy Ebsen, arrived.
>
> Still mounted, an exasperated, soaked, and lost Parker later confronted Marty Sklar. "Help me get out of here," he pleaded, "before this horse kills somebody!"

The purpose of the sprinklers was to lightly soak the dry dust so that it wouldn't cloud up in the air and spoil the shot as the horsemen rode in.

Earlier that morning, a magazine reporter wanted a picture of Fess Parker carrying Crockett's famous rifle, Old Betsy, at a bridge in Frontierland. It was discovered that Disney had forgotten to bring the important prop from the studio. This was a major problem, since there was a big dance number staged to the song "Bang! Goes Old Betsy" written by lyricist Gil George (the pseudonym for Disney Studio nurse Hazel George) and musician George Bruns that was to prominently feature the rifle.

Buddy Ebsen's friend Walter Knott, owner of Knott's Berry Farm, had a display of antique firearms at his park. After Ebsen made a quick phone call, a rifle from Knott's collection was on its way to Disneyland, with a police escort to get through the traffic and protect the valuable artifact.

Miriam Nelson, who choreographed that dance number, also had rifle problems, since they were not ready for rehearsals. She substituted wooden dowels for the inventive dance moves that included the female dancers stepping on the rifles and being flipped over, among other things. When the actual rifles arrived just in time for the performance, they were not as sturdy as the dowels and several of them broke during the lively dance number.

It was so hot during rehearsals that the female dancers wore shorts, t-shirts, and sometimes halter tops. Nelson soon received a personal note from Walt asking her to have the dancers cover up because they were distracting the workmen who needed to concentrate on getting everything ready for the opening.

The next sequence was Bob Cummings talking about the Golden Horseshoe Revue, followed by the christening of the *Mark Twain* Riverboat with Linkletter and actress Irene Dunne.

Walt had asked Dunne to christen the ship because she had starred in the film *Showboat* (1936) about a young woman who lived on a paddlewheel boat with her family that traveled the Mississippi River. She also had relatives who were connected to American steamboats. Dunne told Linkletter:

> This is an authentic sternwheeler. 105 feet long. My father used to be supervising general of steamships in America and my grandfather used to build boats like this. This bottle contains waters from all the leading rivers in America. With these precious waters, I am going to christen this boat...the *Mark Twain*.

The boat was listing because Disney had not yet established the proper ride capacity and often overloaded the *Mark Twain*. In addition, the passengers would crowd on different sides of the boat, resulting in it tipping and water spilling onto the lower deck.

As former 1955 Disneyland cast member Terry O'Brien finally admitted in 2005, he was the one responsible for finally sinking the *Mark Twain* on July 17. One of O'Brien's first assignments was to tend the "holding pen" for the *Twain*, the area where people waited to board the boat. He recalled:

> They gave me a clicker and told me to let people in until the pen was full. The boat would come in and let one group off and we'd put the other group on. No one was sure just how many people would fit, so they said to try and keep it between 200 to 300.

After a few times, it got kind of boring, so O'Brien started talking to the people and the other workers as he clicked people into the pen, not paying much attention to how many there were. The boat came in, and the next group got on. "Pretty soon, we heard the toot-toot signal that meant disaster. And everyone wondered what had happened." What had happened was that the boat, which actually made its way around the river on a rail, had sunk off the track and into the mud. There were too many people on board.

O'Brien continued:

> It took about 20 to 30 minutes to get it fixed and back on the rail and it came chugging in. As soon as it pulled up to the landing, all the people rushed to the side to get off, and the boat tipped into the water again, so they all had to wade off through the water, and some of them were pretty mad.

O'Brien recalled that his boss came to ask him how many people he'd put on the boat:

> "About 250," I said. And he said, "Well, better keep it at about 200." Then I remembered I had the clicker in my pocket. I looked and was shocked to see I'd put 508 people on the boat. I never told anyone until now. Now, I figure, what can they do to me? They can't fire me.

As the ship left from the dock, Reagan talked about New Orleans where such ships were common. Cummings then talked about the area at the end of Frontierland that was supposed to represent New Orleans. Another performance by the dancers also included the Firehouse Five Plus Two and a little black tap dancing boy. Even Aunt Jemima (Aylene Lewis), who would be the hostess of the nearby Aunt Jemima Pancake House, briefly joined in the fun in trying to capture the spirit of Mardi Gras.

Other problems abounded. Just before the filming started, choreographer Nelson was told that her male dancers could not slide down the poles as they had rehearsed because the poles had just been painted and were wet. An area on the ground for part of the dance number was filled with guests who had to be quickly moved out of the way. The little black boy had wandered off to stare at the *Mark Twain* and play with his hand in the water and had to be corralled back to the location.

Tomorrowland

The *C.K. Holiday* freight train leaving the station on its way to Tomorrowland sparked the transition to Walt reading the dedication of that land, after first getting the wrong cue, and the first park release of dozens of pigeons, an idea conceived by entertainment director Tommy Walker.

Author Bob Thomas remembered:

> About ten days before the opening, the pigeons would be released halfway between Los Angeles and Disneyland. Thus, the birds could familiarize themselves with half of the route home. When the pigeon owners assembled at the halfway point early one morning, Walt was there. He interrogated the owners about the birds' habits, and later he developed a television feature about pigeon racing.

The Pigeon That Worked a Miracle aired October 10, 1958, on the weekly *Disneyland* show and was later released theatrically overseas in 1962.

Bob Cummings said that "those doves are, I hope, the harbingers of peace for the world of tomorrow" as they flew in front of the Clock of the World. Tomorrowland was meant to represent an era thirty years in the future: 1986. The date was selected partly to commemorate the return of Halley's Comet. Cummings explained to the audience:

> Tomorrowland is not a stylized dream of the future but a scientifically planned projection of future techniques by leading space experts and scientists.

Walt's friend, actor George Murphy, who would later become a U.S. Senator, was at the star-shaped Court of Flags where proudly flew the flags of all forty-eight states at the time. The flags were raised by Eagle Scouts who did so because they were "the citizens of the future. The world of tomorrow belongs to them."

In the Kaiser Aluminum Hall of Fame in front of a gigantic forty-foot long aluminum telescope, Cummings talked with Dr. Heinz Haber and a group of children. Haber was a German physicist and science author who had appeared on the *Disneyland* TV show episode "Man in Space" (March 1955) and consulted on other installments. He demonstrated how atomic energy was the result of a chain reaction where one neutron would set off the others by using ping pong balls and over a hundred mousetraps, a visual that didn't initially work as planned but did on the second attempt and was later re-created on a *Disneyland* episode "Our Friend the Atom" (January 1957).

Haber ended by saying to young people that this was "an important part of your future: the power of the atom. When you grow up, be certain that you use it wisely."

Linkletter was at the Autopia greeting celebrity guests like Frank Sinatra and his son, Sammy Davis Jr., Don DeFore, Jeanne Crain, Gale Storm, and others.

As Imagineer Bob Gurr told me in 1990:

> So many opening day guests were in a frenzy to ride every attraction that they just went nuts. As the number of available Autopia cars dwindled due to mechanical breakage, guests jumped over the railings and ran up the track. They stopped the returning cars, pulled the occupants out, and drove off right past the ride entrance.
>
> It was possible to spin out the Autopia cars and reverse the direction of the ride. Several super head-on collisions took place while the ride operators were trying to hold back the crowd at the gate. One crash injured two little boys. They came over to me, one of them holding his knocked out teeth carefully in his hands for me to see. As I was escorting them both to the

City Hall first aid, they began to cry. They thought they would not be able to come back and finish their Autopia ride.

Starting out with 40 Autopia vehicles, two of which were police cars and one on display as "'Walt's Car", left 37 for guests. Mechanical failures happened faster than we could fix them. Since all the mechanics were repairing other attractions, which were vitally needed, I pitched in with my own tools to help the lone repairman. Shortly we were down to just two running cars. All the rest were hopelessly wrecked.

Reagan briefly interviewed television producer Jack Wrather and his wife Bonita Granville about their building of a Disneyland hotel across the street while they were standing by the short-lived Tomorrowland Boats attraction.

Because of numerous challenges, including labor strikes and material shortages, the Disneyland Hotel didn't open for business until October 5, 1955, with only seven rooms available for paying customers. On August 25, 1956, the hotel had its official grand opening. The ground-breaking ceremony had been held over a year earlier, on March 18, 1955, at 11:15 a.m.

Linkletter stood in front of the Rocket to the Moon ride entrance with comedian Danny Thomas and "Captain Barton", an actor who had filmed the pre-show segment for the attraction as the head of the command center. The 7x5-inch color certificate given to young Disneyland park guests who experienced the trip to the moon on spaceship *The Star of Polaris* had a place for the signature of TWA Rocket Ship Captain P.J. Collins.

Unfortunately, the attraction was not operating for the broadcast, as Imagineer John Hench recalled:

> We didn't get the ride ready for opening day because some disgruntled electrican sabotaged the electrical work. The control mechanisms in there had to be rewired. On opening day we had to show the filmed portions of the ride on television. It took us about four days [July 22] to get the rocket ride open.

Fantasyland

Once again, Walt read the dedication of the land, after which sixteen costumed medieval performers gathered in front of the drawbridge and a black knight rode up on horseback as a pre-recorded message blared "Open the Fantasyland Castle in the name of the children of the world!" in the deep bass voice of Thurl Ravenscroft, who had done voice-over work for Disney animated films.

Choreographer Miriam Nelson recalled:

> Each [costumed Disney] character was given a specific direction to lead the children to specific rides. The characters couldn't believe their eyes when as they rushed through the gate, there were hundreds of screaming

children. So instead of beckoning the children, the children chased the Disney characters.

Approximately 500 children transported on fourteen steamy-from-the-heat school buses from Anaheim church schools like Grace Lutheran rushed inside. The children were chosen based on their Sunday School attendance. Nine-year-old Bonnie Williams remembered:

> I remember seeing Walt. He looked like a giant. I told him, "I saw you on TV!" The whole day was magical. I felt like a real princess. My favorite rides on opening day were Peter Pan and Dumbo. To this day, I ride them. I continue to love Disneyland. A special piece of my heart is here.

Larry Larsen was also nine years old:

> To me an amusement park was a Ferris wheel and a merry-go-round. Beyond that, I couldn't fathom. When we saw the castle it was literally like walking into a movie. It was unbelievable. I was in awe of the whole thing. I didn't know the word "surreal" then, but that's what it was.

After the children enjoyed some of the Fantasyland attractions for the camera, they were given a box lunch and then it was back on the busses.

Snow White, Alice in Wonderland holding a mirror (a reference to her looking glass), Sleeping Beauty, and Peter Pan (played by a mature woman, as was the tradition) awaken in the courtyard as the Blue Fairy from *Pinocchio* (1940) appeared to bless this land of fantasy.

Children were loaded onto King Arthur's Carrousel and the Mad Tea Party spinning teacups behind the carousel. Throughout this segment only the exteriors of the dark rides were shown, with never a glimpse of the interiors.

Linkletter was outside Peter Pan's Flight (which actor Alan Young rode with Captain Hook). Bob Cummings helped open the Snow White attraction. While it looked like the Casey Junior Circus Train was fully operational (with comedian Jerry Colonna as guest engineer) when Linkletter sang its praises, it was not, and wouldn't open until July 31, 1955, since it had a tendency to tip over as it went up a small hill.

Next, Bob Cummings was on the Chicken of the Sea Pirate Ship with young actor Bobby Driscoll who had appeared in the pirate-themed Disney live-action film *Treasure Island* (1950). Only the side of the ship facing the cameras was finished; it did not open to guests until August 29, 1955.

From his perch on the pirate ship, Cummings announced the arrival of the costumed Mickey and Minnie Mouse who were running to the Mickey Mouse Theater for a performance by the Mouseketeers. He described them as "a group of talented boys and girls who will be on *The Mickey Mouse Club* show this fall, October 3. And I guarantee you that many a future star will be coming out of this group."

Dressed in their Talent Roundup Day attire and along with adult leaders Jimmie Dodd and Roy Williams, the Mouseketeers sang and danced with the only roll call of all the Mouseketeers.

Adventureland

Adventureland only had one ride and several shops, so it was quickly squeezed into a brief final segment at the end featuring a pre-recorded "B" roll of the Jungle Cruise attraction. Bob Cummings stated

> We are now at the beginning of a true-life adventure into a still unconquered and untamed region of our own world.

Closing

After one final commercial break, the cameras return to Art Linkletter standing in front of Sleeping Beauty Castle with Walt Disney. Linkletter says, "Walt, you've made a bum out of [P.T.] Barnum today."

Walt laughs and responds, "I know, but I just want to say a word of thanks to all the artists, the workers, and everybody that helped make this dream come true."

Linkletter then concludes the show: "Let's go into Fantasyland and have some fun. Good-bye folks!" He and a happy Walt turn their backs to the camera and walk across the drawbridge.

Approximately ninety million people, over half the population of the United States at the time, watched the program on TV. ABC produced a short documentary on the making of the production, called *Operation Disneyland*, its title inspired by *Operation Undersea*, the award-winning 1954 Disneyland television show that looked at the making of the movie *20,000 Leagues Under the Sea*.

This roughly fourteen-minute black-and-white documentary was not meant to be seen by the general public, but rather as a special closed-circuit broadcast for over ninety ABC-TV affiliates to laud the ingenuity of the network in handling the *Dateline: Disneyland* show.

It was produced by Dick Brown and narrated by John Fell. Brown, in 1956, operated Cambria Studios with his wife, Margaret Kerry, the live-action reference model for Tinker Bell in *Peter Pan* (1953). They produced animated TV series like *Clutch Cargo* and *Space Angel*.

In 2003, Margaret Kerry told me:

> My husband and I were there working at Disneyland on opening day and I was quite pregnant, a couple of weeks from giving birth to our second child. We were filming a behind-the-scenes documentary of what was going on.
>
> It was a groundbreaking undertaking with miles of TV and sound cables strung throughout the park. ABC did not have enough TV cameras and borrowed many from other local TV stations which is why there is confusion

about how many cameras were actually used. I don't think anyone actually knows. Logistics were made even more difficult because there was no precedent to follow.

The day was hot and chaotic. Dick [Brown, my husband] handled the problems of moving the clumsy TV cameras, sound equipment, cables and some forklifts through the few clogged streets in Disneyland. The cables had to be physically lifted over the top of each heavy truck to allow it to pass. The forklifts were placed in particular areas to be used like camera cranes for overhead shots. It was so exhausting that he slept for about two days straight after the opening. Dick was the one who came up with the idea of having cameras on forklifts so you could get shots over the heads of the crowd.

According to an article in the July 18, 1955, edition of the *Hollywood Reporter* trade newspaper:

> To take in all the rides and attractions, priced at 15 to 50 cents, it would cost an adult $8.70 and a juvenile $5.15; and it is doubtful that all the amusements could be covered on a single visit since it is necessary to walk nearly a mile and a half to take in all the "lands" of Disneyland.
>
> Eating facilities, with 20 restaurants and snack bars spotted all over the lot, can serve 8000 hourly and are designed to accommodate 15,000 visitors daily and a peak of 60,000 on special days. Employees number over 1000.
>
> No doubt stimulated by the expected success of the venture, Walt Disney stock hit another new high on Friday at 58 bid and 62 asked, while the stock of its partner in the enterprise, American Broadcasting-Paramount Theaters, also soared to a new all-time high of $32^{5/8}$, leading all issues on the stock exchange in the day's activity, with a turnover of 46,200 shares.

CHAPTER TEN

Disneyland's First Snow White

JoAnn Dean Killingsworth passed away at the age of 91 of cancer in Brea, California, on June 20, 2015, less than one month before the beginning of the official 60th Diamond Disneyland celebration. She had portrayed the character of Snow White on the *Dateline: Disneyland* ABC-TV special that aired on Sunday, July 17, 1955, to debut the new theme park.

In 1955, Killingsworth, then 31, was hired by Gene Nelson's wife, Miriam, the choreographer for the dancers on the ABC show. Since 1940, Killingsworth had often performed with actor, dancer, and director Gene Nelson in various roles, and was his skating partner in the theatrical ice spectaculars *Hollywood Ice Revue* and *It Happens on Ice*. Miriam recalled:

> I thought JoAnn looked like Disney's Snow White, with her dark bangs She was very enthusiastic, bubbly, and always in good spirits. I knew she'd do a good job.

Killingsworth worked as a professional figure skater and dancer and appeared in nearly a hundred Hollywood films. She didn't remember them all, but the list included *Something for the Boys* (1944), Rodgers and Hammerstein's *State Fair* (1945), Roy Rogers' *Rainbow Over Texas* (1946), Doris Day and Gene Nelson's *Lullaby of Broadway* (1951), where she also appears on the film poster next to Day, and in Rosemary Clooney's *Red Garters*, *Sabrina* and *Nob Hill* (1954).

In Judy Garland's *A Star Is Born* (1954), she stood in for Garland, performing all her songs and dances at the technical rehearsals. She also did some print modeling and advertisements, including one for Chesterfield cigarettes, and from 1953 to 1956, she was a "Redette", one of the dancers on *The Red Skelton Show*.

To mark the milestone 50th anniversary of *Snow White and the Seven Dwarfs* (1937), Disney decided to hold a reunion on Friday, June 5, 1987, of the performers who had portrayed Snow White at the parks. In particular, they wanted to find the performer who was Snow White for Disneyland's opening day ceremonies on July 17, 1955. Snow White rode on a float and later in the televised special she appeared in Fantasyland to inaugurate her dark ride.

No one at the park could match a name to the face in the photos of the opening day parade. Killingsworth's name wasn't in the Disney personnel records, but a friend of hers who heard about the search called the park with the tip that she was in Newport Beach. Killingsworth said:

> I worked for ABC, not Disneyland, so there was no record of me in the park. I didn't know they were hunting for me until a friend read about it in the paper and told me. I really didn't realize Disney was looking for me. If I had I would have called somebody and said, "Here I am. Here's Snow White!" I was living within fifteen miles of Disneyland, working at Neiman-Marcus, and doing some golfing and painting. I was taking some tap dancing lessons.
>
> I had dinner with some people from Disney public relations who told me they weren't actually looking for the first Snow White but some over-eager reporter had written a story that they were and it had gotten national publicity. So when I contacted them, they were excited that they could take advantage of the publicity and announce they had found me.

Two things Killingsworth told me that I have never been able to confirm and probably never will is that because of her extensive theatrical experience, she was also tapped by Nelson to be that surprised young lady kissed by host Bob Cummings in front of the Golden Horseshoe Revue and the feisty little dancer who grabbed Davy Crockett's Old Betsy during that musical number.

She certainly had plenty of time to change into a Frontierland dancer's outfit after the parade and then change back to Snow White before the dedication of Fantasyland, especially since the dressing room was in that area. There were also dressers to help the dancers. In addition, the dancers in those segments do look like her. Here is a short interview I did with JoAnn Killingsworth in 1995:

> It was a different world back then. Of course, I was impressed seeing some of the stars, but it was just a work day. We all did the best job we could do and then went home like any other job. I often spent the evenings roller skating along Hollywood Boulevard.
>
> I adored Gene and we worked well together. He and Miriam knew about the work I was doing and that I was reliable and hard working and never caused trouble, so it was no surprise when she called me with a job offer.
>
> I was five foot three and brunette. I guess they wanted smaller girls because my girlfriends were in the dwarfs' costumes on the float and they were small as well.

We rehearsed for about a month at the ABC Studios on Sunset, and then about another week at Disneyland. In the last three days we worked furiously, as they were rushing to complete the park. We danced over the gardeners planting flowers under our feet.

We couldn't believe this place, all the pastel paints and flowers. It was quite unbelievable back then and still is. We wondered where Anaheim was back then. There was a lot of wondering: "Why Anaheim?" It was the boonies then. We traveled through bean fields to get here. What was surprising is I had no idea what Disneyland was and no idea where Anaheim was. I never watched ABC, either. All of that is funny now, looking back on it.

We all traveled to Disneyland on a bus and were given box lunches. It was all so pretty with pinks, blues, and yellow and these cute little shops. We were all sure they would never be able to maintain it. One day, we got a special treat. We were volunteered to spend a half a day riding the carousel while the engineers tried to balance it properly.

Regrettably, I never got to meet Walt Disney personally. Things were just too rushed and he was running around everywhere. I did see a lot of him. He helicoptered in all the time and while we were rehearsing, everyone always looked up and said, "Oh, there's Walt!"

I later heard he got a pretty good look at me. He wanted to see what I looked like through the camera during a rehearsal. Sometimes someone looks good in person, but on camera it is a different thing entirely. Fortunately, cameras seemed to love me.

Still, I was worried for a minute, because Snow White was his favorite and he was very particular. But he gave me the OK.

Basically, my stage direction in Fantasyland was to "run pretty" and I tried my best. When the drawbridge dropped, we all feared we would be trampled by the children. We had never rehearsed with the children and didn't realize there would be so many of them or that they would be so excited.

We used a dressing room behind New Orleans Street and we sometimes had to run to a location, shouting at people to get out of the way so we would get there on time.

They loaded us on a flatbed truck to be transported behind the buildings to get to some areas. Once, the driver got lost backstage going to the float where I was supposed to be Snow White and we panicked. We barely made it on time. We were yelling at him "Go there!" or "Turn there!"

It was at least 100 degrees that day, so I was glad I was out in the open with a little breeze rather than cooped up inside a coach like Cinderella. She was reacting with her prince, but I had camera experience so I played to where the cameras were.

The reviews weren't great. There was a local radio personality called Dick Whittinghill who was very popular. On his show, he joked he could take his kids to Disneyland or put them through college, but not both.

CHAPTER ELEVEN

When Did Disneyland Open: July 17 or July 18?

For over thirty-five years, the Disney company and international media have touted that Disneyland opened on July 17, 1955. The date appears in books, newspaper and magazine articles, and has been used as the key date for the beginning of all the Disneyland anniversary celebrations in the past few decades.

However, that was not always the accepted date for Disneyland's official opening day. During Walt and Roy Disney's lifetimes, it was acknowledged that opening day was Monday, July 18, 1955, at 10am, and that the July 17 event was merely an invitational press preview and dedication ceremony.

A dedication ceremony is not the same as the official opening day of a theme park. After all, the dedication of Walt Disney World and Magic Kingdom was held on October 25, 1971, nearly three weeks after the park opened to paying guests on the first of October.

The dedication of Epcot Center was on October 24, 1982, again nearly three weeks after the park opened to paying guests and after countless soft openings for both guests and cast members.

The official opening day for Disney California Adventure is February 8, 2001. However, beginning on January 16, Disney annual passholders, media, operating partners, and a variety of other companies and organizations visited the park en masse.

Disney films often have previews or even premieres before their official release dates.

Saludos Amigos premiered in Rio de Janeiro, Brazil, on August 24, 1942. It was released in the United States on February 6, 1943. *The Three Caballeros* premiered in Mexico City on December 21, 1944. It was released in the

United States on February 3, 1945, and in the UK that March. *Song of the South* premiered in Atlanta, Georgia, on November 12, 1946, but did not receive a general release until November 20, 1946. *Treasure Island* premiered in London on June 22, 1950, but did not receive an American release until June 29, 1950.

So, in Walt's mind, a film might premiere early, but it was not "official" until its general release date in America. That was Walt's intention with the July 17 Disneyland press preview. It was a "sneak peek" to generate good buzz for people to come and see the final product.

July 17 was not the first day that guests visited Disneyland. Walt escorted a handful of visitors, primarily reporters like Bob Thomas, through the park to show them what it was going to be like. He also invited large groups to enjoy the park as it approached that fateful day.

On July 4, 1955, members of the exclusive Penthouse Club for the higher-paid artists at the Disney Studio, along with their wives and children, were invited to a special preview of Disneyland.

Walt arranged this preview specifically to see how children and families would react to the park. Up to that time, it had been primarily a handful of adults who had experienced Disneyland.

On July 13, 1955, Walt hosted roughly three hundred guests for the Tempus Fugit Celebration of his 30th wedding anniversary at Frontierland's Golden Horseshoe Saloon and on the *Mark Twain* Riverboat.

Horse-drawn surreys transported guests down glittering, almost-completed Main Street and through the open gates of the wooden fort entrance into Frontierland. The guests were directed across the Frontierland Square to the *Mark Twain* for what was to be its official maiden voyage.

Afterwards, the guests gathered in the Golden Horseshoe for dinner and the first full performance of what would become the longest-running musical stage show in history, with tens of thousands of performances.

Although not all of the things in the park were up and running during these visits, the same could be said of July 17 when many of the key attractions were not operating and wouldn't officially become operational until days or weeks later, like Rocket to the Moon, which didn't open until July 22, and Dumbo, which didn't open until August.

On July 17, Disneyland was supposed to open at 2:30pm after the completion of early morning in-park preparations for the afternoon television broadcast. So, unlike a regular day at Disneyland, the park was not open for its full operating hours.

Tickets were color-coded for the approximately 11,000 guests expected, with each color corresponding to an assigned entry time into the park. Silver tickets had a 2:30pm entry time, green tickets 5:30pm, and white tickets signified entry after 6:00pm. Guests ignored these times.

Disney announced to its invited guests that Disneyland would close at 8:00pm so it "could get the park ready for the official opening the next day" rather than at the usual 10:00pm that was standard for the rest of the year.

On July 17, no admission tickets were sold and all the rides were free to invited guests, so it was a much different experience than a "normal" Disneyland day in 1955. In fact, it was quite an out of the-ordinary type of day.

Advertisements in newspapers as well as radio broadcasts urged people to stay home and enjoy the television show, *Dateline Disneyland*, because the park was only open to invited guests. The millions who tuned in saw Walt Disney delivering his memorable dedication speech and happy people filling the park, so many naturally assumed that Disneyland was open for business, even though July 18 was advertised as the official opening day.

A Disneyland advertisement in the *Los Angeles Times* newspaper on Friday, July 15, 1955, had this information:

> OPENING—Disneyland, Walt Disney's Magic Kingdom, will officially open on Monday, July 18th, and remain open every day during the summer from 10 a.m. to 10 p.m. Beginning in the Fall, Disneyland will be closed on Mondays.

On Sunday, July 17, 1955, a *Los Angeles Times* article entitled "Dream Comes True in Orange Grove: Disneyland, Multimillion Dollar Magic Kingdom, to Open Tomorrow" began with this sentence: "A dream comes true tomorrow—Disneyland opens." Of course, the "tomorrow" is referring to July 18, and this may be one of the first times that Disneyland was referred to as the "Magic Kingdom".

The *Los Angeles Times* for July 19, 1955, stated:

> Plagued by opening-day jitters, Walt Disney's fabulous Disneyland yesterday threw open its gates to an eager and waiting public. Fittingly enough, the first two customers were a seven-year-old boy and a five-year-old girl.

The New York Times for July 19, 1955, reinforced that July 18 was the opening day with 15,000 guests and waiting times of up to an hour for rides, merchandise, and meals.

In the press packet put together by Eddie Meck, the head of Disneyland's public relations, and given to media before the press preview, there is a fact sheet with this announcement at the top: "Opening: July 18, 1955 at 10 a.m."

Another sheet in the packet, entitled "Building a Dream", an essay on the building of the park, begins its second paragraph: "With this July 18 inaugural, Walt Disney realizes a life-time dream in offering Disneyland to the young of all ages."

"We don't even mail a postcard out of here without Walt's personal okay," Meck told newspaper columnist James Bacon, so Walt approved the notion that July 18 was the official opening day.

The July 1956 Disneyland press release prepared by Meck stated:
> Disneyland concludes its first year of operation this week with attendance at the Magic Kingdom in Anaheim nearing the 4 million mark.
>
> At the end of the day on July 17 of this year, 3,642,597 persons had toured Walt Disney's playland, making it the largest single private enterprise attraction in the Western Hemisphere and "a complete success" according to the Park's management.
>
> Guests from the government have included Vice-President Nixon with his family who toured the Park soon after the July 18 opening.

Studying the release, it is clear that the *end* of the day on July 17, not the *beginning*, marked the close of the first year of operation that had begun on July 18. In addition, the release clearly states that July 18 was the opening day.

The *Los Angeles Times* for July 19, 1960, in an article entitled "5th Birthday Mark Set For Disneyland", began with: "Disneyland celebrated the fifth anniversary of its opening yesterday with another new record for attendance." The attendance for the year ending July 17 was 5,238,415 (a 43.6% increase in attendance over its first year and a 15.5% increase of the previous 1958–1959 year). The new year for counting attendance began July 18.

The first issue of *The Disneyland News* sold by newsboys in the park declared in its lead story:
> More than 50,000 visitors were attracted to Disneyland on Monday, July 18, when the Park officially opened its gates.

Some of the confusion over the years has been that things that happened on both days blended together in people's memories.

For instance, on July 18, many of the things that happened on July 17 were re-staged, including the lowering of the Sleeping Beauty Castle drawbridge for the opening of Fantasyland (supervised both times by Bill Martin).

Roughly an hour before this was to happen on July 18, a natural gas line broke under the recently poured asphalt in the castle courtyard. A construction worker casually threw down his lit cigarette and the ground ignited. The Anaheim Fire Department was called in. The gas was shut off, and workers dug up the asphalt and finally capped the pipe.

There was debate about whether Fantasyland should open that day at all for fear that they might be other leaks. The land was closed for a few hours and then opened and operated normally without further incident. C.V. Wood went from building to building carefully testing each area with lighted matches.

How many reports about a gas leak in Fantasyland refer to it as happening on "opening day"? Quite few if you consider July 18 as the opening day.

The *Los Angeles Times* for July 19, 1955, stated (referring to the previous day):

> The man Disney was everywhere on Opening Day. He was at the front gate greeting customers, at the heliport to welcome arrivals, at a drugstore to officiate in a desert contest, at the administration building to iron out ever-present problems and circulating through the crowds signing autographs.

A publicity photo from July 18 shows Walt, broadly smiling and squatting next to Christine Vess (age five of North Hollywood) and her cousin Michael Schwartner (age seven of Bakersfield) who were proclaimed the first guests to enter the Happiest Place on Earth.

David MacPherson of Long Beach is credited with being the first actual guest to buy a ticket to get into Disneyland, and that happened on July 18. The *Long Beach Press-Telegram* for July 18 ran a photo of MacPherson at a Disneyland ticket booth giving an "okay" sign with his fingers to the photographer, reporting:

> Purchase of the First Ticket to Disneyland was made today by a Long Beach man, Dave MacPherson of 2312 Iroquois Ave. He achieved the distinction by getting in line at 2 a.m. By dawn, almost 6,000 others were in line behind him.

One of those others was a young boy who would grow up to be filmmaker George Lucas and who also considered July 18 as the opening day. Lucas recalled:

> I was there opening day with my best friend. It was one of the most amazing experiences an eleven year old could have. I had been to a lot of typical amusement parks, but this was beyond belief.

Roy O. Disney always considered July 18 as the opening day because that is when people paid to get into Disneyland and paid to ride the attractions. The experience on July 18 was like every other day that guests would enjoy at Disneyland in 1955.

At a Club 55 reunion party in July 1968, Roy told the following story, much to the discomfort of his wife, Edna, who was also in attendance.

> The studio's every dollar was tied up in Walt's Disneyland dream. What if we opened the gates and nobody came? Well, on opening day, I left the studio and headed down the Santa Ana Freeway. I was worried. After getting out of Los Angeles, the traffic began to get heavy. It could have been people going to the beach. Because the freeway was not completed, it was stop-and-go most of the way. It must have taken more than an hour to finally get to the Disneyland parking lot, which was jammed.
>
> A young man working there recognized me and came up in a bit of a panic. He wasn't familiar with our first-name policy. "Mr. Disney," he said, "people

have been stalled on the freeway and getting into our parking lot. Children are peeing all over the lot." I looked around at all of these people who were coming here to pay to get in. With a great sense of relief, I said, "God bless 'em, let 'em pee!"

With the death of Roy O. Disney at the end of 1971, his affirmation that July 18 was the official opening date gradually faded.

It wasn't until Disneyland's 25th anniversary in 1980 that the park's opening was officially declared as July 17 with a special 25-hour party that began at 12:01am at Disneyland on July 17 and ended the following morning on July 18. The souvenir program for the event stated:

> Twenty-five years ago today, a dream became reality. A dream that lived in the heart of Walt Disney for most of his adult life. He nurtured and developed it, but most of all, he believed in it.
>
> Today we're celebrating 25 years of making dreams come true for the almost 200 million people who have passed through the gates of our Magic Kingdom. Thank you for being such an important part of our family and for sharing in the proudest moment in Disneyland's history.

Dates in Disney history can be fluid. It wasn't until 1973 that Disney Archivist Dave Smith officially declared that Mickey Mouse's birthday was November 18, 1928. Up until that time, a variety of dates from September through November were used to celebrate Mickey's birthday. After Smith's declaration, Mickey's birth date has remained consistent in books and articles for over four decades.

It is clear why the July 17 date eclipsed the actual opening date of Disneyland as the years progressed. It was that unforgettable *Dateline: Disneyland* ABC broadcast that stuck in people's minds with Walt dedicating the park.

At the beginning of the broadcast, co-host Art Linkletter standing at the train station proudly affirmed that the day was "the opening of the 8th Wonder of the World!" Later, co-host Bob Cummings standing at the Hub looked directly into the camera and said:

> Standing here has been one of the most exciting moments in my life. I think, ladies and gentlemen, that anyone who has been here today will say, as the people did many years ago when they were at the opening of the Eiffel Tower, "I was there!" I am proud to say I was at the opening of Disneyland. It's a fabulous thing to happen.

Despite their authoritative proclamations, it is important to realize that both of these hosts were hired because of their ability to improvise and neither of these statements is in the official script notes.

Linkletter's ad-libs were the source of much misinformation about Disneyland over the years, including the fact that the train, the buildings on Main Street, and Walt's miniature horses in Frontierland were all built to a 5/8 scale.

Bob Cummings, taking his cue from Linkletter, told the television audience that the interior of the Golden Horseshoe saloon was also built to a 5/8 scale.

Where did this falsehood that everything in Disneyland was 5/8 scale originate? Imagineer Roger Broggie said:

> We took the plans of Walt's 1/8 scale *Lilly Belle* from the Carolwood Pacific and just blew them up five times larger...and this was the start of the nonsense that all of Disneyland was 5/8 scale. Both engines were inspired by Walt's backyard miniature engine but were modified (the stack, domes, and cabin). The *C.K. Holliday* was decorated as an 1873 woodburner with large headlight and diamond stack. The *E.P. Ripley* was decorated as an 1880s-era coal-burning engine.

The trains were first tested on July 14, 1955, since there was a delay doing the final track work around the entire park.

Linkletter also told viewers that Mr. Toad's Wild Ride was on a monorail beam. These are just a few of the whoppers and flubs generated under the pressure of the live broadcast, but for decades they were accepted as facts by Disney fans.

In the classic John Ford film *The Man Who Shot Liberty Valance* (1962), one of the premises is that a legend can become so appealing and engaging to people that it eventually supersedes all the facts that contradict it.

"When the legend becomes fact, print the legend."

That is the case with the answer to "When did Disneyland open?"

The answer now and in the foreseeable future is July 17, 1955, even if that is not the answer that Walt or Roy Disney would have given.

CHAPTER TWELVE

The Story of the Disneyland Tickets

When Disneyland opened to paying customers on July 18, 1955, general admission was $1.00 for adults and 50 cents for children. There were special rates for groups and conventions if they contacted the Customer Relations manager ahead of their visit. In addition, students, servicemen, and clergy could get an admission ticket for 75 cents with proper identification.

It was John Gostovich, general manager of the popular tourist attraction Los Angeles Farmers Market, who initially advised Walt to have a high entrance fee to keep out the "loafers and other undesirable characters", something that was not common at other amusement venues who wanted to encourage the largest possible crowd to spend money inside.

Attraction tickets were individually priced. An "A" ticket was ten cents. A "B" ticket was twenty-five cents. A "C" ticket was good for any attraction priced at thirty-five cents. Each attraction required a ticket. There were ticket kiosks in each land so cash could be exchanged for a ticket. No cash was accepted at the entrance of any attraction. Shows like the Golden Horseshoe Revue and sponsored exhibits were free.

Those first Disneyland admission and ride tickets were "stubs" on a roll like the kind of ticket one might purchase at a movie theater or a carnival and not as artistically impressive as the later tickets. That's why the small tickets had a round hole in them, to go through the sprocket dispenser.

The back of the ticket had this disclaimer: "The person using this ticket assumes all risk of personal injury and loss of property. Management reserves the right to revoke the license granted by this ticket." It was the standard waiver on all generic tickets produced by the Globe Ticket Company who later produced the more elaborate A–E tickets in the famous coupon books.

The first tickets to Disneyland were sold on July 18, 1955. While the cost of an adult ticket was a dollar, nine cents of that price went to a federal tax which was later abolished in 1956.

There were no ticket books at first, but that changed on October 11, 1955. Van France, the founder of Disneyland University, recalled:

We had major price increase resistance in 1955. The rumor was that it cost $40 to visit Disneyland. This was impossible unless a person splurged wildly with purchases everywhere!

To combat that rumor, Ed Ettinger, head of public relations, came up with the idea of a ticket book. Then we could advertise: "Admission and eight rides for $2.50." Ed worried and said, "I'll either be a goat or a hero." He was a hero.

Optional "A Day at Disneyland" ticket books were originally just an experimental promotion scheduled through Thanksgiving Day 1955 and advertised in the October 1955 issue of *Disneyland News* as: "Have more fun for less money with Disneyland ticket books!"

Unlike the stubs, these tickets, called "coupons" by Disney, were larger, more colorful and substantial. Each level was printed on different colored paper. In fact, the term "coupon" later was imprinted on the individual slips rather than the word "ride".

Priced at $2.50 for adults, $2.00 for junior and senior high school students (with ID), and $1.50 for children under twelve years old, each book had a general admission ticket and eight attraction tickets—three "A" coupons, two "B" coupons, and three "C" coupons. This was a great bargain since it allowed guests to pay less than face value for the attractions.

One of the advantages of the ticket books was to spread guests throughout the entire park and not have them congregate at the most popular attractions. Having a variety of tickets also allowed guests to experience several attractions that they might not normally have selected, now that they were already "paid for" in their minds.

The primary goal was to have guests pay only once and not have to constantly keep reaching into their wallets for each attraction. Often, guests would return home with unused tickets, which many still have today. They are still valid and can be exchanged for face value.

The ticket books were a huge success and were not eliminated until 1982 and the opening of Epcot Center where every sponsor and country felt they should be an "E" ticket and other entertainment venues on the West Coast were advertising a "pay one price" for their parks.

The "D" ticket worth thirty-five to forty cents was introduced with the opening of the Rainbow Ridge Mine Train ride in 1956. The "C" ticket dropped to thirty cents. The famous "E" ticket worth fifty cents and later seventy-five cents was introduced in June 1959 with the opening of the monorail, the Matterhorn Bobsleds, and the Submarine Voyage.

Over the years, the costs of each individual ticket fluctuated and attractions were sometimes moved to different levels. For instance, the Jungle

Cruise started as a "C" ticket, jumped to a "D" ticket, and finally an "E" ticket, where it remained. Other attractions dropped to a lower level. What an individual ride "cost" depended upon its popularity, expenses that needed to be recovered, maintenance, and other variables.

Walt's brother Roy O. Disney arranged to pre-purchase the first Disneyland ticket sold on July 18, 1955, from Curtis Lineberry, the manager of admissions from ticket booth number 2. Roy thought that the first ticket would be historically important. He did the same thing when the Magic Kingdom opened in Florida in 1971.

That valuable Disneyland souvenir survives in the Disney Archives to this day. Roy had given it to his secretary, Madeline Wheeler, and she kept it safe until she turned it over to former Disney Chief Archivist Dave Smith, who used to keep it in a protective sleeve in his top desk drawer to show to visitors.

The first guest to buy a ticket was Dave MacPherson, a twenty-two-year-old resident of Long Beach, California. There is color newsreel film footage of MacPherson holding up the ticket and smiling as he heads toward one of the tunnel entrances.

MacPherson was trotted out for some publicity in 2005 for Disneyland's 50th anniversary. He was then 72 years old and a retired journalist for a local newspaper living in a cabin in Monticello, Utah, about 240 miles southeast of Salt Lake City. He said he had left "Quakafornia" twenty years earlier, but still visited Disneyland with his lifetime pass.

When Disneyland opened in 1955, MacPherson lived ten miles away from the park. He was a student at Long Beach State University where he worked on the college newspaper.

Watching the July 17, 1955, broadcast of *Dateline: Disneyland* on ABC inspired MacPherson to hop on his Simplex motobike and drive out to Anaheim to be the first person in line for the opening on Disneyland to the general public the next day, thinking he might get a prize. MacPherson said:

> I thought, *Boy, I sure would like to go out there.* I decided I wanted to be the first in line. The first person to go into the park who wasn't a relative of Walt's or some celebrity. The first regular guy to go in through the front door.

He arrived shortly before 1am to take his place in line an hour before anyone else showed up. He selected the nearest ticket booth. MacPherson recalled:

> I had it in my mind to be the first. I would have said "forget it" if someone was already there. But I was the first person.

When he took his place in front of the ticket booth, Disneyland was scheduled to open at its regular time, 10am. As MacPherson stood there for eight hours, he saw Disneyland employees rushing about to get the park ready after the disasters of the previous day. He remembered that he heard Disneyland employees testing animal sounds for the Jungle Cruise.

When the admission booth opened, a photographer for the *Long Beach Press-Telegram* captured the historic moment of him buying the first ticket. Looking at the photo years later, MacPherson realized he had his own camera but never used it. He remembered:

> Well, I had thought that perhaps someone might try to get ahead of me at the last moment. So I had prepared a sheet to the effect that I was first, and had last-minute workers and security people sign it. Sure enough, about five minutes before the gates opened a woman and two little kids tried to get in front of me. So I pulled out the sheet (like a miniature Declaration of Independence!) and showed it to her. It was like Dracula seeing the light shining on the cross and she slunk back!
>
> After I bought the first ticket, the management gave me a special pass to all rides, etc. "This complimentary ticket entitles the holder to be the guest of Disneyland on all rides and amusements in Disneyland for this date only: July 18 1955." [MacPherson has since misplaced that valuable item, but he did save an image of it on microfilm in the 1980s.]
>
> Since the line behind was very long and since it was hot, I thought that someone way back might want to buy my ticket that I had paid a dollar for. As I recall, I foolishly sold it for a dollar to a young man (since the complimentary pass would allow MacPherson to get into the park as well as enjoy all the attractions). I wish I had kept it.
>
> After standing in line so long, the first thing I did was go to the restroom.
>
> I can't remember buying anything or seeing a parade, but as I recall, the attractions had very long lines that first day! It was hot and humid, and I heard that folks standing in the long line to get in were passing out from the heat.
>
> I have no real sharp memories of the various parts of the park. I was very tired from being up all night, so I went briefly around to see at a glance, so to speak, the entire layout. I needed to get some rest because I wasn't thinking straight.
>
> I didn't even go on any rides. I had my camera with me, and I didn't even take any pictures! I didn't realize those pictures would be valuable someday.
>
> I was still in school and I had to get back because I had a class later that day. I was dead tired. I was the most popular guy at the college after the students found out.
>
> And, oh my goodness, it was very, very hot, and I had to get home to get some rest.

CHAPTER THIRTEEN

Disneyland 1955 Highlights

Construction

At the time Disneyland began construction there were 4,000 orange trees on the property and less than 20 houses. Construction included:

- 3.5 million board feet of lumber
- 1 million square feet of asphalt
- 5,000 cubic yards of concrete (roughly 32,000 sacks)
- Over 35,000 cubic yards of dirt was moved
- 8,467 feet of clay pipe for the sewer system
- 4,000 feet of gas line
- 7,000 feet of water line
- 2,000 lineal feet of storm draining piping
- 1,200 full size trees and 9,000 shrubs had been planted, costing Walt about $400,000 and "depleting nurseries from Santa Barbara to San Diego", according to newspaper columnist Hedda Hopper. However, the lot still included much open land, native brush, bare river banks, and unpaved access roads that could be seen by guests from the train.
- Approximately five million square feet of pavement.
- It rained for 21 days during the spring construction period, the wettest spring in Los Angeles in twenty years, slowing the work. Then, when Disneyland opened, the rain stopped, but there were 10 days of 100+ degree temperatures with up to 90% humidity.

Wienie

At night after work, Walt used to play with his pet poodles by waving a hot dog to get them to go where he wanted. He used this experience to explain to his art directors how he wanted things designed at Disneyland to direct guest movement. Imagineer John Hench explained:

> [Walt] used the term "wienie" to describe something at the end of a corridor that beckons [guests] to continue their journey, like the *Mark Twain* or the Moonliner.

Alcohol

Walt banned beer from the park, though breweries made him some tempting offers. Walt was 53 years old and a grandfather. He told Florabel Muir for an article in the July 10, 1955, edition of the *Daily News*:

> I could have got most of my costs back with beer concessions alone. A lot of adults will come here, but Disneyland is primarily for children and I don't think kids and liquor mix.

Guests

Van France created the first Disneyland orientation training program and themed it to "We Create Happiness". On page six of the orientation book, *A Guide for Hosts and Hostesses*, he wrote:

> Meet the King of our Magic Kingdom. The most important person in Disneyland is a guest. A guest is a person who enters Disneyland seeking entertainment. A guest may be white, black, brown or yellow…Christian, Jew, Buddhist or Hindu…Republican or Democrat…
>
> Showoff or wallflower, big shot or small…Rich or poor, healthy or unhealthy… But, from the moment his car turns into the Disneyland parking area until he leaves, he is a guest of Disneyland. How we greet him, how we look, the big and little things, are all vitally important to the enjoyment of his day at Disneyland. A Disneyland guest is to us a King in our Magic Kingdom.

By the end of the first summer, there had been visitors from 61 different countries.

Disneylanders

Park employees were officially known as Disneylanders. The term "cast member" did not exist until Van France created it in the 1960s. Just as people from Iceland were called Icelanders, it seemed logical that the inhabitants of Disneyland (as its own "country") would be called Disneylanders.

At its opening, Disneyland had approximately 950 employees representing 106 crafts, trades, and professions. More were quickly added within the first weeks.

Name Badges

In 1955, only employees of Disneyland, Inc. were issued brass badges stamped with their employee numbers. It wasn't until 1962 that their names were inscribed on them, though some high-ranking WED employees had their names inscribed on them in the late 1950s.

The badges were an oval shape approximately 1-3/4" tall by 2-1/2" wide. The Disney company never kept a record of those numbers and who they belonged to, but it is known that badge number one was assigned to Walt Disney and that the numbers eventually went into four digits. The badges were produced by the Los Angeles Stamp and Stationery Company with a brooch pin on the back attached to the badge with metal riveting.

The First Children

The Schwartner family had no intention of visiting Disneyland on July 18, 1955. Bill and Mildred Schwartner had different plans for their seven-year-old son Michael. They drove their family Buick from Bakersfield on July 17 for a trip to Mexico and stopped in North Hollywood for a brief visit with Bill's sister, Carol Vess, and her two children, Christine (5) and Donna (11).

Michael was able to convince his cousins to plead with their parents to go to Disneyland instead the next day, the official public opening of the park. When they arrived at eight o'clock in the morning, there were more than 15,000 people who had been standing in line for hours—some for as many as six hours.

While her husband and sister-in-law went to buy admission tickets, Mildred went to a wooden awning near the entrance to wait because it was already so hot and there was no shade. Michael was so excited that he engaged in horseplay, doing backflips by the turnstiles, and his cousin Christine was running around so wildly that she tripped and scraped her knee and began to cry uncontrollably. In the famous photo taken of her that day, it is clear that there are two Band-aids below the knee of her right leg.

It caught the attention of a female Disneyland employee nearby. Mildred thought they were all going to be thrown out, but instead the employee asked if she could take the children to meet Walt Disney.

Michael remembers spending almost forty-five minutes with Walt. He told *Orange County Register* reporter Joseph Pimentel in 2015:

> I was just a kid but he talked to me like a real person. He asked me if I could wiggle my ears. I said, "No, can you?" He said, "Nope, but I can wiggle my nose." And he did, mustache and all.

Fifteen minutes before the park opened at 10:00am, Walt walked to the front entrance with Michael and Christine and knelt down and greeted them as the first boy and girl to officially set foot in Disneyland. The families did not have to pay for admission and Walt personally took them around the park aboard the train where he explained about the different areas and what they could go see.

They were given a free pass to all of the rides and for all of the food and drink they wanted, and they didn't have to wait in line for any ride. They stayed until the park closed. Michael and Christine were given lifetime passes.

The Disneyland Marquee Sign

For most people, the huge Disneyland Marquee sign on Harbor Boulevard was a significant landmark. However, from 1955 to 1958, the sign didn't exist. Disney artist Herb Ryman had done a sketch for a sign in 1954 that featured two turrets reminiscent of Sleepy Beauty Castle and a curved ribbon banner stating "Disneyland Entrance", but it was never built. Bill Cottrell, the first president of Imagineering, said:

> We were so anxious just to get the park opened that we didn't have the time, or probably the funds, to put much of a display out on Harbor Boulevard.

Billboards along the Santa Ana Freeway (a huge pink sign with yellow lettering that stated "Right Turn. ¼ Mile at Harbor Blvd. Walt Disney's Magic Kingdom Disneyland") directed drivers to the correct exit, but, after that, the park itself was the only indicator. The Disneyland Hotel erected a big marquee sign in front of its administration building soon after it opened in fall 1955. Each letter of the words "Disneyland Hotel" was on an individual panel, with yellow panels for the "D" and "H". It seems to have been the inspiration for the Disneyland sign put up in 1958 that lasted for thirty years.

One Millionth Visitor

On September 8, 1955, at 2:31pm, five-year-old Elsa Marquez became the one millionth guest to visit Disneyland. Her parents, Daniel and Bertha, didn't intend to go to Disneyland that day, but with Bertha's younger sister, Alicia Ribera, and Alicia's family, including Elsa's cousins Manny and Ann, in town from El Paso, Texas, and all the kids wanting to go to the new park, the families went.

When they arrived at the gates, the children made a dash for the turnstiles. Raul (Elsa's seven-year-old brother) was first, followed by Elsa and then four-year-old Manny who pulled Elsa back so he could get ahead of her. Her younger three-year-old brother, Daniel, stayed with his parents. When Elsa finally made it through, balloons came down and music played. Customer Relations Director Jack Sayers greeted the Marquez and Ribera families.

In an interview with Joseph Pimentel that appeared in the July 17, 2015, issue of the *Orange County Register*, Elsa remembered:

> I was terrified. My mom picked me up and a [Disneyland employee dressed as a] sheriff came over [Frontierland Sheriff Bill Lacy] and was trying to explain something to her, but my mom didn't speak English. So he grabbed me from my mom. Walt Disney bent down and shook my hands. He had a warm

presence. He was a very kind person and sweet man. They put some type of crown or headdress on my head. I remember just feeling like a princess.

During this, officials were able to explain to Mrs. Marquez and the rest of the family what was happening. Elsa received a wicker basket that included a stuffed doll of Lady from *Lady and the Tramp,* a deed to Disneyland, a sealed pouch of dirt from Disneyland's groundbreaking, and also a lifetime pass. There were also gifts from Disneyland's lessees.

She and her brother, Raul, rode with the conductor on the train around the park. She led the Disneyland band in renditions of the Davy Crockett theme song and "Let Me Call You Sweetheart" with a baton. The native Indian dancers supervised by Frontierland's Chief Shooting Star performed around her and she was greeted by Tomorrowland's Space Man K-7 (John Catone).

Both families were guests of the park for all rides and for dinner at the Red Wagon Inn. When Walt Disney passed away in 1966, she was told her lifetime pass was no longer valid and it took over twenty years for that situation to be rectified.

At the end of its first fiscal year of operation, Disneyland had welcomed 3.8 million guests.

The First Christmas December 1955

A large, live, decorated Christmas tree stood to the left of the entrance to Sleeping Beauty Castle to celebrate the Christmas Festival which began November 24, 1955. Another tree adorned the forward deck of the *Mark Twain.*

Twelve costumed Dickens Christmas carolers from the University of Southern California under the direction of Dr. Charles Hirt (who would later create the Candlelight Processional) wandered through the park, warbling Christmas songs and encouraging guests to sing along. Local school bands and youth choral groups also performed, usually at the bandstand (which Disneyland called the Christmas Bowl, inspired by the famous concerts in the Hollywood Bowl). In a 1993 interview, Hirt said:

> I trained the Disneyland carolers. This included teaching the singers how to respond to people in the park. For example, if a little girl walked up to one of the singers, that caroler would sing directly to that child.

A flyer states that "thousands of lights and marvelous festive decorations of every conceivable kind" make Disneyland "a glittering fairyland of fun and thrills".

Parking Lot

Just like Disneyland itself, the parking lot was carefully planned and charged a nominal all-day fee of twenty-five cents. According to the July 18, 1955, issue of the *Hollywood Reporter*:

A 100-acre parking lot provides space for 12,175 cars—a potential load of about 50,000 adults and kids—and an "elephant train" takes guests from the parking lot to the main gate.

Van France said:

> Today's visitor would have a difficult time visualizing what it was like. The Santa Ana Freeway was far from complete. There were still many signal lights. The local roads were all two lane. And, we were in the country. Sidewalks, curbings, and gutters were to come later.

Curbing hadn't been finished and workmen still needed to paint the stripes down the street of Harbor Boulevard. Even though they were on overtime, they threatened to leave, so Van France loaded his car with cold beer and took it out to them to encourage them to finish in time for opening day.

At roughly 100 acres, the parking lot covered much more land than the park it served. WED studied every similar venue they could find to estimate parking needs and determined that the closest example was Forest Lawn Memorial Park.

WED correctly assumed that 92% of guests would arrive by personal car, with the rest coming by bus. At the different venues they studied, like Knott's Berry Farm, they learned that each car averaged 3.7 persons and that attendance during the day would ebb and flow, with a large crowd when the park opened in the morning and then, after many of those guests had departed, a second wave in the afternoon that stayed until the park closed.

Taking the number of potential guests and the number of cars necessary to bring those guests to Disneyland, WED calculated roughly the size of the parking lot. Disneyland originally was considered a daytime activity, so no adjustment was made for any night-time arrivals.

In 1955, the parking lot extended from the Disneyland ticket booths back to about where the Tower of Terror now stands, but only a couple of sections nearest the entrance were paved. The other parking spots were on dirt, which was not uncommon for venues like carnivals and circuses. It was only in later years that the parking lot was paved out to West Katella Avenue. By 1957, management was already debating about raising the price to park in the lot to thirty-five cents.

Forty-five security officers were employed on a full-time basis at Disneyland in 1955, with eight others on call to protect the park and its guests. In the early months, they were kept busy looking for "stolen" vehicles, which almost always turned out to be merely "misplaced" in the Disneyland parking lot.

The original Disneyland parking lot existed from July 17, 1955, to January 21, 1998, when it was mostly closed for Disney California Adventure, Downtown Disney, and Disney's Grand Californian Hotel and Spa.

Closed Mondays
At the end of that first summer, Disneyland started to close on Mondays for maintenance, a policy that continued until 1985. Later, the park would also close on Tuesdays during the off season. In 1955, the first Monday that the park closed was September 12. It did open on Monday, December 26, and on Monday, January 2, for the Christmas Festival. For guests unaware of the Monday closings, Knott's Berry Farm remained open on that day, just as Disneyland was open on the day in the middle of the week that Knott's closed.

It Takes People
- Organ grinder Sam Iezza cranked away on Main Street and the Hub as his monkey Josephine tipped her round red cap that matched her bright red outfit. Sometimes she wore a Davy Crockett coonskin cap.
- Fritz Musser (the photographer who parked his car backstage at Frontierland where it could be seen and got yelled at by Walt Disney for doing so), Milt Hyman, and Amador Acosta were the official photographers of Disneyland during its first years.
- Vern Croft was the manager for Disneyland, Inc. of the many gift stands run by Disney throughout the park. The first Disneyland merchandise director was Bob Burns, who joined the company in December 1954 and left in January 1956.
- James Warrick, who worked at the Long Beach Boat Shop that supplied some of the boats for the park, was brought on board as the captain of the Disneyland watercraft. The Coast Guard required that, due to all the water and boats at Disneyland, a skilled and licensed captain be on site at all times. Warrick served in that capacity from 1955 through 1958, when the Coast Guard removed the requirement. He enjoyed working at Disneyland so much that he transferred to the Maintenance department, where he remained until his retirement.
- John Huffman worked for McNeil Construction Company. After the designers and architects finished with the design of Disneyland, the plans were given out to contractors. Larry and Bruce McNeil gave the plans to Huffman, and it was his job to figure out the dollar cost of excavation, utilities, nuts, bolts, nails, concrete, wood, plaster, and everything else. After he turned in the finished estimate, Huffman was made superintendent. McNeil used sixty subcontractors with materials purchased from several hundred sources in Southern California.

CHAPTER FOURTEEN

These Many Worlds

The weekly *Disneyland* television show began with the announcement:

> Each week as you enter this timeless land, one of these many worlds will open to you.... Frontierland, tall tales and true from the legendary past.... Tomorrowland, promise of things to come.... Adventureland, the wonder world of nature's own realm.... Fantasyland, the happiest kingdom of them all.

On the first show, broadcast October 27, 1954, Walt showed the famous map of the theme park painted by Peter Ellenshaw that matched the four segments of the television show. He said:

> The Plaza or the Hub is the heart of Disneyland. Shooting out from here like the four cardinal points of the compass, Disneyland is divided into four cardinal realms: Adventureland, Tomorrowland, Fantasyland and Frontierland.

Those four lands had been selected because they represented the four most popular movie genres of the mid-1950s.

In 1955, movie studios released nearly fifty theatrical films that were themed to the Old West, among them *Man With The Gun* with Robert Mitchum, *Rage At Dawn* with Randolph Scott, and John Payne in *Tennessee's Partner*. On television, *Gene Autry*, *The Lone Ranger*, *Wild Bill Hickok*, *Roy Rogers*, *Death Valley Days*, *Wyatt Earp*, *Gunsmoke*, and *Annie Oakley* entertained audiences, with many more Westerns soon to come, like *Wagon Train*, *Maverick*, *Wanted Dead or Alive*, *Bat Masterson*, *Have Gun—Will Travel*, and *The Rifleman*.

Exotic jungle adventure on television in 1955 featured Irish McCalla in *Sheena Queen of the Jungle*, Jon Hall in syndicated reruns of *Ramar of the Jungle*, and Johnny Weismuller in *Jungle Jim*. Jungle-themed movies that year included *Phantom of the Jungle*, *Tarzan's Hidden Jungle* (with Gordon Scott as Tarzan), *African Manhunt*, *Simba*, and *Lord of the Jungle* (featuring Bomba the Jungle Boy), with others like *Congo Crossing* and *Safari* already announced for the next year. Notably, the release of the Disney True-Life Adventure *The African Lion* inspired Adventureland.

The golden age of science fiction films that began in 1950 was still going strong in 1955, with such movies as George Pal's *Conquest of Space, This Island Earth, King Dinosaur* (where American space explorers find dinosaurs on a rogue planet), *The Quatermass Experiment*, and *Beast with A Million Eyes* about an alien who controls animals. The following year, the iconic *Forbidden Planet* would be released.

Warner Brothers (Bugs Bunny), Walter Lantz (Woody Woodpecker), Famous Studios (Popeye, Casper), MGM (Tom and Jerry), and UPA (Mr. Magoo) were all still releasing animated theatrical shorts, as was the Disney Studio. Television was showing packages of old black-and-white theatrical cartoons, often with a live host.

Although never officially called a land, Main Street, U.S.A. was the only "land" that every visitor to Disneyland had to visit to enter and exit the park. It acted as a transition from reality to fantasy, and an effective corridor through which to funnel guests to the other lands.

One of the things that made Disneyland a different experience was that it was like a movie set, with guests immersed in it as if they were the actors—which is one of the reasons people behave differently at Disneyland than at other parks. Since Disneyland was such a different venue than a typical amusement park, Walt planned to have a variety of plaques throughout the park to help guests understand the purpose of each land.

The famous plaque that hangs above the entrance tunnel to Main Street, U.S.A. was not installed on opening day because Walt had made some significant changes to the wording.

Originally, the plaque stated: "Disneyland...Where You Leave Today... And Visit the World of Fantasy, Yesterday And Tomorrow". On June 22, 1955, Walt edited those thirteen words to its current version: "Disneyland... Here You Leave Today...And Enter the World of Yesterday, Tomorrow And Fantasy."

The individual "land" plaques were also not installed on opening day, even though Walt read them on the *Dateline: Disneyland* broadcast on July 17, 1955.

TOMORROWLAND: "A vista into a world of wondrous ideas, signifying man's achievements...a step into the future, with predictions of constructive things to come. Tomorrow offers new frontiers in science, adventure and ideals: the Atomic Age...the challenges of outer space...and the hope for a peaceful and unified world." (The plaque was later installed at the entrance of Tomorrowland in 1967 with the opening of the new Tomorrowland. The original wording was approved by Walt on June 24, 1955.)

ADVENTURELAND: "Here is adventure. Here is romance. Here is mystery. Tropical rivers—silently flowing into the unknown. The unbelievable splendor of exotic flowers...the eerie sound of the jungle...with eyes that are always watching. This is Adventureland." (The wording was approved by Walt on June 22, 1955.)

FRONTIERLAND: "Here we experience the story of our country's past... the colorful drama of Frontier America in the exciting days of the covered wagon and the stage coach...the advent of the railroad...and the romantic riverboat. Frontierland is a tribute to the faith, courage and ingenuity of the pioneers who blazed the trails across America." (The wording was approved by Walt on July 5, 1955.)

On camera on July 17, 1955, Walt read the plaque as: "It is here that we experience the story of our country's past—the color, romance and drama of Frontier America as it developed from wilderness trails to riverboats to railroads and civilization—a tribute to the faith, courage and ingenuity of our hearty pioneers who blazed the trails and made this progress possible."

There *was* a plaque at the entrance to Frontierland in 1955. It was given to Walt by the American Humane Association in July of that year and reads: "To Walt Disney in Recognition of Outstanding Assistance and Cooperation in Extending Humane Ideals To Peoples Throughout the World from the American Humane Association". The plaque now sits atop a rock pedestal near the base of the flagpole; in 1955, it was closer to the ground, like a grave marker.

FANTASYLAND: "Here is the world of imagination, hopes and dreams. In this timeless land of enchantment, the age of chivalry, magic and make believe are reborn—and fairy tales come true. Fantasyland is dedicated to the young and the young-at-heart—to those who believe that when you wish upon a star, your dreams do come true."

Walt's experience was in doing animated films, so he organized the creative aspects of the park like his films. His animated feature films would have "sequence directors" in charge of particular scenes in the film and making sure the work of varied artists was consistent in telling the story. For Disneyland, Walt assigned individual art directors for each land who would oversee the contributions of different artists.

Wade B. Rubuttom (Main Street), George Patrick (Frontierland), Harper Goff (Adventureland), Bill Martin (Fantasyland), and Gabe Scognomillo (Tomorrowland) were chosen for those roles. Martin recalled:

> The reason he brought us over was in a way he didn't trust his animators to design the park. Now, they worked on the rides, that's for sure. But he wanted set designers that were used to building false facades. Walt once said jokingly "I don't trust the artists that I've got, because they can exaggerate anything and I don't see what I am getting."

Walt hated what he called "aircraft thinking" that included organizational charts, blueprints, and other forms of institutional planning. This term came from C.V. Wood and his cronies who had worked at Consolidated Vultee, a company that manufactured aircraft in Texas, and that is how Walt perceived they were approaching the challenges of Disneyland.

Wade B. Rubottom was a veteran of the MGM movie studio who had worked as associate art director on a number of films, including *The Philadelphia Story* (1940). He was also a Harvard-educated architect. Walt considered him too stubborn. He only worked for one year at WED. Later, for C.V. Wood's Marco Engineering Company, he designed Freedomland in New York and Magic Mountain in Denver, Colorado. Both entertainment venues had similarities to Disneyland.

Many other artists contributed significantly to Main Street.

Emile Kuri had been Walt's personal interior decorator as well as one of the youngest movie set decorators in Hollywood. Kuri designed the lush interior of Captain Nemo's cabin in *20,000 Leagues Under the Sea* (1954).

Kuri made a trip to Baltimore in 1955 to purchase, at three cents per pound, some 160-year-old gas lamp posts that the city was replacing, for installation on Main Street, U.S.A. In another cost-saving maneuver, when a car knocked over a street light on Wilshire Boulevard in Los Angeles, Kuri rescued it at a cost of five dollars to become the flagpole base at Disneyland.

Those horse-head hitching posts in Town Square at both Disneyland and the Walt Disney World's Magic Kingdom were designed by Kuri from a mold of an original antique hitching post he was given by the grateful owner of an 1840 mansion where *The Heiress* (1949), a film he worked on, was shot. The original resided for many years in the front yard of Kuri's house in Corona del Mar, California.

George L. Patrick was a well-known art director in Hollywood. He had just finished art direction on the Western *Siege at Red River* (1954) and would go on to do art direction for Western television series like *Cimarron City, The Restless Gun, Laramie, Riverboat, Whispering Smith, Frontier Circus*, and *The Virginian*.

Patrick was recruited after construction on Disneyland had started and was responsible for creating the overall theme for the Frontierland and New Orleans areas. Harper Goff and Sam McKim contributed significantly to the design of Frontierland.

Bill Martin was responsible for Fantasyland. He was working at 20th Century Fox when Walt asked him to join the Disneyland project. He was primarily responsible for the interior layout of all the dark rides.

Walt liked Martin and he remained with the Disney company. He later became the vice president of design at WED Enterprises, overseeing layouts at the Magic Kingdom.

Such Disney artists as Ken Anderson and Claude Coats contributed significantly to Fantasyland's dark rides.

The earliest ideas for Tomorrowland were inspired by the popular science fiction B-movies and were pitched by Gabriel Scognamillo, the art director for the land. He had recently finished *Tobor the Great* (1954) for Republic Pictures, about a robot who would supposedly take the place of astronaunts for outer space voyages.

Scognamillo had proposed a dark ride where guests would travel over the surface of Mars. However, Walt's vision for Tomorrowland evolved as he consulted with leading space experts on the episodes for his television series. Walt wanted the land to be a more "science factual" experience of the future just around the corner rather than a Flash Gordon-Buck Rogers type of science fantasy.

As might be expected, Walt and Scognamillo repeatedly fought over the design direction of Tomorrowland. Walt fired him before the park even opened, claiming that Scognamillo was too egotistical and was more concerned about commemorating his own vision rather than what was best for Disneyland.

John Hench, Peter Ellenshaw, and others contributed to Tomorrowland.

Harper Goff had a career as a set designer for Warner Brothers, working on films like *Captain Blood* (1935), *Charge of the Light Brigade* (1936), and *Sergeant York* (1941). He art directed Disney's *20,000 Leagues Under the Sea* (1954) and came up with the iconic design of the *Nautilus* submarine for the film. Goff was also the banjo player in Ward Kimball's Firehouse Five Plus Two jazz band.

The 1955 Disneyland Guide Map stated:

> Welcome to Disneyland. This is your personal map for the Kingdom of Happiness—Walt Disney's Magic Kingdom—Disneyland. This is the kingdom that was created for YOU—and your personal happiness. All of us—Disneyland's Hosts and Hostesses—are dedicated to making your first—and subsequent visits—a very pleasant and treasured experience.
>
> Disneyland was created and designed as a new concept in family entertainment—something for everyone, of every age. Here is the world of Tomorrow, and Yesterday—Fantasy and Adventure skillfully blended in every detail for your pleasure and enjoyment. As Disneylanders we are proud to play a part in creating happiness for you and your family. Whatever we can do to make this visit more enjoyable—won't you please let us help you.

The next five chapters give a glimpse at some of the facts, stories, secrets, and forgotten magic of the five primary areas of Disneyland. Each land is deserving of a full book of its own, so these chapters are not definitive but rather snapshot reference of some of the things that were there in 1955.

CHAPTER FIFTEEN

Main Street, U.S.A.

The 1955 Disneyland Guide Map gave this account of Main Street, U.S.A.:
> Described by Walt Disney as the "heart line of America", Main Street, U.S.A. is an exact replica of a small town main street in that happy era from 1890 to 1910. Complete in every detail, from the horse-drawn streetcars which trundle up Main Street to the fire department's turn-of-the-century hose and chemical wagon "powered" by real fire horses. You'll see and visit all of the 1900 period business enterprises on Main Street, the photographer's shop, ice cream parlor, bakery, meat market and grocery, bank, music shop, drug store and many others—all operating exactly as they did 50 years ago.

City Hall
- First Aid Station
- Lost Children
- Police
- Lost and Found

Food and Refreshments
- Carnation Ice Cream Parlor
- Coca-Cola Refreshment Corner
- Maxwell House Coffee House
- Plaza Pavilion Restaurant
- Red Wagon Inn (Swift)
- Puffin Bake Shop (General Mills; Manager George Means)

Shops and Exhibits
- Bank of America (Manager Leo Wagman)
- Bandstand (Plaza Hub)
- Book and Candle Shop (Manager Pat St. George for Disneyland, Inc.)

- Blue Bird Shoes for Children
- Candy Palace (Manager Vera Connel for A.R.B. Corporation)
- Ellen's Gifts (Wynegar)
- Emporium Department Store (Managers Earl Phillips and Bob Erickson for Emporium of Orange County)
- Fine Tobacco Shop (Manager Howard Rogo for Random Parts, Inc.)
- Gibson Greeting Cards (Manager Dorothy Tierney for John McInnis of Gibson Art Co.; shared space with Stamp, Coin and Pen Shop)
- Global Van and Bekins Storage (storage lockers cost twenty cents)
- Grandma's Baby Shop (closes in September 1955)
- Hollywood Maxwell's Intimate Apparel Shop
- Jewelry Store (Manager Dwight Long)
- (Eastman) Kodak Camera Center (Manager Herb Reich)
- Print Shop (Managers Joe and Ray Amendt for Castle Services)
- Ruggles China and Glass Shop (Manager Phil Papel)
- Silhouette Studio (Managers Alex De Conslar and Nemo Markey)
- Stamp, Coin and Pen Shop (East Center Street entrance; shared space wtih Gibson Greeting Cards)
- Sunny-View Farms Jams & Jellies (Manager Don Wehrli)
- Swift Market House (Manager Myrt Westering)
- Town Square Realty (Manager Wally Pifer)
- Upjohn Pharmacy (Manager Leo Austin)
- U.S. Time (Timex) Watches and Clocks (Manager Vera Hanson)
- Wonderland Music Store (Manager Mildred Maley for Disneyland, Inc.)
- Wurlitzer Music Hall (Victorian and modern displays)
- Yale & Towne Lock Shop (Manager Jan Williams)

Shows
- Main St. Cinema

Rest Rooms
- City Hall
- West Center Street

Telephones
- East Center Street
- Outside of the main gate

Rides and Amusements
- Fire Wagon (horse-drawn hose and chemical wagon; "A" ticket)
- Santa Fe & Disneyland Railroad Passenger Train ("C" ticket)
- Horse-drawn Street Car Trolley ("A" ticket)
- 1905 Horseless Carriage ("A" ticket)
- Main Street Arcade
- Penny Arcade and Shooting Gallery
- Main Street Cinema ("A" ticket)

Other Points of Interest
- The Opera House was not open to the public.
- The Plaza Hotel/Plaza Apartments (INA Carefree Corner in September 1956) was located at 222 Main Street. During the first year, more than 900,000 people signed the Disneyland Guest Register located at the Plaza Apartments, giving their home towns and addresses.
- There was no post office in Disneyland, but there were mail boxes throughout the park for the convenience of guests. The mail was picked up on a regular basis and delivered to the Anaheim Post Office.

Gurrmobiles
The term "Gurrmobiles" referring to the "authentic reproduction antique" cars on Main Street first appeared in an issue of *Mickey Mouse Club Magazine* in 1957. One of Bob Gurr's friends had built a custom radiator for the Carnation Milk Company delivery truck parked in front of the Carnation Ice Cream shop and had playfully included an emblem naming the truck "Gurrmobile".

Imagineer Bob Gurr knew that the vehicles needed to appear to be "old and rickety", but actual antique machinery would not survive the daily operational demands of the parks nor meet safety and efficiency requirements. So, his creations were composites that included things like drive trains, suspension, and springs from 1950s cars. Some of the exterior items suggesting vintage cars were crafted at the Disney Studio shops. Gurr used the book *Treasury of Early Automobiles* by Floyd Clymer for reference.

Postcards
During the first year of operation at Disneyland, there were approximately 65 different postcards of the park produced and sold. The first twenty-two were reproductions of the concept art done by Disney artists. The remaining forty-three were photographs taken during 1955. Referred to as the "P-Series", they were published in "Plastichrome" by the Colourpicture Publishers, Inc.

Lessees

Lessees are today known at Disney as operating participants. C.V. Wood was the person responsible for getting a variety of companies to lease space inside the park. These companies would have to sign fixed, five-year leases, with the first and last years' fees due upon signing, so Walt could use that money to help build his park. Disney would build the shop structures and exterior ornamentation.

Companies like Coca-Cola and Swift agreed to lease space at Disneyland with an annual rent of twenty dollars per square foot on Main Street and fifteen dollars per square foot in the other lands. Lessees were expected to pay both this minimum fee and a percentage of their profits. They also had to pay the construction costs for the interior and the salaries for their own staff.

The Disneyland Inc. Supplementary Specifications for Lessees stated:

> All interior architectural drawings are to be done by a competent registered architect or approved display house of lessee's choice. All designs submitted by lessee's architect whether the buildings or construction of interiors in Disneyland must be approved as to the theme and general plan of Disneyland as established by WED Enterprises. Three sets of preliminary drawings are to be furnished to Disneyland, Inc. as soon as possible after signing of the lease. Two sets are retained by Disneyland and one set is returned to the lessee's architect with any revisions.

Eastman Kodak paid roughly $28,000 up front to lease shop space, Upjohn $29,000, Kaiser Aluminum $37,500 (with the added assurance that aluminum would be used extensively throughout the park, like the bumpers on the Autopia cars and on the Clock of the World), while TWA and Richfield Oil each paid $45,000.

Pete Clark, who was involved with Participant Affairs for thirty-six years, recalled:

> All the lessees were there because they knew they could make a profit from their individual businesses in the Park. The larger sponsors were there to showcase their product, to showcase their services.

Fire Department

The *actual* fire chief of Disneyland at that time was Thomas Jefferson "Mitch" Mitchell. The real Disneyland fire department was staffed by firefighters employed by Anaheim's fire department, with their salaries paid by the park. The fire department was housed in the old white administration building backstage.

Disney acquired a 1954 Willys Jeep with a front-mounted pump for fire protection. It included fire-fighting equipment made by General Fire apparatus of Detroit, Michigan.

In keeping with the theme, Mitch was attired in a turn-of-the-century uniform which he wore when he went about his daily duties of checking on fire hazards. Primarily, his role was "preventative", which was challenging because of the complexity and variety of the park.

Vintage fire equipment and accessories were needed to furnish the fire station that guests saw on Main Street. To help with that, someone located a firehouse supply catalog from the Carrens Company, a long-time supplier of such equipment. The magnetic electric fire gong was first used in Boston in 1851 and was obtained from a private collector who was convinced it would be an important addition to the new park.

Yale and Towne Lock Shop

The store featured a display of antique locks, keys, and safes. Outside the door was a giant key. A guest could get a souvenir key with the Disneyland castle on one side and Yale logo on the reverse. Disneyland's doors all used Yale and Towne lock sets. The collection of antiques was compiled by Charles Courtney and is currently on display at Yale's corporate headquarters in North Carolina and at the Lock Museum of America in Connecticut.

W.K. McGreevy was the West Coast general manager for Yale during the construction of Disneyland and lived in Anaheim to be closer to the project.

Candy Palace

When Paul Adams and Emmert Brooks opened their Los Angeles store in 1932, they sold just one treat: caramel popcorn. Over the years, they developed other confections like Whirly, Twirl, and Unicorn lollipops, P'Nuttles, Fairtime Taffy, and Coffee Rio (made with real coffee and cream).

Al Brooks, who operated a theatrical ticket agency in the Statler Center Hotel, became aware that Disneyland wanted a candy-making exhibit on Main Street. The Adams and Brooks candy shop was just a few blocks away on Pershing Square, so Al saw an opportunity to partner with the duo in a 50/50 arrangement. A.R.B. (Al Brooks' initials) Corporation held the lease for the candy shop for three years, and then Adams and (Emmert) Brooks bought him out in 1958.

Walt was especially impressed with the cleanliness, product quality, customer service, respect for employees, and imaginative merchandise presentation at the shop. It was Walt who suggested having a window facing the street so that guests could see candy being made. Emmert Brooks was responsible for the operation of the Disneyland store while Adams handled production in the Los Angeles factory.

The 1955 souvenir candy box from the Candy Palace had an image of the castle, Tinker Bell in the sky, and at the bottom a smiling Jiminy Cricket wearing a blue badge that said "Be My Guest". Other Disney cartoon characters decorated the sides of the box lid intermixed with line drawings of Disneyland attractions.

Ruggles China and Glass Shop

Phil and Sophie Papel were the proprietors of the shop. Phil had a lifetime of experience in the giftware industry as well as a vision of how to innovatively stock and sell his product. He became known in the industry for his respect and kindness to customers and vendors.

When asked to come up with a name, Phil recalled a favorite film entitled *If I Had A Million* (1932) where different characters were each given a million dollars by an anonymous benefactor. In one sequence, character actor Charlie Ruggles played a shy, accident-prone employee of a china shop who is constantly being fined for breaking merchandise. He used part of his newfound wealth to smash all the expensive china and glass in his workplace with his cane. So Papel decided to use the Ruggles name.

Unlike in the film, where any breakage had to be paid for, Papel's shop had a sign promising: "Relax. We do not charge for accidental breakage."

WED's Harry Johnson did the interior sketches for the design of the shop. The select merchandise featured Wright Glass, Smith Glass, and a large selection of imports from England and West Germany. The Papels' success with this shop led to a twenty-store chain of retail gift shops in Southern California

Trinidad Ruiz

Trinidad Ruiz was a White Wing, one of the custodians on Main Street who were dressed in white linen suits and pushed large trash carts. Trinidad was a small, thin, older Spanish man with a distinctively large white mustache.

The term "White Wing" was the popular name for a street sweeper (especially one who gathered horse droppings) during the early decades of the 20th century. It was coined by Colonel George Waring Jr., head of the New York Sanitation Department, who dressed his garbage men in white duck-cloth uniforms and tall hard white hats that looked like the type British soldiers wore in South Africa during the 19th century. Waring's aim was to instill some badly needed martial order in what he saw as a rag-tag crew.

In *Window on Main Street*, Disneyland University founder Van France wrote:

> Walt not only insisted on having a White Wing for his Main Street, but he personally cast Trinidad for the job. At Walt's demand, Trinidad received extra pay, and for good reason. For several years, Trinidad was the most photographed person in the park, and, on his days off, he would come to the park just to make sure that his replacement was doing the job.

Balloons

Andrew Beard started working at Disneyland on July 17, 1955, when he was thirteen years old, selling colorful helium balloons. In my interview with him, he said:

> Helen Smith managed the balloon concession. She was the sister-in-law of Nat Lewis who operated the balloon franchise at Disneyland for about two decades or so.
>
> Nat Lewis was a smaller man. My memory says he was probably 5-foot-4 inches tall and slender built. I believed him to be in his mid- to late 60s. He was always well dressed wearing a nice suit with a bow tie. Nat was very gruff and abrupt in his demeanor. His name was spelled "Nat" but pronounced "Nate". A good way to picture what Nat looked like is to visualize a thin Peter Lorre. Nat had those same droopy eye lids and could have played as Peter's double, if he would have gained the weight.
>
> If people would ask how much the balloons were selling for, we were instructed to *never* say $0.26, but *always* $0.25 plus $0.01 sales tax. We all wore change aprons and had a certain amount of change given to us that we would have to account for at the end of the day. As a side note, there were only four selling locations: Fantasyland, Tomorrowland, and two at the main gates. We weren't allowed to go up and down the Main Street areas carrying a bunch of balloons. Park officials were adamant that the balloons would frighten the horses pulling the carts.
>
> The various balloon costumes were a sort of clown outfit for Fantasyland, dark pants and a white shirt with the Disneyland emblem for Tomorrowland, and a black-and-white striped shirt, black vest, and a black top hat (or sometimes a flat-rimmed straw hat) for the front of the park.

Disneyland News

There have actually been several publications over the decades called *Disneyland News*. The earliest was a tabloid newspaper published in the park on a monthly basis from July 1955 through March 1957. Home subscriptions were available ($1.20 for twelve issues from Castle Services, Inc. mailed in "special Disneyland wrappers") and some copies were distributed to motel and hotel operators in the Southern California area to help encourage tourists.

It was replaced by the quarterly magazine *Disneyland Holiday* in Spring 1957 and later renamed *Vacationland* when *Holiday* magazine threatened to sue over the name.

Marty Sklar, the original editor of the newspaper, recalled:

> The Amendt [Joe and Ray] Brothers had a concession on Main Street, with strollers and wheelchairs, and they sold the *Disneyland News*. They also had a place on Main Street where you could have your name printed in the

papers, in place of the headline we had done. We printed up a number of copies without the main headline for that purpose. The first summer, we sold 75,000 copies of the *Disneyland News* at ten cents. That's what Walt wanted. He wanted people to have an inexpensive souvenir and to get the word out about Disneyland promoting the attractions, events and businesses.

At the age of 21, Marty Sklar was about to become the editor of the *Daily Bruin* newspaper for UCLA, but he needed a summer job. Johnny Johnson of the UCLA Alumni Association recommended Sklar to Card Walker, then head of marketing at Disney, because Walt wanted a 1890s-style newspaper to be distributed on Main Street to help acquaint guests with the park. Sklar interviewed with Card, who hired him on June 15, 1955, and two weeks later he had to show Walt the final product.

Sklar had worked on the college newspaper for three years, so understood how to produce the tabloid. He recalled:

> I was a college student, had never worked professionally, and believe me I was scared as hell. I've told people many times since then, the good fortune is that Walt liked what I presented, and that's why I lasted for all those years at Disney.

The specialty headline printing was done at the park on antique linoscribe presses with Cheltonham Old English type that had been used to print show card window signs at the turn of the century.

The Disneyland employees and lessees had their own magazine, *Disneylander*, that featured coverage of new additions to the park, but primarily had articles about employees in different departments, including promotions, weddings, childbirths, and bowling leagues. It began on January 1956 and ran monthly through 1963. It was later replaced by other publications.

Disneyland News was revived in 1959, but only printed sporadically, roughly quarterly, until around 1968. There were special issues printed in 1985 to tie-in with Disneyland's 30th anniversary and in 1985 to promote Splash Mountain's opening.

Strollers

The Amendt Brothers were also responsible for the stroller rentals. Ray Amendt's wife commented to him that mothers were not going to last long carrying a baby in the park, so the brothers created the baby stroller rental at the front of the park. Regular strollers cost a dollar a day. They also rented double and reclining strollers, as well as wheelchairs.

Main Street Cinema

In the summer of 1955, select movies ran on the six screens in a circular room inside the Main Street Cinema, often in edited, shortened versions, and promoted as: "Six different pictures on six different screens. All for ten cents. Continuous and Simultanteous." The movies were:

- *A Dash Through the Clouds* (1912), an aviation comedy with Mabel Norman
- *Fatima's Dance* (1896), directed by Thomas Edison, in which Fatima, well known for her belly dancing shows at the World's Exhibition in 1893, performs for the camera
- *The Noise of Bombs* (1914), a comedy with the Keystone Kops
- *Dealing for Daisy* (1915), a Western with W.S. Hart; it was an edited version of *Mr. "Silent" Haskins*
- *Gertie the Dinosaur* (1914), the first animated cartoon with personality animation hand drawn by Winsor McCay
- *Shifting Sands* (1918), a melodramatic thriller with Gloria Swanson

The selection was changed constantly during the early years to feature films by Will Rogers, Valentino, Blanche Sweet, Buster Keaton, Ben Turpin Charlie Murray, Lon Chaney (*Phantom of the Opera* from 1925, with a real costumed Phantom haunting the front of the theater), and others.

Red Wagon Inn

In the 1950s, Swift Foods was one of America's largest producers of prepared meats. They also became one of the largest lessees at Disneyland, running the Market House on Main Street and the Plantation Chicken House in Frontierland (where an entire Plantation House "tender-grown chicken dinner" could be purchased for $1.65), as well as the Red Wagon Inn.

The restaurant was called the Red Wagon Inn because the icon for Swift Premium Foods at the time was the red, horse-drawn delivery wagon from which the founder started the company.

The menu originally offered a varied selection of food, such as steaks and chops and Swift's quality meats. The restaurant served a lot of sandwiches and some fish, as well. Reportedly, Roy O. Disney was especially fond of the split roast chicken served there.

General Manager John Mueller remembered:

> [The Red Wagon Inn] featured entrees of chicken pot pie, Swift's premium baked ham, Swiss steak, traditional chef's salad and a fruit plate. We served thousands of meals. However, eventually, after Swift and Co.'s lease ran out, the restaurant was converted to a cafeteria.

The restaurant featured ornate interior woodwork, chandeliers, stained glass, and tile floors that were something of a rarity in a restaurant that offered reasonably priced foods.

The back of the menu provided the following historical information:

> The Red Wagon Inn on the Plaza in Disneyland offers elegance and glamour reminiscent of famed eating houses of yesterday.
>
> Turn-of-the-century furnishings are authentic mementos of the 1890s. The leaded cut glass entrance doors to the Red Wagon Inn, as well as the stained glass ceiling and back panel of the lobby, were taken from the mansion at No. 20, St. James Park in Los Angeles.
>
> This home was built in 1870 and was one of the luxury homes of the era. Walt Disney purchased this home and removed all the hand carved paneling, newel posts, grand stairway and stained glass that has been used here in the Red Wagon Inn.

Walt wanted a sense of authenticity in the original restaurant as an example of his commitment to "theming". Imagineer John Hench explained:

> Swift's Red Wagon Inn is a good example of authentic theming. Even the interior had a color scheme of wood that was finished in a yellow-brown that was like tobacco. And naugahyde seat covers that were like chipped beef—a dried blood color. The place was authentic and also kind of depressing. We learned from that.

In 1955, the restaurant hosted a Disney Artists Exhibit display of oil and watercolor paintings by Disney artists like Harper Goff, Walt Peregoy, Bill Mahood, and Bruce McIntyre.

The Intimate Apparel Shop

One of C.V. Wood's personal friends, Herndon Norris, was president of the Hollywood-Maxwell Brassiere Company in Los Angeles, which is why Norris got a lease for a shop on Main Street. Herndon proudly proclaimed his business, established in 1934, to be "the largest bra manufacturer west of the Mississippi", with ten plants in America, one in Canada, and multiple licensing contracts with companies overseas.

It was the only shop on Main Street with a front porch and three small steps to enter inside. The reason has been debated, but possibly because the steps prevented children from looking into the showroom and the porch provided a place for men to wait while women shopped for their under garments.

An exhibit hosted by the Wizard of Bras (a mechanical figure with a tape-recorded spiel) presented the evolution of intimate apparel from corsets and pantaloons to "modern-day" marvels of bras and petticoats. The shop closed within the first six months.

Hollywood-Maxwell had a good reputation for supplying "who-can-tells" (handmade full false breasts) to Hollywood leading ladies to enhance their glamorous silhouettes. Stiff competition and labor disputes caused problems, and the company was finally acquired by Munsingwear, Inc. in 1958.

Kodak Camera Shop

In payment for his participation in the opening day broadcast, Art Linkletter was paid "scale" (the minimum wage established by the union) and given the concession to all film and cameras at the park for ten years. He was officially a sub-lessee to Kodak. Linkletter owned and operated a camera store in Los Angeles known as Royal Tone Photo Services. In addition to the store on Main Street, there were gift stands throughout the park.

The shop featured only Eastman Kodak cameras, film, and camera equipment. It rented both still cameras to guests for a dollar a day and movie cameras for two dollars a day, in the hope that doing so would increase the sale of film for both. Guests could leave both movie and still camera film to be developed and then mailed anywhere in the United States. Minor camera repairs were also offered.

Kodak posted plaque stands in the park of recommended locations to take a good picture known. These locations, as Kodak Photo Spots, each featured an example of a good composition. It was actually a marketing idea to increase the use of film. When Walt was asked why he wanted brands like Kodak, Carnation, and Coca-Cola on Main Street, he replied to a reporter, "They make the fantasy real."

Upjohn Pharmacy

Walt was good friends with Donald S. Gilmore, the chairman of the board and managing director of Upjohn. Eighty tickets for the July 17 event were given to West Coast Upjohn employees and their families. On that day, two ribbons were cut in front of the entrance to the Upjohn Pharmacy, one by Upjohn Sales Director Fred Allen and the other by four officers in the California State Pharmacists Association.

Disney initially designed the interior as it did for other lessees. When Upjohn saw the mock-up, they protested, saying Disney's design did not reflect the layout of old-time drugstores. Upjohn then hired well-known graphic designer Will Burtin to design the store. The building was ultimately constructed according to Burtin's plans.

The front half of the store had a reproduction of an old-time apothecary shop based on three New York pharmacies that were in existence before 1886. In the back was a contemporary display with four revolving photo columns showing phases of present-day manufacturing; on a nearby wall was large aerial photo of Upjohn's Portage plant with descriptive captions. Two clerks and two registered pharmacists worked the store under manager Leo Austin. The final rental cost turned out to be $37,720 per year.

Of course, it was not a real pharmacy, even though two real pharmacists (Fredrick August Eckstein and Philip Milton Harvey) were in the shop and dressed in period costumes. Instead, the location hosted an exhibition which traced the origins of pharmacy back to its early beginnings. The shop featured apothecary jars, show globes, scales, and other equipment commonly used in drugsores of that period.

The shop gave away free postcards as well as a free square miniature glass bottle of orange-colored Unicap Vitamins inside a red box with a white silhouette of the Disneyland castle logo containing a pamphlet entitled "A Souvenir of Disneyland Upjohn" with a history of Upjohn. The bottle was an inch and a half tall and contained twelve vitamins with an expiration date.

In the April 1955 issue *The Overflow*, the company's sales magazine, Upjohn reported:

> But Upjohn is in the drug, not the entertainment business, so the inclusion of the Company sponsored drugstore may seem a bit unique and illogical. Our only reason for sponsing the store is that its presence in Disneyland constitutes sound, inexpensive, advertising with exciting possibilities. As Disney reaps the profits of his latest work, Upjohn will get full advertising value. Furthermore, none of our competitors may sponsor an exhibition unless they either get our permission or sponsor the million-dollar Disney TV show. Why does the drugstore constitute good advertising? Of primary importance is the fact that it will be seen by the public. Secondarily, it's inexpensive.
>
> Year after year, Disneyland will present the name Upjohn to the public, much as an ad in *Life* presents the Company's name. But an ad in *Life* does the job once. Disneyland does it many times. The cost? Once construction is finished, the annual costs will be about the same as one page in one issue of *Life*. How many people will see Disneyland? Present estimates indicate that six million people will see Disney's fairyland every year.
>
> It's a new form of advertising, but Board Chairman Donald Gilmore and Advertising Manager Jack Gauntlett have expressed enthusiasm concerning it. All of the sponsors in Disneyland will be top-flight Companies.

Garrard MacLeod, M.D., editor of *Scope* (a pharmaceutical industry magazine) and an antiquer by avocation, helped in the historical research and the procurement of the some nearly one thousand authentic pieces of apothecary equipment.

The stove from 1900 was found in a New Jersey shop. The leaded glass chandeliers came from the attic of a Kalamazoo druggist who bought them in the 1890s and used them in his shop until 1918. The herb grinder at the time was seventy-five years old. A collection of antique microscopes dating back to the 1700s were purchased from a New York collector. Dr. MacLeod fixed some of the parts so that each was usable and vintage slides were included for guests to view. A collection of syringes dated from 1850.

Interestingly, there was a glass jar of live leeches on display. At the turn of the century, leeches were used to draw blood from infected parts of the body.

Many of the artifacts from the Upjohn Disneyland Pharmacy are now in the Pharmacy Museum at the University of Arizona in Tucson. The university received the Upjohn Disneyland collection in 2006 from the California Museum of Science and Industry (now called the California Science Center). The exhibit was designed using old photographs and primary documents to re-create the original back-counter display as faithfully as possible.

Bank of America

Bank of America had been a long time supporter of Walt Disney beginning with its help in financing *Snow White and the Seven Dwarfs* (1937) and subsequent Disney animated features. It also supplied loans for the construction of Disneyland.

The bank building on Main Street was a functioning bank used by the guests, Disneylanders (to cash their checks), lessees, and Disneyland, Inc. It claimed that except for escrow services and safe deposit boxes, it offered all the services of the statewide banking firm. For many years, it was the only bank in the United States to be open on a Sunday or on holidays.

Walt located an original 1904 bank vault and had it installed inside the building where it still exists today. The interior of the bank had hardwood teller windows, a brass hat rack, shiny cuspidors, an old fashioned settee with matching chair, a roll-top desk for the manager, and an 1880 typewriter still in working order. Tellers were dressed in vests and string ties.

The bank also offered collectible souvenir money orders in one-dollar (with the side image of a train engine), five-dollar (image of the front of the Disneyland Bank of America) and ten-dollar denominations (a sidewheeler riverboat, not the *Mark Twain*, since the illustration was based on early concept art) convertible into cash at banks and stores everywhere.

When the park first opened, the bank's business hours were 11am to 5pm, but the hours later adjusted to 10am to 4pm. Bank manager Leo Wagman arranged for fifty bags of silver dollars to be shipped from the central cash vault in Los Angeles to Disneyland for opening day.

Penny Arcade

Albert Clifford Raney had a large collection of mechanical music machines. Raney passed away in 1949. In 1953, Walt Disney bought thirty prized examples from his widow, a friend of Bud Hurlbut who was working with Walt at the time. They were stored in the Disney Studio commissary until their later move to Disneyland. Some went into the Penny Arcade, some to the music store, and one was placed on the *Mark Twain* dock. Walt gave some of the smaller machines to his wife, and one ended up in his apartment.

Walt's Apartment

Walt needed a place to stay while Disneyland was being completed, and so a small studio apartment was built over the firehouse on Main Street. It was decorated by Emile Kuri to suggest the Victorian era. A rose motif was used extensively, on everything from furniture to dinnerware.

Although small, the area included a small dressing area with a mirrored closet, a tiny bathroom complete with enclosed shower, and a living room with a kitchenette behind louvered folding doors. There were also two fold-out bed couches. The room was filled with items that Walt and Lillian had acquired on their travels as well as purchased at Disneyland locations like the Ruggles China Shop. There were also two antique music boxes.

Since the apartment was above the firehouse, there was a fire pole that according to legend was covered up after a curious child climbed up the pole and poked his head into the apartment while Walt was sitting there reading the newspaper. The apartment served as a refuge for Walt when he visited the park as well as a location to entertain friends and celebrities, sometimes on the small outdoor patio with white wicker furniture.

On April 18, 1986, Lillian notified the Disney company that she wanted to remove "all personal items of Walt Disney and mine from our apartment at Disneyland". The first set of personal property (family pictures, hairbrush, portable radio, raincoats, scarves, and similar items) was removed in May, with the remainder of the larger antiques and collectibles taken out that summer. Lillian's last known visit to the apartment was in December 1984.

Harper Goff and Main Street, U.S.A.

One of the primary contributors to Disneyland's Main Street was Imagineer Harper Goff, who was born and grew up in Fort Collins, Colorado, where his dad owned a newspaper. As Goff told the Janzen brothers in the Winter 1992–93 issue of *The E Ticket* magazine:

> I grew up there. It was a very prosperous town. We had banks that looked like banks, you know, and there was a Victorian city hall. I was born in 1911 and these buildings were around when I was a kid. When I started working on Main Street, I had photographs of Fort Collins taken. I showed them to Walt and he liked them very much. Disneyland's City Hall was copied from Fort Collins; so was the bank building and some of the others.

Disneyland's City Hall includes elements from the turn-of-the-century courthouse in Fort Collins, which at the time had a grassy "roundabout" in the street like the one near the entrance of Disneyland's train station.

However, if Main Street, U.S.A., was not an actual re-creation of Walt Disney's Marceline, Missouri, neither was it an exact re-creation of Fort Collins, Colorado, but featured some of the same elements.

CHAPTER SIXTEEN

Adventureland

The 1955 Disneyland Guide Map gave this account of Adventureland:

> Those romantic, tropical far-away places that all of us yearn to see, await your visit in Adventureland. A Tahitian trading post provides an exotic threshold for this wonder-world of Nature's own design. Here you'll marvel at the display of tropical flowers, birds, fish and native handicraft gathered from all latitudes. An adventurous cruise in an explorer's boat, over the tropical rivers of the world is a highlight of Adventureland. On this exciting trip, you'll thrill to the life-like wild animals, reptiles, birds, monkeys and even native savages. Your boat ventures under a real waterfall as you admire the tropical plants and foliage gathered from all over the world. Truly, an adventure to remember is Adventureland.

Rides and Amusements
- Explorer's Boat Ride / Jungle River Boat Ride ("C" ticket)

Restaurants and Refreshments
- Pavilion Restaurant
- Tropical Bar

Rest Rooms
- Adventureland entrance

Arboretum

There are iconic architectural structures that Walt used to call "wienies" for every land except Adventureland. The height of the TWA Moonliner and the Sleeping Beauty Castle capture the attention of guests and draw them deeper into their respective areas. Today, the Disney company claims that Adventureland's lack of a similar elevated structure was part of Walt's plan to keep the mystery of adventure and encourage discovery. Actually, Walt did have plans for a wienie in Adventureland. Next to the two-story Jungle

Cruise building was to be a massive spiked, glass-enclosed arboretum as tall as the castle and filled with exotic plants and birds. It appears as both a line drawing and a concept painting in the first souvenir guide book. It is also shown as the icon of Adventureland on Bank of America's 1955 free "*Your Guide to Disneyland*" eight-fold map. Unfortunately, as costs continued to rise, planned items for the park, including this one, were eliminated.

Adventureland Bazaar

There was only one attraction in Adventureland, the Jungle Cruise, when the park opened, with the rest of the area occupied by a "tropical community" that was originally going to be a Tahitian Village but evolved into a generic Hollywood jungle outpost. Guests could get food and beverages at the Pavilion Restaurant on Main Street and then move to an outdoor terrace in the back to eat and listen to Hawaiian music as they viewed the jungle.

Since the area was to represent many different locations, from the Caribbean to the South Pacific to Africa to India and elsewhere, the architecture was a standard exotic mix of bamboo, dried palm fronds, carved shields, native spears, canvas-covered sections, even a "human" skull or two, as well as a large, rough plaster and weathered main building.

The bazaar, operated by Lawson Engineering and managed by Jack Schrecengoal, sub-leased locations to individual vendors:

- Lee Brothers Enterprises (managed by Bill Wong, and selling imported Chinese novelty items, china, and clothing)
- Hawaiian Shop (managed by Waltah Clarke, and selling Hawaiian apparel like shirts and swimwear)
- Island Trade Store (managed by Eli Hedley, selling bamboo spears with rubber tips, plastic leather necklaces with a jeweled eye tiki, rubber snakes, shells, plastic reptiles, and the occasional black rubber shrunken head)
- Guatemalan Weavers (managed by Ed Jeffries and Marta Cordon, and selling hand-woven fabrics)
- Curio Hut (managed by Berncie De Gonslar)
- Tiki Tropical Traders (managed by Merlen Poemocoah, and selling "South Sea Island apparel in a colorful assortment of unusual fabrics")
- Here and There Imports (managed by Leal Brenner, and selling brassware, jewelry, silks, and cottons)

In addition, there was a giftware stand managed by Vern Croft for Disneyland Inc., and a Tiki hut souvenir stand sat comfortably in the area between the entrance to the Jungle Cruise and the entrance to the bazaar.

Electro-Mechanical Animals

Imagineer John Hench explained:

> Walt wanted every person who came through there to get a full show. The only answer was mechanical animals. Real animals sleep during the day. Walt's idea for the animals was really a form of his basic honesty—he wanted the audience to get the same full performance every time.

In fact, a 1955 Disneyland postcard talks about animals lurking in the Adventureland bushes, but the word "animals" is in quotes.

Disney artist Harper Goff recalled:

> Walt and I had both seen the film *The African Queen* (1951) and the animals were never completely visible. They were partially hidden in the underbrush on shore or just under the water. So we began to think of hippos and other animals whose mechanics and tracks could be hidden and still have animated elements. We brought in Bob Mattey who later created the shark for *Jaws* (1975) to engineer the original animals.

The models for the animals on the Jungle Cruise were sculpted by Chris Mueller who had a previous career working at Universal Studios as well as sculpting the giant squid for the Disney feature film *20,000 Leagues Under the Sea* (1954). Mueller used clay to build figures for molds that were later cast in fiberglass.

Then Bob Mattey installed a mixture of spring steel, rubber, flexible tubing, and other things on rocker arms or hinged joints that were operated by cams and levers connected to electric motors. The movement was done in an on/off fashion, sometimes on a support carriage that followed a track or swung around a pivot. Mattey recalled:

> Walt said he wanted mechanical animals that looked real, animals that wiggle their ears and open their mouths.

It took three different sets of cams to operate the hippos so they could move forward and back eight feet, up and down, and open and close their mouths. In the early months, these devices soon became clogged with sand and mud and water damaged, so a water-based hydraulic system was installed in 1956.

While many of the animals were built and tested at the Disney Studio, some of the larger ones were made right at Disneyland. The African elephant stood eight-feet six-inches tall at the shoulder. It weighed nine hundred pounds and the day before opening, as a crew attempted to install it, it began to sink into a mound of fill dirt. The black rhino was nine feet long and the hippo over twelve feet in length.

Live Animals

Walt felt he needed live animals in Adventureland as well. So he stocked a small pond near the front of the Jungle Cruise queue with baby alligators. Walt probably got this idea from The Los Angeles Alligator Farm, a major city tourist attraction from 1907 until 1953 in the area that later became Lincoln Park. In 1953, it relocated near Anaheim to become the Buena Park Alligator Farm, with gators shipped in from Florida.

However, Walt's gators kept escaping and were removed within months. In addition, Walt explored purchasing some exotic waterfowl like crown herons to mix with the mechanical animals on the attraction, but with money quickly running out, that order was canceled.

Disney artist Herb Ryman recalled:

> The Jungle Cruise Ride was to be filled with live animals and we gave serious thought to where they would live and how they would be cared for. We thought there would be monkeys, elephants, crocodiles, etc., until the zoo people said, "You'll have a time taking care of them. Besides, if you run people through on boats, these animals are going to hide. Someone from one boat will say, 'How did you like the chimpanzees?' And someone from another boat will say, 'We never saw anything. There weren't any animals. We got cheated.'" So, it was obvious, we would have to simulate animals, which disappointed me, because I thought it would look phony. But the talents of the men involved made it look convincing.

The Jungle Cruise Launches

The Jungle Cruise Explorer launches were designed by Imagineer Harper Goff to be reminiscent of the one used by Humphrey Bogart in the film *The African Queen* (1951). They were among the first, and the biggest, to be built out of the recently perfected fiberglass material. The boats were constructed by the Wizard Boat Company in Costa Mesa, California.

The original seven boats were all named by Walt's brother-in-law, Bill Cottrell: Congo Queen, Swanee Lady, Amazon Belle, Ganges Gal, Nile Princess, Mekong Maiden, and Irrawaddi Woman.

Their candy cane-striped canopies were not just for "show" but served the purpose of narrowing the guests' vision so they could not fully see the still-growing foliage and the buildings that the landscaping would eventually hide.

The river averages a depth of about five feet and is dyed brownish to hide its shallowness. Out of desperation at the monotony ("That's something you don't see everyday...unless you are a Jungle Cruise skipper..."), and in keeping with their natural showmanship, the skippers began adding humorous commentary so that the trip became less and less of a nature documentary.

Sound Effects

Radio &Television News reported in its August 1956 issue:

> One entire section of the park is a simulated African jungle in which three types of sound effects are required. They are: intermittent localized effects which must come in on cue such as the trumpeting of a mechanical elephant as visitors approach on one of the riverboats; continuous localized effects such as a constant chattering of monkeys in one area of the jungle; and continuous overall effects which would be heard virtually anywhere in the jungle at all times such as the roar of lions, bird sounds, and the noises of crickets and frogs at night.
>
> All the sound effects are on magnetic tape and various types of control devices such as photoelectric cells, times and the magnetic tapes themselves turn the effects on and off automatically.... To heighten the illusion, a different sound track is used during the evening. This second track was actually taped in the African jungle at night and brings authentic evening sounds to the listener.
>
> For instance, as the riverboat nears the "rhino land" area of the jungle tour, it interrupts a photocell beam reaching across the river. Infrared filters keep the beam invisible. The signal from the photocell trips relays which are located in the mechanical rhinos, thus setting them in motion and also starting the tape in one of the 150 cartridge type repeating tape players in the control room for the jungle area.
>
> The third type of sound effect to provide the continuous overall effect of typical jungle sounds for the entire area is recorded on a portion of a 4800-foot reel of one-quarter-inch magnetic tape. Used on a self-reversing tape player, it is fed into a 50-watt amplifier and then sequentially to five groups of loudspeakers (eight speakers to a group) by means of the "continuous automatic fader" designed for that purpose.
>
> This device was developed specifically for use at Disneyland by Mr. James Hervey, general manager of the project for the Ralke Company, Los Angeles, California, contractors for audio-visual effects at the park.

CHAPTER SEVENTEEN

Frontierland

The 1955 Disneyland Guide Map gave this account of Frontierland:
> Frontierland is where you'll actually "live" America's colorful and historic past. You'll enter Frontierland through the gates of an old log fort—past leather-stockinged frontiersmen and Indians of many tribes, gathered at the entrance. All the stores and buildings, reminiscent of this period, line the boardwalk of the town. At the blacksmith shop, you'll watch ponies being shod—next door you'll see the harness maker at work and across the street the ever-famous general store.
>
> How about "hopping" a freight train? At the Frontierland station, you can board a scaled-down version of an old-time Santa Fe and Disneyland "iron horse", and ride in the freight car (comfortably provided with special seats) for an exciting ride around the perimeter of the park. You can board a buckboard, Conestoga Wagon or Concord Stage to ride by the Marshal's office, the jail, assay office and other frontier enterprises, including an exciting trip through the Painted Desert. The Golden Horseshoe, "longest little bar with the tallest glassful of pop", faces a river dock in Frontierland. From here you can board a 105-foot paddle-wheeler steamboat for a cruise on the rivers of America.

Exhibits
- Davy Crockett Museum

Shops
- Assay Office (Jemrocks; manager Darcey Hines)
- Bone Kraft (Manager Richard Swenson)
- Pendleton Woolen Mills Dry Goods Store (Manager Harv Johnson)
- Frontier Trading Post (Manager Eve McFadden)

Shows
- Golden Horseshoe Revue
- Indian Village

Rest Rooms
- Plantation Restaurant
- Frontierland entrance

Telephones
- Left of fort entrance

Food and Refreshments
- Aunt Jemima's Pancake House (Quaker Oats)
- Casa de Fritos (Mexican food from Frito Lay)
- Golden Horseshoe (Pepsi Cola)
- Swift's Chicken Plantation Restaurant
- UPT Concessions food and beverage stands

Rides and Amusements
- Conestoga Wagon Ride ("B" ticket)
- Mark Twain River Boat Ride ("C" ticket)
- Mike Fink Keel Boats ("C" ticket)
- Mule Pack Ride ("C" ticket)
- Santa Fe & Disneyland Railroad Freight Train ("C" ticket)
- Shooting Gallery
- Stagecoach ("C" ticket)
- Surrey Rides ("A" ticket)
- Yellowstone Coach Rides ("C" ticket)

Indian Village

Walt wanted Frontierland to be representative of the wild frontier rather than a settled town. Original concept art had the Indian Village located in front of the entrance, but when the park opened in 1955, it sat near the border between Adventureland and Frontierland as a collection of teepees on dirt with a dance circle. The tribal symbols were done by Sam McKim based on reference books from the Disney Studio library.

In 1956, the village moved to the area now occupied by Critter Country. The "villagers" displayed traditions and dances of nearly seventeen different American Indian tribes, including Apache, Comanche, Hopi, Navajo, Sioux, and Pawnee. Disney publicity proclaimed that the "authentic dances from such tribes were performed with the permission of the respective tribal councils and the U.S. Bureau of Indian Affairs". The Indian Village closed in 1971.

Walt felt that the Indian Village was a celebration of the cultural heritage of Native Americans, especially since his wife, Lillian, was born in 1899 on an Indian reservation in Idaho, the tenth and last child of Jeanette Short Bounds and Willard Pehall Bounds. Lillian grew up in Lapwai, Idaho, on the Nez Perce Indian Reservation. Her father worked for the government there as a blacksmith and federal marshal. Lillian's mother enthralled Walt with stories of coming to the West in a covered wagon and Western history involving the Indians she met.

In Frontierland, in 1955, there was a building near the Miniature Horse Corral and the entrance to the Mule Pack that had a placard proclaiming it was the location of "Williard P. Bounds Blacksmith and Marshal's office". Later, in 1956, it was replaced by Casa de Fritos.

Eddie Adamek sold trick ropes out of the blacksmith shop. Comedian Steve Martin learned how to do rope tricks from Eddie when he worked at the park. At a press conference for his film *The Three Amigos* (1986), Martin said:

> I met a guy named Eddie Adamek who was a trick roper. I was working at Disneyland, and he was twirling ropes and taught me how to do it. You don't learn it overnight. It takes two nights.

In Sam McKim's design for the Indian Village, he had placed "human scalps" up on the top of teepee poles drying in the wind. Walt immediately told him to remove them as not being an accurate portrayal of Indian culture.

At the Indian Village, guests were sometimes given souvenir wooden nickels with an image of a Buffalo reminiscent of the real nickel coins produced by the U.S. Mint from 1913–1938 that had the head of an Indian on one side and a buffalo on the reverse.

Eddie Little Sky

Prominently featured in the Indian Village and in early publicity photos was Eddie Little Sky (also known as Edward Little), one of the first Native Americans to play Native American roles in films. He was a member of the Oglala Lakota tribe and had parts in three-dozen feature films and over sixty television shows. He was not the chief, just an Indian brave.

When Disneyland opened its gates, Eddie and his artist wife, Dawn, went to work there. She was a narrator hired to explain dances she also performed. Dawn danced in the traditional style in the Indian Village, along with other tribes who had moved to the Los Angeles area during the work relocation era. Dawn had previously spent four years working in the Ink and Paint department at the Disney Studio. They had five children and lived in Anaheim during the time they worked at Disneyland.

The Wild West

According to a December 1955 Disneyland newspaper ad:

> You will ride the Conestoga Wagon in Frontierland—one of the most picturesque and vital vehicles in history. It was the Conestoga, not the Covered Wagon that developed the West. The great wagons were first built in the Conestoga Valley of Pennsylvania, with water-tight bottoms that permitted safe crossing of rivers. You will also ride authentic stage coaches, pack trains, and buckboards in this remarkable re-creation of the old West.

After new scenic landscaping, the stagecoaches were renamed the Rainbow Mountain Stage Coaches in 1956. Unfortunately, the stagecoaches were still prone to tipping over and their horses being frightened by the *Mark Twain*.

Disneyland maintained around 200 head of horses, ponies, mules, and burros. The horses and ponies were kept in individual tie stalls, with the mules and burros having their own corrals and lots. Gear was kept clean, polished, and in good repair.

A full-time farrier was on hand (Charles Heumphreus handled all the horse-shoeing chores for Disneyland), and barns, stalls, tackrooms, and corrals were kept spic and span. All animals at Disneyland and their quarters were inspected regularly by officers of the SPCA.

Because of the special skills necessary to manage the pack mule trains, only professional animal handlers were allowed to be trail bosses. Disney executive Ron Dominguez said:

> You had to know your horses to do that. Some of the handlers were ex-jockeys and really knew how to handle the horses and mules. They were exclusive to this ride and not interchangeable.

Walt fought as long as he could to keep those horse-related attractions in Frontierland because they added so much authentic atmosphere. However, they were low capacity, high maintenance, and high cost. The horses were unpredictable, occasionally unsafe, and some even considered it cruel to have these animals burdened with so many guests, even though Disneyland promoted the fact that the animals only worked limited hours each day.

The wilderness navigated by these attractions had cacti, windswept cliffs, natural bridges, poison waterholes, "graves", dried bones, desert animals and reptiles, and indications of Indian pueblos high on the mesas. In summer of 1956, this area expanded its offerings.

In its September 1957 issue, *Western Magazine* reported:

> From a horseman's standpoint, one of the highest possible compliments was passed along by an officer from the Society for the Prevention of Cruelty to Animals. After an inspection, he said, "If there's anything to this reincarnation stuff, I'd like to come back to Disneyland as a horse someday!"

Walt had found two little Sardinian donkeys that he was going to name Snow White and Prince Charming and have them pull a brightly painted cart through Frontierland. His plans changed when one of the donkeys, while it was being kept at the studio, took a nip at Walt's hand.

Golden Horseshoe

The Golden Horseshoe Saloon was pretty much an exact copy of the Golden Garter Saloon from the Warner Brothers' movie *Calamity Jane* (1953). In the film, the frontier saloon (located in Deadwood City) hosted traveling actors and actresses who performed light musical fare on stage. The Disney version has greater ornamentation, even though both saloons were designed by Harper Goff. Warner Brothers later refitted its saloon set with different curtains for *Phantom of the Rue Morgue* (1954), where it became the Moulin Rouge with a can-can dance sequence.

The original performing cast at the Golden Horseshoe was Wally Boag, Don Novis, and Judy Marsh. The Golden Horseshoe Girls who did the can-can were Shirley Towers, Gloria Watson, Glenda Guilfoyle, and Susan Reed.

The actual show was put together by Boag and musical director Charles LaVere (who had written some of the songs for the show with lyrics by Tom Adair), along with contributions from Don Novis. Wardrobe mistress Ruby Watson also kept her eyes on the young female dancers. Marsh only lasted about six months in the role of Slue Foot Sue until she was replaced by Betty Taylor who shone in the role for decades. Marsh was a nightclub singer and the cause of her dismissal is still a topic of speculation.

Walt loved the show, highly recommended it to others, and would often take guests to see it. He would always sit in the box on stage left. If word got out that Walt was in the park, they'd keep that box reserved for him. Other fans who would frequently see the show included Cary Grant and Lucille Ball.

From the Pepsi Cola in-house promotional campaign book for Disneyland from spring 1955:

> We hope that from the photographs on these pages, you will be able to visualize this Park, but please be assured by those of us who have seen the actual site and scale models of the various components that this will without doubt be the greatest single tourist attraction in the United States, and we are exceptionally happy that we have been able to complete our negotiations with Disneyland on such a dominant scale.
>
> While there will be competition in the Park, there is little doubt that Pepsi-Cola will over shadow everyone else. [The Golden Horseshoe] will be the largest, single concession area [4,500 square feet] in the entire park and one of the very few places where people can refresh themselves and also have an opportunity to rest! In addition to this marvelous Pepsi center, we have extensive distribution throughout the rest of the Park.

Rivers of America

The riverbed had to be created by bulldozers plowing the necessary trenches. The first time water was pumped into them, it immediately seeped through the coarse soil. Eventually, a hard clay bottom mixed with gunite (cement, sand, and water applied through a pressure hose) was installed with a metal framework. The river ranges from eighty to a hundred feet wide, but just a few feet deep.

According to Disneyland publicity at the time:

> Flocks of wild geese, mallards, and other birds have found Frontierland's River a safe retreat in their pilgrimages south. The birds pause to rest here and in some cases stay for several months.

There were as many as four dozen forest animal and "friendly Indian" figures on the rivers. Some of the animals were stationary, as if caught in the moment of sensing humans in the forest. In the earliest months, real birds often attacked the stuffed birds because they felt their territory was being invaded. Other birds pulled out the hair from the fake animals to build nests.

The most prominent Indian figure was a stately Plains Indian chief in full head-dress astride his horse. He slowly raises his right arm in greeting as if granting safe passage to the ship and its passengers. Blaine Gibson sculpted the head and ended up doing all of the Indian heads that were placed on bodies molded from actor Woody Strode, who also provided the castings for the natives in the Jungle Cruise. Gibson and Herb Ryman painted every Indian personally.

Mike Fink Keel Boat

The last new attraction of 1955 was introduced December 25, 1955. ABC had just aired the final two episodes of the Davy Crocket saga: *Davy Crockett's Keelboat Race* (November 16) and *Davy Crockett and the River Pirates* (December 14). Davy and his friend Georgie Russel poled the *Bertha Mae* and their competition was Mike Fink and his rowdy crew on the *Gullywhumper*.

Walt realized that these two thirty-eight-foot long movie props might be great additions to the Rivers of America. Both of the keelboats were brought to Disneyland in August 1955 after the filming on the episodes had been completed so that they could be converted with seats and windows. The original *Bertha Mae* was actually redecorated as the *Gullywhumper* and introduced to the park in December. The original *Gullywhumper* required more work. When it made its appearance in May 1956, it was dubbed the *Bertha Mae*.

Both boats were built entirely out of pine, cypress, redwood, and Douglas fir. They lasted for about ten years, after which they were quietly replaced with new fiberglass boat replicas that were stronger, lighter, and had electrical systems.

The boats were "free floating", meaning they were not on a rail so they had more freedom in terms of the trip, often visiting both banks of the river. Collector Richard Kraft bought the *Bertha Mae* for $15,000 from Disney Auctions in December 2001.

Davy Crockett Museum

Located just inside the Frontierland stockade entrance, the Davy Crockett Museum was a shop that hoped to capitalize on the popularity of the Disney version of the character with various merchandise. Inside it was decorated like part of the Alamo with adobe walls and rough wooden framing. On the walls were some of the drawings used in the television program to illustrate the various verses of the famous song.

There were many small themed retail locations inside, including a leather shop, rock shop, and souvenir area, as well as a display of historic guns showing the evolution of firearms sponsored by the National Rifle Association. It was assembled by author James E. Servern, an arms historian and consultant, and featured actual weapons from the Revolutionary War, Colt pistols from the 1930s, and even some "Kentucky" rifles like the kind associated with Crockett. Sam McKim designed the display.

In October 1955, the museum was renamed the Davy Crockett Frontier Arcade. The coin-operated shooting gallery, B'ar Country, challenged guests to test their skill with Crocket's Ol' Betsy, with the rifles holstered in a tree stump. In addition to trees that had owls and squirrels that moved once they were hit, the panorama also included little mechanical grizzly bears that moved back and forth. If a marksman hit the dot on their sides, the bear would rear up and swivel toward the shooter, revealing another dot on its stomach, and would remain standing as long as the shooter kept hitting that dot.

In addition, the museum had life-sized wax figures of Davy and his friend Georgie Russel as a photo opportunity. They were sculpted by Katherine Stubergh, who had created the wax figures for the film *House of Wax* (1953). They were posed against a backdrop of the Texas plains, and guests could borrow a coonskin cap and long rifle to pose with the pair for their official Disneyland photo.

Sheriff Lucky

A familiar figure in Frontierland who also appeared on Disneyland postcards was Burl Fauntz, who played Sheriff Lucky. Fauntz preferred going by his nickname of "Lucky", which is how the sheriff got his name. He had been a Los Angeles police officer and a San Bernardino deputy and was a big man with a black mustache. Besides interacting with guests and being a photo opportunity, the sheriff participated in up to four gunfights a day. In the beginning, he did this with comedian Wally Boag on his breaks from his shows in the Golden Horseshoe, and then later with card sharp Black Bart. Over the years, several different people took the roles of lawman and outlaws.

Mule Pack

There were thirty mules that traveled a loop out into the wilderness that was also traversed by the Conestoga wagon and the stagecoaches. The mule train consisted of a trail boss on a horse and seven or eight mules of varying sizes. The smaller ones were up front for younger guests so they could be monitored by the trail boss. There was not much to see except for three Indian teepees, a few horses, the frontier vehicles, and lots of dirt, but the thrill for urban children was riding a real mule like a cowboy. In June 1956, the experience became more elaborate with the expansion into the Rainbow Ridge theme.

Lafitte's Anchor

On a warm day in August 1955, the celebration started with the Disneyland Band, under the direction of Vesey Walker who led the dignitaries that had gathered on Main Street to a bandstand in Magnolia Park on New Orleans Street. Following the band was actress Dorothy Lamour (not in a sarong, but in a long, white, short-sleeved dress and heels) accompanied by her husband William Howard, riding in a Main Street surrey.

She was followed by the Disneyland stagecoach carrying the Frito Kid, the mascot of the Casa De Fritos eatery. Casa de Fritos debuted the month after the opening of Disneyland in 1955, next to Aunt Jemima's Pancake House.

Since this was in the days before costumed mascots made such public appearances, the Frito Kid was portrayed by a "little person" actor who wore a Frito Kid outfit, including the name Frito Kid in huge letters on the front of his shirt, but his real face was clearly visible.

The parade was still not over, because there were now members of the United States Marine Corps from New Orleans who happened to be in the area because of training at the El Toro Marine base near Disneyland. Finally, bringing up the rear of the parade was the original cast from Slue Foot Sue's Golden Horseshoe Revue.

Lamour, to loud cheers from the gathered crowd, approached an ancient anchor laying on its side, but tilted slightly up at an angle. According to Disneyland publicity, the anchor was believed to be a part of one of the pirate ships that sailed the Gulf of Mexico in the days of pirate Jean

Lafitte, and it remained displayed at Disneyland for at least four decades. Lamour christened the anchor by breaking a bottle filled with water from the Mississippi River and the Gulf of Mexico. "We found it in an antique store near New Orleans," Walt told the press.

The plaque near the anchor stated:

> Lafitte's Anchor. Said to be from a pirate ship commanded by Jean Lafitte in the Battle of New Orleans, January 8, 1815. It is also said that Lafitte's privateering ships left a wake of blood from the Mainland to Barataria Bay, but don't believe everything you read.

Walt Disney on Frontierland

In its May–June 1958 issue, *True West* magazine ran an article entitled "Frontierland", under Walt Disney's byline:

> Of course, all the realms of Disneyland intrigue me but Frontierland evokes a special response because it reminds me of my youthful days when elements of the frontier were still visible in rural Missouri.
>
> One of the biggest joys of my life is sitting on the levee in the Frontierland section of Disneyland. As I gaze to the north, I can see the smokestacks of the steamer, *Mark Twain*, belching smoke. When I was growing up in Kansas City, there were still two stern-wheelers plying out of that town.
>
> As you can expect from a Missouri-bred boy, I wanted the *Mark Twain* to be authentic. Our staff did extensive research on river boats of the past before it came up with a design. Like most of Disneyland, the boat is under-scale to give a fantasy-like appearance. That meant the engines had to be specially built to fit into a smaller craft.
>
> The Frontierland entrance is the log stockade. Those logs are the real thing. They were felled in the mountain region near Lake Arrowhead, California, and hand-hewn by carpenters who were specially chosen for their experience in log cabin or ship building.
>
> Inside, you'll see some gnarled pine posts. Those were my own discovery. When I was on a trip to the Jackson Hole country in Wyoming, I came across some logs with unusual burls on them. I figured they were just the thing for Frontierland and had sixty of them shipped down to California.

CHAPTER EIGHTEEN

Fantasyland

The 1955 Disneyland Guide Map gave this account of Fantasyland:
A world of imagination—come to life. You'll cross a drawbridge to enter Fantasyland through the portals of a medieval castle with towers and parapets rising dizzily above you. In Fantasyland you'll take the Peter Pan ride aboard a pirate galleon that soars over moonlit London to Never Land, home of Mermaids, Buccaneers, Indians and Lost Boys, and flit through the Darling home, take the Snow White ride and meet the Seven Dwarfs, the Wicked Witch who will offer you a poisoned apple, and all the other characters of this immortal classic.

Mr. Toad's Wild Ride runs through a series of misadventures in a 1903 vintage automobile, knocking over a cow and crashing into a barn, you travel through the "Pearly Gates" to the sounds of heavenly music. Other gay, novel amusements of Fantasyland are based on cartoon or story book characters that Walt Disney has brought to screen life. Dumbo, the Flying Elephant, a breath-taking aerial ride, the Mad Tea Party, King Arthur Carrousel with 72 gorgeous steeds, the Casey Jr. circus train, Canal Boats of America, England, France and fabulous attractions.

Shops
- Merlin's Magic Shop (Managers Bud and Merv Taylor for Taylor and Hume Inc.)
- Toy Shop (Manager Bob Erickson)
- Don Frank's Fantasy of Disneyland (children's clothing)

Show:
- Mickey Mouse Club Theater ("B" ticket)

Rest Rooms
- West side of the Mickey Mouse Club Theater (identified as "Prince" and "Princess")

Telephones
- West side of Fantasyland

Food and Refreshments
- Pirate Ship (Van Camp Chicken of the Sea)
- Welch's Grape Juice Stand (adjoining the Mickey Mouse Club Theater)
- UPT Concessions food and beverage stands

Rides
- Canal Boats of the World ("B" ticket)
- Casey Jr. Circus Train ("B" ticket)
- Dumbo, the Flying Elephant ("B" ticket)
- King Arthur Carrousel ("A" ticket)
- Mad Hatter's Tea Party ("B" ticket)
- Mr. Toad's Wild Ride ("C" ticket)
- Peter Pan Ride-Thru ("C" ticket)
- Snow White Ride-Thru ("C" ticket)

Sleeping Beauty Castle

One of the original concepts of the castle was that it was to be Robin Hood's castle to tie in with the Disney live-action film *The Story of Robin Hood and His Merrie Men* (1952), starring Richard Todd. In the documentary *Disneyland U.S.A.* (1956), Robin Hood and his men are sitting on the drawbridge welcoming guests into Fantasyland. One of Imagineer Marvin Davis's first diagrams identifies the structure as Robin Hood's castle.

The turrets for Sleeping Beauty Castle were made out of fiberglass and were created at the Disney Studio and then shipped to Anaheim and assembled. It was discussed having a "camera obscura" in the highest tower, but Eustace Lycett said there was not enough light for it to be effective.

Artist Eyvind Earle told Walt that the turrets should each be different colors like pink, red, purple, and yellow. When Walt talked with his art director for Fantasyland, Bill Martin, about Earle's suggestion, Martin replied that all the turrets should be blue, like slate, and Walt agreed.

In the episode *Man in Flight* (03/06/1957) from the weekly Disney television series, Walt identified the castle as Snow White Castle, obviously remembering a previous concept.

Chicken of the Sea Pirate Ship

The mermaid figurehead (meant to resemble the mascot of the food brand) on the bow of the ship was sculpted by Chris Mueller from designs by

Imagineer Marc Davis, his first work for Disneyland. Mueller was also responsible for the twenty-foot wide fantail of the ship. The restaurant opened August 29, 1955.

Van Camp Seafood used the phrase "Chicken of the Sea" to describe the taste of the tuna as being mild and having a white color just like chicken; it was so successful that soon it also became the company name. Bruce Bushman came up with the original drawings for the eighty-foot-tall wooden ship, intending it to Captain Hook's vessel from the Disney animated feature *Peter Pan* (1953).

Instead of being an accurately scaled sailing ship, it was meant to be more fanciful with its oversized crow's nest on four tall masts and the red-and-white striped canvas sails to fit in with the Fantasyland theme. The entire ship was built backstage at the Main Street Opera house mill and then lifted by crane to be put in Fantasyland.

Guests entered by crossing a pier-like bridge of planks. In the earliest days, a peg-legged pirate with an eye patch and a live parrot interacted with guests. The specialty served at the counter in the hull was tuna sandwiches (along with tuna burgers, tuna pies, and tuna salad) which guests could take upstairs to the main deck to eat or to one of the many canvas awning-shaded tables outside at the port side of the ship. The upper deck gave an unobstructed view of all of Fantasyland at the time. Skull Rock Lagoon was added in 1960. In 1969, ownership passed to Disneyland and it was officially renamed Captain Hook's Galley.

Peter Pan's Flight

There were originally nine ships, with a tenth held in reserve. These fiberglass vehicles (from a mold created by Chris Mueller) were each seven feet long and four-and-a-half feet wide and weighed 250 pounds. The monorail track system was obtained from the Cleveland Tram Rail Company, which built overhead conveyor systems for industrial sites. The ships were attached to the overhead rail by their front and back masts. The small sails helped obscure vision and direct guests where to look so they didn't notice what was holding up the ship. The highest point of the attraction, sixteen feet nine inches, was when the ship circled the Big Ben clock tower.

Construction of the fleet of flying galleons, and the creation of their intricate details, was handled by Bob Jones, who had made the miniature reference models and marionettes for *Pinocchio* (1940) and who had later started a plastics company.

King Arthur Carrousel

This carrousel (the double "r" is an old spelling variation meant to evoke medieval times and also appeared with that spelling on Harper Goff's

1951 drawing of the Mickey Mouse Park) was an 1875 merry-go-round with a menagerie of giraffes, deer, cats, and horses built by Dentzel in Philadelphia and had run for decades since 1922 in Sunnyside Beach Park (also known as Sunnyside Amusement Park) in Toronto, Canada. The park was demolished in 1955.

Ross Davis, through his amusement park connections, located the attraction for Walt and saved it from destruction. Walt paid $22,500 for it. Davis had been in charge of the famous 1926 Spillman merry-go-round at Griffith Park that Walt loved so much and that had helped inspire the creation of Disneyland.

Walt never saw the carousel in person until it arrived in Los Angeles. The outer row horses were all "standers", but Walt wanted them to be all jumpers and to have nothing but horses on the carousel, so Bruce Bushman, who designed the concept art for the attraction, was assigned to make the adjustments, including the creation of a fourth row to accommodate more riders.

According to *Disneyland News* Volume 1, No. 2 August 1955:

> In its original state, the carrousel consisted of lions, elephants, tigers and other wild animals, as well as horses. But the Disneyland castle was intended for visitors to Fantasyland's medieval castle, and King Arthur never rode anything but a horse. And so it was necessary to stick solely to the Dentzel mounts. Other horses were acquired from old merry-go-rounds, their legs subsequently broken by Disney artisans and reformed into jumpers of the type used by King Arthur and his Knights of the Round Table.

Arrow Development did all the work refitting the mechanical elements like crankshafts. Bud Hurlbut helped a few years later with the bull gears since parts no longer existed for machines like this one when they broke.

Bushman located some vintage horses underneath the Coney Island pier and installed them along with some additional Dentzel horses he obtained from Whitney's Playland in California. There were a total of 72 horses on the attraction with over a dozen other hand-carved horses as back-ups. In 2003, a wheelchair accessible bench and ramp were installed, so today the carousel has only 68 horses. Wurlitzer model number 155 played music until replaced with speakers in the 1983 renovation of Fantasyland.

As was true of carousels from this era, there was detailed ornamentation like court jesters and cherub carvings. Some of the ornamentation, including a chariot bench, was refitted to the Casey Jr. train's calliope and passenger cars.

In the early years, the horses were in traditional shades of black, tan, gray, and brownish red. They did not become all white until John Hench made that change in 1975. Other changes at that time included the canopy and the addition of nine hand-painted mural panels to tell the story of Sleeping Beauty.

In 1955, there were approximately 4,200 operating carousels in the United States. Today, it is less than 200.

Mr. Toad's Wild Ride

Bill Martin came up with the track layout. He worked with Ken Anderson and Claude Coats (who was responsible for the color styling on the original cartoon) to create the gags. Bob Mattey assisted with some of the mechanics in such scenes as the balancing crates and barrels in the warehouse.

The idea of going through the devil's mouth into hell was approved by Walt, who felt there should be consequences for reckless driving. This fate was foreshadowed on the mural at the front of the attraction. A hell's mouth dates back to medieval theater. No such scene exists in the original cartoon. More gags were added in 1961. In the beginning, the cars actually bumped into the doors to open them, but that was eventually changed.

Mr. Toad's Wild Ride was designed to last one minute and thirty-eight seconds in order to accommodate nearly 700 guests an hour. There were a total of twelve cars built by Arrow Development from Bruce Bushman's concept sketch. They were the first items produced by Arrow for Disneyland. Each weighed two hundred pounds and was composed of fiberglass and sheet metal.

There were individual cars named Mr. Toad, Mac Badger, Moley, and Ratty with two cars each named Toady, Cyril, Winky, and Weasel. Bob Gurr rode mock ups of Mr. Toad and Peter Pan at the Burbank studio in October 1954.

When a Disneylander called Walt "Mr. Disney", he smiled and replied, "There is only one 'mister' at Disneyland, Mr. Toad."

Fantasyland Buildings

The ride show buildings were 60 x 100 foot pre-fabricated buildings made by Soule which Disney purchased and had installed. It took awhile for this to happen, so by late 1954, a test track and ride mockup for Fantasyland attractions like Peter Pan and Mr. Toad's Wild Ride were set up in the Special Effects building at the Disney Studio for testing.

Ken Anderson and Claude Coats were responsible for the artwork on the interior plywood flats, often just painting directly on them without any pre-planning because of the frantic rush to meet the deadline. Black light, still a novelty in 1955, was used in the Fantasyland dark rides. The two men were also responsible for the colorful murals in the loading areas.

The tent-like tournament exteriors were meant to shade the queue area and give a festive medieval fair atmosphere, with signs and placards made from swords and shields (which, more importantly, were relatively inexpensive and quick to install).

CHAPTER NINETEEN

Tomorrowland

The 1955 Disneyland Guide Map gave this account of Tomorrowland:
> The daring land of dreams and hopes, upon which the future rests. You'll see the giant pylon-like TWA space rocket, visit buildings of advanced architectural design, participate in American industries' imaginative and exciting exhibits—all demonstrating what the future holds for everyone.
>
> Among Tomorrowland's exhibits will be an advance motion picture development, Circarama, consisting of continuous images focused on a 360 degree screen, the three-billion year story of the universe from the time the earth was a flaming globe whirling endlessly through space, and a story on oil production with a 40-foot diorama of the Long Beach area for the setting. You'll see an enormous kaleidoscope of color, a gigantic aluminum telescope, a futuristic conception of American home appliances and installations.
>
> A court of Honor will grace the center of Tomorrowland, flying flags of each state and the American flag. Tape recordings will be used instead of the customary register to identify guests. The Jules Verne Exhibit (20,000 Leagues Under the Sea) will also be an attraction in Tomorrowland.
>
> Here young drivers-to-be will learn future driving techniques on freeways of the future and enjoy speedboat excursions through an island-dotted waterway. From Tomorrowland you may have an aerial view of America by boarding a space station which, theoretically, travels in an orbit 500 miles above the earth's surface, or you may be a passenger in a TWA Rocket making a round trip to the moon.
>
> In short, all of man's dreams of the future are realities in Tomorrowland at Disneyland.

Exhibits
- Circarama (American Motors)
- Clock of the World (Timex)
- Aluminum Hall of Fame (Kaiser Aluminum)
- Hall of Chemistry (Monsanto)

- The World Beneath Us (Richfield Oil)
- Art Corner

Shows
- 20,000 Leagues Under the Sea ("A" ticket)
- Hobbyland Flight Circle

Restrooms
- Alongside exhibit buildings

Telephones
- Near exhibit buildings

Restaurants and Refreshments
- Space Bar
- Yacht Club

Rides
- Autopia (Richfield; "C" ticket)
- Rocket to the Moon (TWA; "C" ticket)
- Space Station X-1 ("A" ticket)
- Phantom Boats ("B" ticket)

The Kaiser Aluminum Hall of Fame

This pavilion was a self-guided walkthrough exhibit showcasing the best of Kaiser's aluminum products. It was one of the last attractions to be constructed before the park's grand opening, and was completed just days ahead of time.

Guests began the tour by learning how Kaiser makes aluminum. The pen for the guest book was made out of aluminum. On display was the Kaiser Aluminum Pig (KAP), a reference to pig aluminum (the unmilled rough form of aluminum). He wore overalls and carried an aluminum wrench. Most impressive was the polished 40-foot aluminum telescope at the entrance.

After guests traversed a series of hallways filled with various aluminum structures, appliances, and showcases, they arrived in an open hall containing the two highlights of the attraction: the Time Sphere and the Brightest Star in the World of Metals.

The image of the goddess Venus, the "historic symbol of beauty", was re-created life-size in a futuristic setting to represent the welding of art and industry, and the inherent beauty of aluminum. The statue, draped in aluminum yarns and bathed in colored lights, was surrounded by a huge multi-colored aluminum star, beneath which were fanciful settings of possible future uses of Kaiser Aluminum, like space suits.

The Time Sphere, a massive aluminum ball, projected images of ancient knights, 1950s firemen, and an imagined futuristic spaceman, all proudly using or wearing aluminum.

As guests exited the attraction, they received a commemorative card:

> (Fill in Your Name) has been ALUMINATED by "The Brightest Star in the World of Metals" at the Kaiser Aluminum Exhibit at Disneyland and is aware of all the benefits pertaining thereto.

The Clock of the World

What is a prominent icon on a main street, even in the future-around-the-corner? A large clock that can be seen by residents and visitors. When the park opened, this structure was often used as the major icon of Tomorrowland.

The Clock of the World was a seventeen foot, two-and-a-half-inch tall pedestal sponsored by Timex (U.S. Time). Its design mimicked the look of an hourglass to reinforce that the out-of-the-ordinary looking structure was indeed a clock. It rested on a concrete foundation surrounded by a floral setting of the points of the compass.

The dominant blue Italian glass tile on the icon was flecked with silver tiles to suggest the stars in heaven. Early park guests were indeed fascinated that with a little effort it was fairly easy to tell the exact time for any location on Earth twenty-four hours a day, but some locations were particularly emphasized, like New York, Moscow, Paris, and even Disneyland.

When Tomorrowland opened, there was a big planter shaped like an eight-pointed star with flags from all 48 states. In 1956, the flags and their poles were moved to the entrance of the land and became the Avenue of the Flags leading up to the clock arranged in the order of their admittance to the Union. On each flag pole there was a plaque with the name of the state, the date it was admitted, and its motto.

Three years later, two more flags were added. The American flag was placed directly in front of the clock. Both the Avenue of the Flags and the Clock of the World disappeared in September 1966.

At the top of the clock was a half-sphere gold-anodized aluminum sun and a silver crescent moon with a stylized man in the moon face. At night, lights from within the sun illuminated the moon. These figures rotated clockwise while the numerical band underneath rotated counter-clockwise.

Disney animator Blaine Gibson said:

> Herb Ryman had done some drawings for this clock of the future and I did the moon based on the sun Herb had done for the other side of the clock.

TWA Rocket to the Moon

The project leader for this pavilion and for the iconic Moonliner was Imagineer John Hench in consultation with Willy Ley and Wernher von Braun, who had both been advisors on the *Disneyland* television episodes about outer space. Their input influenced the design of the rocket ship with its white fuselage and red highlights to look similar in shape to the infamous V2 rocket. However, Hench included his own design elements, like the three twenty-two-foot long steel pylons flaring out at the base for support.

The rocket was 76 feet tall (taller than Sleeping Beauty Castle) and was considered to be one-third the size of an actual rocket built to hold 102 passengers. The exterior featured 15,000 square feet of aluminum.

The *Los Angeles Times* reported:

> Wednesday, July 6, 1955. Early risers along a twenty-mile route between Hollydale and Anaheim were startled this morning to see an 80-foot Rocket ship moving through the streets. In order to prevent a gigantic traffic tie-up, the ten-ton aluminum and steel "Air Ship of Tomorrow" was trucked before sun-up, from Hollydale where it was built, to Disneyland where it will become part of the TWA exhibit as well as the theme of the Tomorrowland section of the park.

The animation inside the attraction of the take-off and landing appearing on the two circular screens was done by Hench himself, cleverly putting in clouds and static to disguise cuts. The attraction with its simulated flight to the moon and back was narrated by the fictional Captain Collins, pilot of the Star of Polaris rocketship.

Originally sponsored by Trans World Airlines ("The Official Airline to Disneyland"), the sponsorship shifted in 1962 to McDonnell Douglas. In 1956, Howard Hughes, the owner of TWA, added a 22-foot-tall version of the Disneyland Moonliner to the top of the TWA corporate headquarters building in Kansas City, Missouri. In 1955, TWA served 60 U.S. cities and 21 world centers abroad.

Walt Preston was the civil engineer who developed the structural engineering drawings necessary for the assembly of the rocket pylon. Waldrip Engineering was put in charge of acquiring materials and doing the actual construction and contracted with Preston to do the detailed shop drawings and, with his assistant, Jim Block, overcoming the challenges of the expansion and contraction of the exterior in the heat and cold as well as the overturning forces of wind and earthquake.

In the July 10, 1955, issue of the *Daily News*, Walt Disney told reporter Florabel Muir:

> The rocket symbolizes the scientific achievements that will be as familiar to the young people of tomorrow as Main Street is to you and me. Kids and

grown-ups too can take a trip to the moon from here. Well, at least they can board a passenger rocket and have all the thrills of such a trip—and in accord with the latest scientific theories on interplanetary travel.

The Phantom Boats

The distinctive looking fiberglass Phantom Boats with their dual shark fins and seemingly jet engine air scoops at the back were cast from a sculpture created by Chris Mueller. They were originally dubbed just the Tomorrowland Boats in the Tomorrowland Lagoon, and there were fourteen boats in the fleet. They were planned as an aquatic version of Autopia, with no guide rail, and would let young drivers maneuver through a marked course around three islands.

Fiberglass was new at the time, but enclosing the motors inside it caused them to overheat and die, leaving guests stranded and having to be towed back to the dock.

On August 16, the boats were rechristened the Phantom Boats to make them seem more futuristic, and a white-costumed driver with a snappy captain's cap was assigned to each boat to help prevent overheating or guests driving the boats too fast. No one seems to know if there was any other story behind the name change.

They were shut down by the beginning of 1956 (although brought back temporarily that summer to have more rides available to guests after an alternative air boat proved unworkable) and so have the dubious honor of being the first original Disneyland ride attraction to disappear.

Autopia

Forty Autopia cars (referred to as everything from roadsters, sports cars, and cars of the future in publicity releases, and prominently sponsored by the Richfield Oil Corporation) were made of fiberglass by the Glasspar Company in Costa Mesa. These shells were shipped to Mameco Engineering in Newport Beach for final assembly over a 160-pound frame of cast iron. The cars weighed 475 pounds each and could easily accommodate an adult.

Thirty-seven were put into service for guests. Two cars that had no speed governors were transformed, at the suggestion of consultant George Whitney, into black-and-white police cars with flashing lights and sirens. Originally meant to help control the traffic and overtake reckless young drivers, they were more often used to give rides to small children unable to meet the size requirement for the regular cars. They were later repainted and incorporated into the attraction. Bob Gurr also drew up plans for a small bus (with the image of a dachshund rather than a greyhound on the side) to transport small children along the expressway, but it never left the drawing board.

Gurr insisted that one car be a "special" show car painted a distinctive maroon color and it came to be known as "Walt's Car". Gurr said:

> The standard cars didn't have windshields, but Walt's car had a plastic windshield and luxurious upholstery. We made special spun wheel covers and that car's bumper was an actual 1953 Pontiac upper bumper bar that we sliced, re-welded and re-chromed to look like a new bumper. It was often shipped off to other cities as a promo car for Disneyland in parades and events like at the Hollywood Bowl. When it wasn't being used for anything else, it sat on a special turntable in Tomorrowland.

Helicopter

A unique way of getting to Disneyland was by helicopter. By May 1955, TWA advertised that a person could soon buy a ticket from New York City direct to Disneyland, with the last leg of the flight completed by helicopter. Those Disneyland flights were managed by Los Angeles Airways, a company that offered helicopter service to nearly a dozen Southern California locations, including Los Angeles International Airport and Long Beach.

In 1955, a helicopter flight to Disneyland cost roughly four dollars a person each way. There were four flights daily from Los Angeles International Airport to Disneyland, each carrying seven to nine passengers.

The helicopter pad was located just outside Tomorrowland, on a little strip of asphalt not far from where the Skyway station would be built. Thousands of guests used this service, but private and military helicopters also landed in the heliport transporting high-profile celebrities and political figures.

A fatal crash in May 1968 killing all eighteen passengers and three crewmen ended the operation by 1969.

Public transportation to the park also included a variety of buses, including Metropolitan Coach Lines, Tanner Gray Line Motor Tours, Pacific Greyhound Lines, and the Orange County and Long Beach bus systems.

Stratosnak

This never-built food and beverage location was advertised with full color concept art in the local newspapers:

> DINNERTIME 1986. You will enjoy a delicious dinner of the future delivered to you from an immaculate, fully-automatic food service. Just push a button of your selection—seconds later you will have a complete, piping hot meal. Then you eat "midst all the splendor of Walt Disney's 'Tomorrowland" at family-sized tables in a shaded resting place overlooking the freeways of tomorrow.

It became the much simpler Space Bar.

20,000 Leagues Under the Sea

This exhibit was a late addition to help fill out Tomorrowland. Walt hoped to save money by reusing the beautiful sets from the film and entertain an audience that had never seen movie sets up close, especially from a film just released the previous December. It was intended as a temporary filler to last six months to a year at most, but remained for eleven years.

Entering the circular exhibit, the deep voice of Thurl Ravenscroft announced:

> You will see the Academy Award-winning motion picture sets actually used in the filming of Walt Disney's *20,000 Leagues Under the Sea*.

As guests wandered the corridor, they heard in the background the tune "Whale of a Tale" from the film. Available rooms included the Power Supply Room, Fitting Chamber, Diving Chamber, Pump Room, Wheelhouse, Chart Room, Professor Aronnax's Cabin, and as Ravenscroft announced, the Salon:

> Here Captain Nemo entertained his guests at the organ…through the starboard viewing port you will see the giant squid which was actually used in the movie.

The squid's arms had been refitted with a more easily maintained cable system. A tin shed had to be built outside the main building to house the massive prop.

In the center of the exhibit, guests could peer through windows to see the last resting place of the *Nautilus*. Walt had wanted to have guides costumed like the crew of the ship take guests through the exhibit, but as costs rose that idea was abandoned.

Oceanic props used in the movie and in this exhibit were rented from Marine Props and Rentals in Culver City, California. Extended rental for Disneyland became so expensive that the items were gradually replaced with replicas made at the studio. The lenses for the bank of lights in the Power Supply Room were actually the bottoms of glass salad bowls. When the exhibit closed, the organ found a new home in Disneyland's Haunted Mansion.

Hobbyland

To help fill out Tomorrowland, Walt contacted a local hobby club, the L.A. Hobby and Model Club, to put on demonstrations of their homemade motorized models of planes, cars, and boats (in a small pool inches deep) in a flight circle. Problems with scheduling, unreliability in starting the models, and other issues resulted in a professional, Leroy Cox, being brought in to take over when Walt saw that the Cox engines were the only ones that started reliably.

Hobbyland had shiny work counters (made of Kaiser aluminum) where model kits were sold. At the time, Disney had an exclusive deal with Strombecker Models to create models based on Disneyland attractions like the stagecoach and the TWA Moonliner.

Art Corner

The Art Corner opened on September 5, 1955, in Tomorrowland. Originally, it had been in a temporary location in a tent near the Red Wagon Inn. The inside was designed as if it were an outdoor art market in Paris. Big Mooseketeer Roy Williams spent time here doing quick sketches of Disney cartoon characters for guests.

Merchandise included squeaking postcards, flicker buttons, flipbooks, how-to-draw books, art supplies, the beloved Walt Disney Animation Kit, and more. The real treasure was original animation cels that sold for roughly a dollar forty-seven (larger cels with backgrounds or ones with multiple characters could cost up to five dollars) and had been rescued from the dumpsters at the Disney Studio by Jack Olsen.

Circarama

It was called Circarama not only as an allusion to the new movie technique called Cinerama, but also because the film was sponsored by American Motors. The original sign outside the attraction had the word "Circarama" in large dark black letters except for the word "car", which was in red.

Ub Iwerks designed a set-up of eleven 16mm Cine Kodak Special cameras with two hundred feet of pre-threaded film magazines that were mounted on a circular platform covering 360 degrees of arc. The drive shafts of all the cameras were linked mechanically by means of a single sprocket chain.

This unique camera set-up was strapped to the top of an American Motors Rambler to record a travelogue down the new Los Angeles freeways to Monument Valley, the Grand Canyon, and even a visit to Las Vegas.

Peter Ellenshaw was the art director of the original twelve-minute film, *A Tour of the West*, that ran from 1955 to roughly the beginning of 1960.

The audience stood in an asphalt-paved circular area forty feet in diameter with the eleven eight-foot-high screens elevated about eight feet off the floor. There were no "lean" rails in those early days.

William McGaughey, Jr. remembered:

> George Romney [American Motors chairman] and Dad [Romney's assistant William McGaughey] were hosts of the opening of the Circarama Exhibit which opened at 8pm on the preview day. A line of people were standing at the door. Dad spotted Frank Sinatra and invited him in. After viewing Circarama, Sinatra remarked to Dad that this was the ultimate in motion pictures.

CHAPTER TWENTY

Mickey Mouse Club Circus

For the first two seasons after the original *Mickey Mouse Club* premiered on television October 3, 1955, every Thursday was Circus Day. These shows proved to be the most expensive and difficult to produce, and so were eliminated for the third season.

The Mickey Mouse Club Circus opened at Disneyland near the area where the Matterhorn now stands on Thanksgiving Day, November 24, 1955, giving three 75-minute performances every day (the longest live-action show in Disneyland history), including Christmas Day and New Year's Day, for roughly the next six weeks.

During the week, shows were at 1:00, 3:30 and 7:30pm. On weekends, shows were offered at noon, 2:30 and 7:30pm. General admission was fifty cents, but there was also a reserved section of seats that could be purchased for a dollar.

The circus was part of the Christmas Festival at Disneyland. Of course, there was a daily circus parade down Main Street as well, but in keeping with the Christmas theme it included the three wise men and their camels. Because of a shortage of performers, Disneylanders like Van France, the founder of Disneyland University, were recruited to dress up in costume and join in the character parade. Some of the mothers of the Mouseketeers did so as well.

The show closed January 8, 1956, for a number of reasons, including poor attendance, high cost, and the fact that guests did not come to Disneyland to see a circus that required a separate admission.

In his book *Window on Main Street* (2015), Van France wrote:

Walter Knott warned us about the weeks before Christmas. He said that the public seemed to forget at that same time each year that there was a Knott's Berry Farm. Well, we didn't want the public to forget Disneyland, so Walt came up with an idea for changing that pattern of visitors.

After Disneyland opened in July 1955 and proved to be such a success, Walt was flooded with many offers for new things or to sell him odd items. Showman R.E. Anderson approached Walt about the idea of doing a Wild West show in Frontierland.

Walt liked the idea of a live show, but decided it would be fun to do a circus and to tie it in to promote *The Mickey Mouse Club* TV show. Walt had always loved the "mud show" circuses (small traveling circuses that would set up in a vacant field for a few days, and if it rained, the ground turned to mud) since he first saw one as a young boy in Marceline, Missouri. Walt had even told a few people that his dream was to run a circus some day.

At a meeting on October 4, 1955, to formalize a concept with Imagineers Dick Irvine, Bruce Bushman, George Whitney, and a few others, Walt stated that the circus would go through Christmas, and then early in 1956, it would be reconfigured into a new theme, The Mickey Mouse Club Wild West and Wild Animal Show.

Under Walt's supervision, these Imagineers storyboarded the circus show and oversaw the design of signage and midway booths where guests could purchase peanuts, snow cones, cotton candy, hot dogs, and other items, just like at a real circus. Joe Fowler, the former admiral who Walt hired to help him build Disneyland, told reporter Bob Thomas:

> How [Walt] loved [The Mickey Mouse Club Circus]! And it was a damned good circus, too! But, the problems!

The Mickey Mouse Club (MMC) Circus was not a slapped-together, poorly done entertainment, but featured many legendary circus performers at the peak of their abilities. Its failure was not connected to the value of the show being presented.

Ted DeWayne, who owned and operated the DeWayne Brothers Circus, which had its main quarters in North Hollywood, was brought in to coordinate the circus acts. DeWayne was much beloved and respected by the circus community, and was responsible for helping many performers over the years. He was a performer himself known for his extraordinary skill on the teeterboard.

The DeWayne Brothers Circus included eight ponies, an elephant (Bimbo Jr., who at county fairs would water ski on fifteen-foot long, three-foot wide, and one-foot thick skis, and who also appeared on TV), llamas, a bear, a kangaroo (who once escaped down Main Street and used his feet to keep people from grabbing him), three monkeys, and several performers.

The troupe included Mike Foster and Ben Myers (trampoline and tight wire), Cecil ("Peanuts") Kestler, and Todd LeRoy (clowns who did the Atomic Hair Grower act and revolving ladder), Paula Dell and Bobbie DeWayne (web act and teeterboard), and Bill Maynard (elephant trainer).

Also appearing was Fay Alexander, one of the few flying trapeze artists to master the triple somersault. Fay was part of the four-person Flying Alexanders act composed of Bob and Dorothy Yerkes and Fay and Rose Alexander that performed at the Mickey Mouse Club Circus as well.

The infrastructure and additional expertise for the circus were supplied by the Gil Gray Circus owned and operated by Guy Gilbert Gray (1904–1989). John Herriott was contracted to present the painted pachyderms, each dyed a different solid color. Herriott (1931–2015) was a respected equestrian, animal trainer, and circus owner, the third generation of one of the few truly American circus dynasties. When he died, he was lauded as the last true ringmaster (originally, ringmasters didn't just speak; they also did a horse act).

The cover of the View-Master reel entitled Mickey Mouse Club Circus Visits Disneyland features a very young Mouseketeer Karen sitting on top of an elephant. The colorfully costumed gentleman standing next to her was Herriott.

The very first act that was signed for the Mickey Mouse Club Circus was Professor George Keller, who spent thirty years teaching visual arts at the Bloomsburg State Teachers College in Pennsylvania.

In 1932, a friend knowing of Keller's love of animals, shipped him a mountain lion and dared him to train it. He did, and acquired other big cats. Beginning in 1937, he exhibited his growing collection of trained big cats and turned them into an act.

Starting with local fairs and picnics, Keller expanded to carnivals and circuses during his summer time off from teaching. After his final academic year of 1949–50, he made it his full-time work.

It was while performing on tour with the Polack Brothers Circus in 1955 that Keller was spotted by two men from the Disney Studio who convinced him to film a segment for the upcoming television *Mickey Mouse Club* show on his one day off, June 29. On that day, he also met Walt Disney and talked to him about displaying his animals at Disneyland.

Walt had grander ideas, and Keller left the Polack Brothers Circus on November 20, 1955, after an engagement in Springfield, Illinois, and headed to Anaheim for the Mickey Mouse Club Circus. Walt had suggested that Keller wear a black hairpiece so he looked younger and more dashing, and Keller did so for the rest of his career. Before then, he wore a cap in the ring that hid his baldness.

A Disneyland promotional release stated:

One of the most unusual performances, according to Walt Disney, will be that of George Keller, who walks into a cage of wild animals without a gun, whip, chair, or other defensive apparatus. "I think Keller hypnotizes the beasts," Walt said. "He's really amazing!"

Keller's girlfriend, Ginny Lowery, who would soon become his wife, worked at the Disneyland Hotel answering phones and letters. Primarily, she told prospective guests that there were no vacancies, because the hotel was so small in 1955. Decades later, she would donate to the Disney Archives color film footage taken of the Mickey Mouse Club Circus.

When the MMC Circus ended, Walt signed Keller to a new contract. Opening on February 19, 1956, Keller's act reverted to its original name, Keller's Jungle Killers, and continued to be performed under the big top. For MMC Circus performances, the act was given the gentler, more family-friendly name of Professor George Keller and His Feline Fantastics.

The contract had been open-ended, but on March 27, it was extended through Labor Day, concluding September 7. It now cost twenty-five cents (or a "B" ticket) to see the act. Keller performed four shows a day, with no days off.

Keller was eventually relocated to a smaller canvas tent near the Red Wagon Inn as Tomorrowland needed to be prepared for the Junior Autopia attraction and the bigger tent would be stored and re-assigned to the forthcoming Holidayland area.

According to the back of a 1956 Disneyland postcard featuring Keller:

> George J. Keller, a former college professor turned wild-animal trainer, demonstrates for the first time the unarmed subjugation of a group of African Lions, tigers, leopards, mountain lions, jaguars, black panthers and a cheetah.

Keller told reporters:

> My cats are not "tamed" but merely trained to perform. At any moment, they might revert to their natural jungle habits and the results could be a catastrophe. It has happened to me before and it it could happen again.

Additional performers at the circus included two six pony drills in the end rings; Chief Shooting Star (from the Frontierland Indian Village); Beatrice Dante and Charlie the Chimp; Nolly Tate with his balancing white dog, Pal; Bergs seals and Reynolds seals (in the end rings as well); and Hazel King's horses from her liberty drill of Roman marching horses.

Owen Pope's signature act that he performed at rodeos was restaged with a small Cinderella pumpkin coach drawn by six Shetland ponies that raced into the tent. On opening night, Joe Fowler noticed that one of the coach wheels had caught in one of the diagonal posts that held up the tent and pulled it out, but apparently, no damage was done.

Kinko the Clown, also known as the Human Pretzel, would make his entrance inside "the world's smallest car", a midget car 31 inches high and 41 inches long. On the side door it said "Squat Car" as a parody of "Squad Car". Billy Burke was the "boss clown" coordinating all the different clown acts.

Possibly because of the ABC connection with the park, Charles M. Runyon, who as Chucko the Birthday Clown was a popular Los Angeles children's TV show host on the local KABC-TV Channel 7 (the same station airing *The Mickey Mouse Club*) from 1955 to 1963, apparently also appeared and is visible on the View-Master reels.

Adolph Del Bosq performed with his daughter Clara (who styled the act) to present the talented horse Serenado. The feather-plumed horse would dance to music and played musical tunes (including the "Ballad of Davy Crockett") by nudging with his head on vertically hanging strings of sleigh bells tuned to different notes. The bells were later given to John Herriott who occasionally filled in as the handler. Herriott recalled that the horse was "high strung" and jokingly referred to the animal as Tornado.

Of course, the show also featured "The Mouseketeers in Person!" with Jimmie Dodd attired as a ringmaster and Roy Williams as a strong man just as they appeared on the Thursday Circus Day episodes on the television show.

Prominently featured from the show as well was Bob-O the Clown, performed by the talented Bob Amsberry who did a variety of character roles on the series, such as an elderly soda jerk. Like the other clowns, between shows Bob-O would wander through the park and talk to guests, trying to spark attendance at the performances.

In his autobiography *Ears and Bubbles* (2014, Theme Park Press), Mouseketeer Bobby Burgess recalled:

> That was so much fun, we had a great time! My mom and Sharon's [Baird] mom were Chip & Dale. They got $6.00 per day for two shows. We got to ride elephants; we got to ride horses; we were in a aerial act. We dressed up as Peter Pan and Tinker Bell and they turned off the lights and we glowed in the dark as we swung the girls through the space. It was a blast. They even made some 3D pictures of us [for View-Master reels].
>
> It wasn't a big success, but it was put on by the Ted DeWayne Circus, which was a professional circus troupe. They had camels, and zebras, a lion and tiger act, and elephants...it was a big deal. We had fun on that one. I was called a web setter for my part in the flying act. Mouseketeer Bonnie would climb to near the top of the tent on a rope, and I would twirl her around and around on a ladder.

In his autobiography *The Accidental Mouseketeer* (2014, Theme Park Press), Mouseketeer Lonnie Burr remembered having a less pleasant experience:

> I found that riding on an elephant's or camel's back was fun, but their long, tough hairs would poke through most costumes or clothes and hurt. And the camels sometimes spit at you.
>
> Since our contract guaranteed twenty-two weeks of pay out of twenty-six for each six-month option, they made damn sure we were used all twenty-two

weeks and all six days, which gave rise to our performances in the [Mickey Mouse Club] circus. This venture was to make sure our pay was not wasted and to enhance both the park and our own show for fans...Disney synergy in action.

After the opening parade around the ring, we changed costumes and midway through the circus acts we did our insipid specialty. The girls struck various ballet poses on a suspended ladder which the boys carefully swung back and forth. Not very creative, but nerve-racking since the girls could easily fall and be hurt badly. They would mount the ladders and then be pulled up to about nine or ten feet to do their routine.

I heard Cubby and Karen did a small bit with one of the big cat acts, but I don't remember seeing it. I have no idea what Roy did as a strong man other than appear in the parade. Jimmie did more as the ringmaster. The controlled tawdriness of the environment did not please me. It was like being around a lot of convicts without guards. The men and women were rough-edged and tough.

One of the perks was that before the park opened we got to go on the rides for free and as much as we wanted. The cars on the Autopia always had to be warmed up in the morning, so we would drive them around the track with the governors off.

Lonnie and Mouseketeer Tommy Cole got into a shoving match behind the tent that ended with two punches, the only recorded physical fight between the Mouseketeers, with parents worried Walt might fire them all.

The lifestyle of circus performers was vastly different than the behavior and attitude that Walt was expecting of Disneyland performers. The circus folk would gamble, drink, walk around in various states of undress, and curse strongly and often, even with the young innocent Mouseketeers nearby.

The tent raising was held at Disneyland on November 11, 1955, with Walt and a dozen or so of the Mouseketeers. The candy cane-striped tent was a 150-foot big top with the center ring 50 feet in diameter and on either side two thirty-foot rings, making it a three-ring circus.

The red- and white-striped tent was made of vinyl, not canvas. Disneyland promoted it as the largest striped tent ever made, and it was advertised as being heated inside.

Next to it was a menagerie tent where guests could visit the animals up close (an experience included in the admission). The tent also served as a dressing room area for the Mouseketeers, since it was about thirty feet from the back flap of the main tent.

The total cost of the tents was $48,000 and the performance area could seat up to 2,500 guests on bleachers, but it was common that less than a quarter of the seats were filled. Some estimates put the attendance at significantly less than that number, but that is still hundreds of Disneyland guests at each performance.

When the filming for the first season of *The Mickey Mouse Club* was completed in early November, the Mouseketeers (including some who had already been eliminated) were sent to rehearse for the show. The Mouseketeer segments for the circus were staged by Hal Adelquist who had apparently contacted some of the circus acts personally as well.

Walt purchased nine authentic circus wagons from the Bradley & Kaye Amusement Park at the corner of Beverly and La Cienega boulevards in Los Angeles that had been sitting there as a sort of backdrop for the entertainment venue. David Bradley had purchased them in 1949–50, and they had previously been part of Ken Maynard's Diamond K Ranch Wild West Show.

Later, Walt purchased an additional five wagons in Venice, California, that had been used in the Jimmie Wood Los Angeles-based circus that had fallen into disrepair. Walt had the wagons carefully restored. For instance, the Swan Bandwagon had wood that had rotted in some places from being displayed outside in all sorts of weather over the years. A few carvings and panels were missing and had to be reconstructed using existing pieces as templates.

Unfortunately, a few of the wagons that Walt purchased were in such an extreme state of deterioration that they were simply used for parts for some of the other wagons. Walt wisely saved everything that he could.

Walt's intent was to use the wagons as part of the circus parade down Main Street and then to have them fill out and decorate the Mickey Mouse Club Circus area.

The Dragon Calliope, a long staple of circuses, was a fabrication (at a cost of $50,000) using the twenty-whistle steam calliope from one of the Bradley and Kaye collection. The Disney Dragon Calliope was based on a Marcus Illions wagon and adorned with pieces from other wagons Walt had purchased so that it looked completely authentic.

The Disneyland News of November 10, 1955, detailed the rich history of the various wagons, some dating back to the 1880s or earlier. A publicity photo from the same time period shows Walt supervising the restoration at the Disney Studio. The program for the Mickey Mouse Club Circus stated:

> Researchers, artists, designers, special craftsmen and wagon builders were enlisted by Walt in his dream for authenticity in their rebuilding. Circus historians and "old-timers" were brought in as consultants.

The wagons were featured prominently in Walt's live-action feature film *Toby Tyler, or Ten Weeks with a Circus* (1960).

For the MGM film *Billy Rose's Jumbo* (1962), Walt loaned twelve of the reconstructed wagons. Other wagons for that film were supplied by Louie

Goebel, one of the best-known importers of wild animals in the United States. He owned the famous zoo Jungleland in Thousand Oaks, California.

Later in 1962, Walt would donate most the Disney-restored wagons to the Circus World Museum in Baraboo, Wisconsin, where they are taken care of and displayed to this day. In 1962, Baraboo High School honored Walt with a ceremony and the presentation of a certificate of gratitude.

In 1966, Walt sent the museum two calliopes along with seventeen crates of carvings that had been rescued from the wagons.

The Dragon Calliope was kept and used in Disneyland and Walt Disney World parades. It was eventually converted from steam to a fifteen-horsepower air-driven instrument operated by forty six-volt batteries. However, a set of additional dragon carvings that had been rescued in the original restoration effort made it up to the museum.

The rare printed program from the Mickey Mouse Club Circus had the face of Bob-O the Clown on the front cover and this introduction from Walt:

> Everyone loves a circus and I'm no exception. I've been fascinated by the clowns and the animals, the music and the excitement ever since I worked in one of these wonderful shows for a few days as a youngster.
>
> While we've had a number of circus themes in our pictures through the years—you will remember *Dumbo* as an example—we've never had a real honest-to-goodness live circus until now. It seemed to us that Disneyland was just the right spot for one.
>
> We are happy to present, in their first personal appearance, the Mouseketeers from *The Mickey Mouse Club* television show. And in the show, you will also see the old circus wagons we have collected—interesting show rigs which have rolled all over America and which are now restored to their original state.
>
> I hope the Mickey Mouse Club Circus will add many pleasant memories to your visit to Disneyland. My best wishes to every one of you.
>
> — Walt Disney

The opening day parade had Walt Disney and actor Fess Parker, well known at the time for his portrayal of Davy Crockett on the weekly Disney television show and attired accordingly, riding two of Walt's polo ponies down Main Street. Because the horse was so small and Parker so tall, his legs could not comfortably fit in the stirrups and so hung down the side of the saddle. They were followed by several horse-drawn wagons, a band, elephants, clowns, and more.

In the Carl Hagenback Split Cage wagon that had been built in 1905, there was a wooden partition in the center to separate the animals. There was a tiger on one side and a panther on the other. The tiger managed to wedge its paw around the partition and the panther chewed it off.

Joe Fowler recalled:

My boys tackled the panther with two-by-fours to get him off. By the time we finished, we destroyed fifteen thousand dollars worth of cats.

The official souvenir program listed the following acts:

- On Parade
- George Keller and His Feline Fantastics
- Clowns and Follow the Leader
- The Mouseketeers in an Aerial Ballet
- Animal Varieties
- Kinko the Clown
- The Camels and the Llamas
- The Ted DeWayne Troupe
- The Clowns and the Mouseketeers
- Serenado, the Musical Horse
- The Baby Elephants (featuring the world's only twins)
- The March of the Clowns
- Flying Trapeze Number
- March of the Toys from "Babes in Toyland"
- With a Christmas Tree Finale

The show began with an introduction from ringmaster Jimmie Dodd, a fanfare, and the circus parade coming inside the big top and circling around and exiting. For the grand finale, Dodd proclaimed:

> It is a time when even the toys seem to come to life. Walt Disney, from his realm of fantasy, presents the March of the Toys.

Billed as the Santa Claus Parade, Mouseketeers dressed up as toys, animals, and characters from nursery rhymes marching to the music of Victor Herbert's "Babes in Toyland" mixed with some Disney cartoon characters in costumes from the Ice Capades. Annette Funicello was dressed as Snow White. Other Mouseketeers moved robotically as toy soldiers.

After that parade, the music changed to "When You Wish Upon A Star" as "The Magic Christmas Tree! 40 feet in 10 seconds—most spectacular and mystifying circus finale in the history of the Big Top" took place. A white fabric tree rose up from the ground to a shining star at the top of the tent.

This was followed by Jimmie Dodd and the Mouseketeers ringing bells and leading the crowd in a rendition of "Jingle Bells" as Santa Claus (Imagineer Bruce Bushman who would perform the same role in the early years of the park) and his sleigh arrived.

The official production credits listed in the program were:

- Produced by Walt Disney
- Staged by Hal Adelquist and Roy Williams (Williams supplied some of the gag ideas)
- Art Direction by Bruce Bushman
- Production Manager: Ben Chapman
- Musical Director: Tommy Walker
- Ringmaster: Jimmie Dodd
- Wardrobe: Chuck Keehne (who had done the costumes for *The Mickey Mouse Club* TV show and made the first sets of Mouseketeer ears from Roy Williams' design)
- Additional Costumes Courtesy of Ice Capades (these were the same Disney character costumes borrowed for the July 17 *Dateline: Disneyland* special.)

As Van France remembered:

> On opening night, the female trapeze artist lost her brassiere while flying through the air with the greatest of ease. [Joe Fowler remembered that she split her tights instead of losing her top. Jack Lindquist said, "This well-built trapeze artist whizzed back and forth completely topless." Basically, it was a "wardrobe malfunction" with the embarrassed woman having difficulty getting back down to the ground while preserving her modesty.]
>
> The llamas would not only spit but would also attempt to escape down Main Street.
>
> The lions in Professor Keller's famous lion act had been de-clawed and tranquilized. The Professor's greatest fear was that one of them would go to sleep and fall on him. Although almost any circus is usually a good draw, this was a very expensive learning experience, losing an estimated $375,000."

Joe Fowler recalled:

> If I never see a circus again, it'll be twice too soon! I want to tell you, running that Park was simple compared to running that damn circus. You'll excuse my language. The circus played to tents that were never more than a quarter full. That was the one time we learned this lesson: people come to see Disneyland.
>
> I can remember Dick Irvine's children coming down and Dick saying, "You're going to see a circus." The kids would say, "We don't want to see the circus. We want to see Mickey Mouse!"
>
> Walt loved that circus, but he finally gave in and said, "I've got to get that circus out of here, because I need it over at the studio to make a picture." And we all said, "Thank God!"

In this book *In Service to the Mouse* (2010), Jack Lindquist remembered:

> Professor Keller wore white gloves and claimed he hypnotized the animals. He got the four lions up on stools and would direct them as a typical lion tamer does: to roar, sit up, snarl and look mean and menacing. But behind each lion was a guy with a sharp stick. He also told me that the only danger in the act is that the lions could fall asleep, stumble off their stools, and crush him. So, for about a year after the circus closed, we had good ol' Professor Keller who performed everyday at one o'clock and four o'clock.
>
> Walt wanted to do the circus. We had less than two million visitors at the time. We could put the circus at Fairfax and Beverly Boulevard in Los Angeles, and it would have been a huge hit. At Disneyland, it was a yawn because people wanted to see Disneyland. The rides were bigger and better than any circus.

After the circus ended and the tents were pulled down, the site was cleared to make way for the Junior Autopia attraction, which opened on July 23, 1956, covering the area occupied by the Mickey Mouse Club Circus (and additional land besides). It was designed to alleviate some of the huge lines for the original Autopia in Tomorrowland, though the track was smaller.

The vehicles looked and drove the same as those at the Tomorrowland Autopia, but wooden extension blocks were placed on the foot pedals and booster seats added to accommodate smaller drivers who had been unable to drive on the original. The track was only one car wide which helped reduce accidents, unlike the double-wide lane of the original.

Some of the circus wagons still stood in the background to "fill out" the view for the first two years that the attraction was open before being moved to the Disney Studio for the filming of *Toby Tyler*.

The new version became an instant hit and was expanded in January 1959 as the Fantasyland Autopia. Later, it would be combined with the Tomorrowland Autopia track.

CHAPTER TWENTY-ONE

In Their Own Words: Memories of Disneyland 1955

In order to belong to Disneyland's Club 55, you had to have started working at Disneyland in 1955, or in the case of some members, even earlier during the planning and construction phase.

In addition, you had to have been paid by Disney, which meant that people who worked for lessees were not eligible since their paycheck came from the lessee.

On July 17, 1970, the 15th anniversary service awards ceremony (the Castle Awards Banquet) was held. A bronze replica of Sleeping Beauty Castle along with a castle pin that had a small pendant hanging beneath it that said "Charter" was given to those original cast members who were still active.

Shortly afterwards, two hundred cast members were notified that Disneyland University Founder Van France was organizing a special group known as Club 55.

John Catone designed a club logo that he copied from the logo for the special VIP restaurant at Disneyland, Club 33. He just changed the numbers from "33" to "55". In 1995, Bob Penfield changed the logo to an image of the castle with "Club 55" above it so that the logo would be more unique.

Each year a special reunion was held of both active and retired cast members who had worked at the park in 1955. The parties were held in a variety of locations, from the Balboa Bay Club and Turnip Rose Restaurants to the *Queen Mary* and Catalina Island.

Starting in 1985, only active cast members were invited. At the last dinner party, held in 1996, only Ray VanDeWarker and Bob Penfield were still working at Disneyland.

In August 1997, the last person from Disneyland's opening day staff still working at Disneyland retired. For his more than 42 years of service, Bob Penfield was given a window on Main Street that says: "Club 55 School of Golf, Bob Penfield, Instructor".

Today, less than ten members of Club 55 still survive. Many of them, as well as those who worked at Disneyland in 1955 but were not members, have shared their impressions of the first year of Disneyland over the decades.

The following quotes come from a variety of sources, including personal interviews, excerpts from *Disneyland Line* anniversary issues, Disneyland press material, commentary from television specials, and obscure publications.

Ray Van De Warker

Bob Penfield and I were friends and got hired at the same time.

They brought us in the park and none of the attractions were finished. None. Main Street was just dirt and some of the buildings didn't even have facades on. The *Mark Twain* was just a shell. Anyway, one of our jobs was to test out the new attractions. We sat for about two days behind the castle because it was the only cool spot and there wasn't anything else to do.

But I'll never forget the first ride we got to test out. I can't think of the name of the thing, but it was some sort of satellite and you got on this conveyor belt that took you around to what was supposed to be a look down at Earth. [Space Station X-1] It didn't impress me and we had to test that thing nearly all day and we got sick of it.

But the night before the park opened, Bob and I were asked to work overtime because they had just finished Peter Pan's Flight and we were the only ones who were being trained on it.

When we started training that night, we looked at the pirate ship and it still hadn't been painted. We practiced all night and we knew we had to come back the next day for a full shift for opening. Well, we got out around 2:00am and the pirate ship had been painted! At least the side facing the guests. The next day, we basically trained the night crew during the day.

Fantasyland was the last area to open that day. Boy, when they lowered that drawbridge, it seemed like all 30,000 kids came in at once. And there were so many people that they had to close the carousel a few times because children climbed over the chains and we couldn't control them.

We had to post employees around the perimeter to stop them from trying to get on the attraction while it was in operation. As I was helping one little boy onto a horse, lifting him by putting my hands under his arms, he punched me in the nose, bringing tears to my eyes and bloodying my nose. Apparently, he didn't want to be helped onto his horse.

I was the first lead in the Indian Village. I was known as the Great White Fur Trader, the only Caucasian employee in the village.

Earl Anderson

In July 1955, I came to Disneyland and my first job was helping to build the lumber storage building. I would get down on my hands and knees in the rain and mud to work on the foundations. On opening day, John Yarber and I got a call that the gate had fallen off the Mule Pack Ride, and that we were to go and fix it. We had not the slightest idea where the Mule Pack Ride was. I had many little chats with Walt, but I particularly remember one time when I suggested building an animated Holy Land. He said, "I'm a religious man, but here, at Disneyland, we have no religious confinements. All religions are welcome."

Dave Bartchard

We moved to Anaheim in 1931 and when I was 16, I bought my own tractor with money I saved from working in the orchards. I worked my tractor taking care of the groves until Walt Disney moved in...then I came over and worked here. I started with the McNeil Construction Company and the job was supposed to be for just half a day. It got stretched out a little, didn't it? When I started to work here, Main Street was nothing but two by fours, stakes, and chalk marks. I was hired to drive a truck hauling paint all over the place, but I also hauled Walt Disney everywhere, as well as the paint. He rode with me a lot and he became a real, nice friend of mine. Walt was there every day, and he always treated a man like a man. I was on the job 24 hours per day for the last two months before opening. I slept a little in the truck and only went home on Sunday. Opening day was my day off, and I guess that I must have slept all day.

Roy Brem

I was living in Whittier and while watching television, I saw them building this place. I wrote to Walt Disney and told him what I could do. He wrote back and said, "Take this letter to Fred Newcomb at the park." So I came over with the letter, talked to Fred, and he put me to work. Opening day the movie star kids were, to put it mildly, unruly! I started on the steam trains as a conductor. We had a great crew, with Jim Cashen, who was the fireman, and Harley Elgin was the engineer. One day Roy Disney jumped aboard and I didn't know him until he showed his pass. He was smoking a big cigar!

Rima Bruce

I started the day before the park opened. I was going to go to Arabia to work with the railroad and while I was waiting to hear from them, I took a drive over toward Anaheim with my mother. I saw a formation of what was to be the train station. So I made out an application, was interviewed by Chuck Whelan, and started work the same day. I started with Jim

D'Arcy in Food. All food was lessee, and I was typing memos and menus and trying not to mix up the two. The phone never stopped ringing with everybody trying to get a food lease in the park. The railroad tracks went right by the office window and as the train passed by, it would blow its whistle with a tremendous noise...scared the wits out of me.

On opening day, bedlam! Nobody knew their way around the park...took an hour to get from Personnel to my job. Then we turned our offices over to the press and I went out to watch the celebrities. Hawaiian Abe was in front of the Bazaar in Adventureland, making palm frond hats for Debbie Reynolds and Eddie Fisher. Things settled down after a few months. We were really experimenting. What hours to stay open. Which days to close.

Jim Cashen

I went to work in the Round House on July 18, 1955, as a junior engineer. I was a glorified helper, polishing the engine and sweeping the floors. I had never seen engines so dirty. Two or three weeks later, they put me on the engines as a fireman. Walt and I were fellow steam train engineers. Walt liked to run the trains, but he drove a little too fast. At the beginning, Walt dressed like a construction worker. One time he looked at my eight-dollar work shoes and asked me where I bought them. He said that his old Marine shoes were wearing out and he needed a new pair of work shoes. One time Walt committed a "no-no" and blew the whistle in the tunnel. It made an awful noise and actor Walter Pidgeon turned to him and said, 'Please don't do that!"

John Catone

I read about Disneyland in the newspapers. My first day was on the Autopia. There were wooden planks for curbing, backed up with sand bags. Autopia was a two-lane highway, wide enough to handle three cars abreast. The next day I was in a space suit, doing promotions with the guests...one day 13,000 pictures were taken! As a space man, I was also used as a crowd "mover". I would go right past a long waiting line, the people following me like they followed the Pied Piper. At a small line, I would stop to start some business there. There was pure oxygen in the space suit at first. Sometimes a kid would turn the tap in the boots and drain the oxygen to the head. I would feel like I was on Cloud Nine. Walt was a down-to-earth person. He would always take time to talk.

I sure remember Black Sunday. There was a plumbers' strike and very few toilet facilities were ready. Roy Disney said, gently, that he didn't mind if the people urinated in the bushes! Walt was like a little boy with a new toy!

Hank Dains

I remember the first day we had paying guests in the park and Walt was over at the fire station. And I heard him say, "Paying guests. I love you."... and threw them a great big kiss!

Boyd Diaz

I was working on the loading dock of the Casey Jones Jr. railroad when in came the train with actress Marjorie Main riding in the wild animal cage. She was wearing one of her great big fancy hats and as she got out of the cage, she knocked her hat off onto the dock. As I bent over to pick up her hat, my Casey Jr. overalls spilt from top to bottom. I had to stand with my back to the wall until quitting time! Walt would come around two or three times a week and talk to me in Spanish. He spoke the language pretty well. He was a remarkable, wonderful man...but very humble.

Jim Harman

I first went to work at the Richfield Exhibit, an animated show consisting of a diorama of Long Beach with a professor giving a speech. He was describing how water was being pumped into the oil fields to prevent the depleted land from sinking. The Moon Ride was quite a mess! You would push the button and nothing would run ... or it would run backwards or upside down! At that time, the sound speakers on the Rivers of America were hidden in false rocks and the gophers would fill the speakers in with earth. They sent me into combat with the critters. I remember how, during the course of a season, the ants would eat the real fur off of the animated birds and animals.

Homer Holland

Opening day? It was wonderful! I was loading jungle boats and Bob Cummings' microphone wire kept getting wrapped around my neck! I was supposed to be working on the *Mark Twain*, but they didn't have my uniform by opening day. Well, the *Mark Twain* had too many operators and the jungle didn't have enough, so I went to the jungle for a year. There were no microphones on the boats then and you shouted yourself hoarse with a megaphone.

Joyce Belanger

A couple of days before we opened, I had my costume fitting. The seamstresses must have worked 24 hours a day getting costumes ready. I had one day of cash handling and then the night before the park opened, we got to see inside the park. Nothing seemed finished. But the castle...that was impressive. It belonged and looked like it had always been there.

I couldn't believe how everything looked so chaotic the 16th and then the next day it was sparkling clean and ready. I had lunch that day at Carnation.

Sitting at the next table was Ronald Reagan. Who'd have known? I do remember he was putting on his contacts.

I can still see Walt strolling through the park. He didn't talk down to the children. He'd bend down so they could talk to him at their level. Kids always came up to talk to him. He'd pose for pictures and always had time for them. And they loved him. They'd follow him all over the park. He was like the Pied Piper and wherever he went, the kids followed. He had a very child-like quality about him and never seemed to tire of the park.

Jim Barngrover

On July 10, 1955, the local musicians' office got a call for musicians at Disneyland. It was to last for two weeks and a 16-piece band was wanted. The band was put together by Tommy Walker and Tommy's father, Vesey Walker. He soon became the first Disneyland Band director. We used to play on a gazebo in what is now Plaza Gardens. There were no seats for the guests and there was no shade. So nobody came to listen! That's when we started marching and became a marching band.

Chuck Boyajian

We had open trash cans then, and we had trouble getting the trash removed. It piled up in a gigantic heap behind City Hall...trash was overflowing everywhere.

Imogene Brinkmeyer

I spent opening day at home in bed with a strep throat. Anyway, I came to work the next day and it was hot as hades...you couldn't get a drink anywhere. There had been no training for the ticket sellers, but everyone pulled together and everything fell into place. I still don't know how it all worked out!

Stan Gomez

Don't even mention it! The day before opening I worked from 6am to 6pm and then came back at midnight. I had to distribute 500 or more lockers all over the park. Then I went on foot to check each key against the locker. That look till 7am. After that I left and spent opening day at home asleep.

Frank Martines

I didn't get much of a view as I was at the main gate. We all looked like bellhops, with Eisenhower yellow jackets, green trousers, gold "overseas" caps... we were pretty proud! At the end of the summer, I went to Main Street as foreman and then I became an assistant supervisor. The company bought the supervisors grey suits with orange ties...the better to be seen in the area!

Gunter Otto

I had worked many hours in the Jungle with Joe Delfin. The work skiffs had no motors, then, and were too heavy to paddle, so we put on tennis shoes, jumped into the river, and pushed the boats, laden with their cargoes of plants and flowers. On opening day, I was to turn on sprinklers at a signal given by a television director. He gave a wrong signal and I turned on the sprinklers just as Fess Parker and Buddy Ebsen came riding out of the Living Desert. They got soaking wet and I was sure that I'd get fired for that one!

Cora Lee Sargent

Bob Cummings stopped and talked to me and I wasn't any good for three hours after that! Being fitted for costumes, a wardrobe girl suggested that the "not-so-well endowed" wear falsies. There were no lockers. We just hung our clothes on poles with our names on them. There was just a huge make-shift open-topped tent and sometimes airplanes would swoop down to try to catch a look. The first winter we wore our own coats. There were no requirements on shoes and I wore tennis shoes sometimes.

Marion Schawacha

Opening day? Hectic! Painters still painting. Carpenters still sawing. The waiting lines were all mixed up and criss-crossing each other. The line from Autopia would end up at the Space Bar and vice versa. All you could see in Tomorrowland was people! The guy who was supposed to be the manager almost blew the place up. He turned the gas on for the big oven and then went down the corridor to get a match. BOOM! He later became a treasurer.

I worked at Coke Corner and I can remember seeing Walt in the early morning in the arcade. He'd come by and always order a plain hot dog and get a box of popcorn. He was a fantastic man and he always made us feel like we were all one big family.

Peter Ellenshaw

Walt had us all down there for Disneyland in 1954. Animators. Everybody. We had to do our work at the studio and at the same time still go down there and do other work.

He came into my office and said, "I want you to devise something that will show America. You get on a platform and start on one side of America and you go all the way round until you get to the other side. And during that time it will play "America the Beautiful". It turned out to be called Space Station X-1, not "America" as Walt originally planned.

One hundred feet across it was. They had already decided how big it was going to be. I had a model made and put it in one of the rooms next to my room. I was gradually painting it and thought it would work.

You can paint it trompe l'oeil so you think you were seeing it in the round and that's the way I was doing it. I got halfway through and thought, *What an awful job!*

We did get it finished. I painted the whole thing so it was designed that we could make a slice to see if it would work. We made a huge slice and painted and lit it and it looked terrific. Then we had to show it to the background painters who did a rough of my sketch, squared it up, and got it just so.

Then it was pasted down on this huge disc. I had to get on my hands and knees.

Then we put the lights on it. I put luminescent paint on the towns at night so when it got dark they would glow. It was very effective. Looked wonderful.

After about a year, after the lights had been redone, it was a terrible thing to keep going. We decided it should be called the Dust Bowl of America. We couldn't keep the dust out. So it was eventually abandoned. It never had a sponsor like some of the other things. It was a lot of work for nothing, really.

I was also involved with the Circarama 360 films for American Motors. It was a travelogue in the round of Southern California and the West. They mounted eleven cameras on a circular platform atop a station wagon. I was the art director.

My greatest problem is I would find this lovely composition, just beautiful, but the cameras behind this vista would show all this trash and junk. It was horrible. I had nothing to do with the mechanical side of the process. That was all Ub Iwerks.

On Wilshire Blvd. we ran the cameras at half speed so when it was run at normal speed it seemed like we were demons going at tremendous speeds and somehow amazingly stopping just in the nick of time. That's the scene most people remember. That film lasted until around 1959 and then they replaced it.

Margaret Kerry

Tinker Bell was just going to be a fun secondary character that Disney was going to have in one movie like so many others.

I'm told that so many of the people at the studio thought Disneyland was going to lose money or even go bankrupt that they went to Roy and said, "Roy, would you tell [Walt] that we're asking him not to use our big characters that we can license and make money off of, so when Disneyland flops, we can get the money back?"

That's how a secondary character like Tinker Bell became the one used so often to represent the park and on so much of its merchandise.

Marc Davis

Actually, the first thing I did for Disneyland was the mermaid figurehead on the Chicken of the Sea pirate ship. I designed that and Chris Mueller sculpted it. I know it was supposed to look like their mermaid mascot, but everyone told me I had done it so that it looked like my version of Tinker Bell.

Later, Walt had asked me, "Hey, Marc, think up some things that the people on the train could see on the outside of some of these attractions." I did several sketches like cannibals cooking a guy in a pot with a Mickey Mouse hat. Over by Tomorrowland I had a flying saucer that had crashed and little green hitchhiking spacemen. None of those ever got built.

When I did the sketch of the trapped safari and the rhino, he saw that and he laughed like hell. "That's too good to go outside." So he put it inside as a major part of the attraction. With the Jungle ride we were trying to make it more exotic, a little more interesting than just the boring travelogue that it was in 1955. I made a drawing of this huge man-eating plant gag, but I was never able to get Walt to buy off on it.

There was no real humor on any of the Disneyland rides when it first opened and I wanted to put some in there and I did.

Ken Anderson

There was never anything like Disneyland. Disneyland was going to be an answer to all these other kiddie park things around at that time. Walt was fed up. He had two little girls who loved these amusement places with roller coasters, gum on the floor, wrappers all over, and messy, junky gunk.

You felt ugly when you left the place because there were people who made you feel this was an ugly thing. It was Walt's idea to upgrade the experience with clean streets, clean toilets, clean everything. No liquor on the premises. He wanted it to be a place for all people for all time.

He gave up all his money to build Disneyland. Every bit. He sold all his insurance. Sold his new house in Palm Springs. Had nothing left. Put everything he could beg, borrow, or steal into Disneyland.

They hadn't even finished the freeway to Disneyland. Six miles of it from Buena Park and Tustin wasn't finished. It was just dirt. They had contracted to finish that thing that year, but when we opened Disneyland, you had to take all these detours down dirt roads. Still, people came, and we were astounded.

He spent his time going around in old clothes and meeting people and finding out how they felt about Disneyland. He would ride in the ride vehicle with them. They didn't even know it was Walt. He was so nice that they would want to know who he was and he would say, "I'm Walt Disney." He astounded all sorts of people.

The first ride I worked on for Disneyland was the Snow White Ride-Thru for Fantasyland. I designed it so the audience, each person, going through there would think of themselves as Snow White herself, but they didn't. They all wondered where Snow White was in the ride. It took us fifteen years to back up and redo it and put in a Snow White figure.

For Tomorrowland, Walt wanted to use the squid in the 20,000 Leagues exhibit.

It was a very nice exhibit. This big iris glass would open up and you could see this huge squid that was supposed to grab the submarine and sink it. It had big tentacles coming at you.

The only way we could do it was to build this building on the outside. Walt told me to go ahead and do it. So I built this building and went to see Bob Mattey who was the special effects man in the studio to help.

We didn't have to build it from scratch because we had the one from the movie. But we had to have one that we could make work for Disneyland. There were two nights left where we could paint the whole inside of this building where the squid was going to be. We didn't know the spray paint was poisonous.

We were just spraying away having a wonderful time with all this poison in the air. Walt came in about two in the morning on opening day. We were still spraying away and Walt said, "I'd like to work with you," so we gave him the paint and he worked squirting paint just as much as either of us. Unfortunately, it still wasn't ready for the opening.

Royal "Mickey" Clark

Opening day at Disneyland was a nightmare. Money was coming in faster than we could handle it. The park was not prepared for the very large amount of cash generated on the opening days. All of the money had to be counted and there was so much of it. We worked throughout the night. Everything was in control by the end of the week. The bank would send an armored truck to pick up the money for deposit each day in the afternoon.

Michael Broggie

Bill Cottrell was involved with cash control in the beginning. They had these little kiosks that sold tickets with little drawers for the money. That wasn't enough. They had to start bucket brigades because there was so much change. They got some buckets and run them out to the kiosks and fill them up with coins and run back to Cash Control, dump the bucket, and run out for another load. They'd put it into piles and weigh it to calculate the totals.

Charles Ridgway

I was on the staff of the *Los Angeles Mirror-News* and so my wife and I were invited to the grand opening celebration. We lived only two miles away from the park and realized this would be a historic and important occasion. I arrived with my wife, Greta, at 9am and I don't think they were happy to see me show up that early. I picked up the press credentials and wandered around and had a wonderful time. Everything you heard was true. They ran out of food. Rides broke down. After 5pm, the park was almost completely empty, but they had the rides back up and running so my wife and I rode everything. I loved the experience and that's the story I filed. I was surprised to see all the negative stories that appeared the next day.

We decided to have an early lunch and ate prime rib at a table near Debbie Reynolds and Eddie Fisher. I recall a chunk of window from the *Mark Twain* steamboat crashed on the head of an invited guest who happened to be a state senator. I saw people get into fist fights to get a ride on the Jungle Cruise. I watched as Walt Disney messed up over and over in rehearsals as he prepared for the live television coverage of the opening later that afternoon.

James Bacon

I was a writer for the Associated Press and got invited to the opening on that hot day in July.

Walt was flabbergasted the next day when he saw the adverse media reaction to his opening. Headlines like "Disneyland Premiere Is Disaster" and "Walt's Dream a Nightmare" are hard to take after what Walt went through to get his park built.

"I probably opened it before it was ready," he told me. "I'm making a list of all the complaints, especially the lack of water fountains, and the next time people come back, you'll see everything fixed. I take all this criticism as constructive criticism. And I'll learn from it." That was Walt.

What I remember most about that day is that wonderful sense of awesome nostalgia I felt when I got my first look at Main Street. I could have sworn I was walking down Main Street in 1920 in Jersey Shore, Pennsylvania, the town I grew up in. What, in effect, Walt had created was something that struck a nostalgic chord in all of us—even grown up kids from big city streets and ghettos.

I once asked Eddie Meck, Disneyland's long-time publicity director, what made Disneyland the greatest man-made tourist attraction of all time. I fully expected him to give me a long spiel. Instead, he said: "I can give it to you in two words—Walt Disney. We don't even mail a postcard out of here without his okay."

Bill Martin

In 1954 we got the go-ahead to build Disneyland, but we didn't know what we couldn't do in those days. We had nothing to go on because nothing had ever been built like Disneyland before. We toured "amusement parks" as they were all around the country in those days, but they had little creative impetus to offer us, so we went to work on something entirely new using the Disney movies, of course, for the way to tell the story.

The pirate boat was painted on just one side, the side facing the cameras on opening day, and they laid cables and water lines in such a hurry that they had no time to go by the drawings and we're still discovering where they put everything years later.

I was the art director for Fantasyland. The castle was the main thing and it went through quite a few transformations before the design was finalized. It was a composite dream castle.

Every Saturday for about two years, we [the Park Operating Committee] would meet Walt in Joe Fowler's office, downstairs in City Hall, at about nine in the morning. There would be Walt, Joe Fowler, John Hench, Dick Irvine, Tommy Walker, Bill Evans, Truman Woodworth (who was in charge of construction), and me.

We'd walk through each land before the park opened and each area manager of Operations would be there. Walt would have a few ideas before we started walking around and that's how we'd find out about them. Walt was always looking for ways to make the park better. About noon, we'd go out to Harley's lunchwagon and have hamburgers. Walt loved hamburgers. We'd eat there and then all go home. We would take the ideas and in the next day or two do up some drawings to take back to Walt

Bob Penfield

I started to work at Disneyland on July 13, 1955, four days before opening. I had just turned 18 and graduated high school, and it was my first real job, the only job I ever paid taxes on. Before that I had only worked on a farm at a dollar an hour. Disneyland paid $1.65. I was in heaven.

I was a ride operator assigned to Fantasyland, specifically the Peter Pan ride. Because so many of the rides were not ready, we trained on others, plus test rode many in other lands.

I also was assigned to George Whitney, who was in charge of the construction and implementation of Fantasyland. He would have me run around Fantasyland with messages to other personnel, plus at times over to Adventureland, which I did not even know where it was. I had to ask.

On opening day, it was a total mess. The Storybook Land ride at that time was known as the Canal Boats of the World and was basically just the canal with nothing on the banks, mostly weeds, some of which were marked as to what kind of weeds they were.

They were operated by all men operators, and used Johnson 10 horsepower outboard motors which were inside the aft compartment. They would vapor lock constantly, and had to be towed into the storage area. The operators actually actively discouraged the guests from riding, but they still wanted to.

When the drawbridge was lowered all of the children came rushing in, climbed over the chains around the carousel and overwhelmed us. We had to shut down the ride to keep control. Another thing was that we were really learning our job on the job that first day.

After three days I was made foreman of the afternoon shift of the Snow White ride, and had mainly school teachers and young Marines from Camp Pendleton working for me. One of the things we used to do for fun when things were slow at night was these guys would get on the teacups and we would compete as to who could spin it the fastest. They always won.

There was a place backstage near the staircase to Walt's apartment that we called Walt's Garage where he always parked, so we made sure nobody parked there. For many years after Walt died, people still didn't park there.

The area behind Main Street there was a bunch of old buildings used as offices and we used to call it Tijuana Row because it was so run-down. In the early days, a guy named Harley would park his lunch wagon back there and we used it as the employee cafeteria. There were picnic tables. Sometimes you'd go over and lie down on a picnic bench and try to take a nap. It turned out that Harley was some sort of a bookie as well and some of the Disneylanders were gambling there.

William "Sully" Sullivan

I started working at Disneyland on July 27, 1955, about a week and a half after the park opened.

They made me a full-time ticket taker for the Jungle Cruise attraction in Adventureland. In those days, there were individual tickets for each attraction, so you had someone take them and rip them in half and dispose of them. I didn't request any particular job. I just wanted to go to work at Disney and that's what they gave me.

It was a much different atmosphere in the park in 1955. People came dressed up, especially on Sunday after church. Men would wear ties and hats. Women would wear gloves and high heels. Even kids would be dressed up nice. It was like coming to an event, not a dirty carnival.

You had to be a showman to get people to come over and ride the ride. Nobody knew what the ride was about and it was the most expensive ride. So I would shout out a spiel so people would get excited about trying it.

We had a ticket distribution box where we put the torn half of a ticket. You had to tear the ticket in half so it couldn't be used again. We had problems in the park of some guys not always tearing the tickets and then giving them to their friends. They all got caught, eventually.

In the first few months, they were like those small, stubby tickets you would get at a carnival, not like those fancy color tickets that people remember.

I did that for a couple of weeks and Charlie Thompson, my first boss out there, says, "I'm gonna train you on the boats." So he turned me over to Pete Crimmins who ran the boats on Catalina Island. I had told him I really wanted to be a skipper.

Great guy. Pete says, "Here's your script and this is how you run the boat. I want you to learn the script and we're gonna put you on the boats."

No other training. I just watched what the other skippers were doing and they said "off you go".

I guess they just liked my personality. I took public speaking in high school and I think I flunked it.

I started out at $1.56 an hour. We were all extroverts because we had to put on this good show.

In fact, most of us sometimes took our lunch with Aylene Lewis who played Aunt Jemima over at the Pancake House restaurant in Frontierland. She was a sweetheart and she always loved it when Walt came in for a breakfast. She'd sit with him and they would talk.

One of the skippers was Don Weir who was frail and had this big beard. He was a little bit weird. On slow nights, he would do things like drive the boat backwards through the jungle or silly stuff like that.

He would come to work wearing live chameleons. He had tied monofilament around their necks, and he'd wear three or four of them around his neck on his shirt. Really took the guests by surprise and made them feel as if they were in the wild jungle.

One evening we were driving the boats and it was a very quiet evening. Bob Carbonell and I loaded up two .38s, the blank pistols, and went out to the jungle in the village area and hid behind the pepper tree.

When Don Weir came around he fired at the natives and yelled at them, and we fired back and scared the hell out of him. It took him by surprise and he was so unnerved he fell to his knees. A guest had to bring the boat back in to the dock.

We weren't given any training on how to use the blank pistol, but then I had been hunting all my life so I was familiar with guns. We just shot at the hippos and the natives and it was fun.

I let my hair grow long for four months and it was down around my shoulders and I had a Van Dyke goatee beard. I looked like I belonged in the jungle. There weren't the "Disney Look" grooming standards. I think they started all of that because of how we looked.

Walt kept looking at us and says, "I want the wholesome, young, American guys and gals working out there at the park. So nothing of any extreme, so clean it up!"

That's when the grooming standards started. We all got haircuts and we shaved. The girls, the bouffants went away and all that good stuff. The way you dressed was black shoes, no white socks, good stuff like that.

Sometimes for lunch, we would go backstage and there was Harley's tent. It was a real roach coach type of thing with a tent over the area where you could sit and eat. Walt was the one who put up the green tent to protect us from the sun and rain.

He'd come out there and eat off the roach coach as well. He loved hamburgers. He loved chili burgers. Later, they built the Inn Between that was between the Red Wagon Inn and backstage as an employee cafeteria. Walt would eat in the employee cafeteria as well. He had no airs about him. Just one of the guys.

As I recall, it wasn't really what you would think of as a script, it was just kind of a block of words. Here are the animals you're going to see and this is what you can say, maybe. It was pretty boring stuff so we started tossing in our own jokes.

Things would change and we would change the narration. That first year Walt took out the monkeys that were on the temple in the beginning because they were awful, scraggly little things. Walt would come down to the boats all the time and bring guests.

He'd never take the wheel. He'd let us do our job. He'd usually come on a Saturday or Sunday morning and just want to take a look. Make sure everything was being kept up and the guests were happy.

When it came to learning about Disney culture and how things should be done at the park, we learned that through Walt being there and watching him and what he did and said. He was there almost every weekend and he was there every Wednesday for the Park Operating Committee meeting.

We'd have to catch the baby alligators that we had there because they'd climb over the fence and get out, so we'd catch them every once in a while and put them back in their pen.

In the beginning there was a little pool by the entrance to the Jungle ride that had baby alligators in it because Walt wanted real animals, not just the mechanical ones. I guess it made it all more exotic or something or gave the guests something to look at that they hadn't seen. It didn't last long because these babies kept getting out and it was a pain.

There were four gators and it was fenced with poles and fishnet. They would climb the fishnet and get out. There was a guy who worked with us who was from Florida and he could call them. He could make this sound like an alligator and that would help us catch them.

Tom Nabbe

At the age of twelve, as part of my newspaper route, I was selling the Sunday edition of the *Los Angeles Herald-Examiner* at the employee gate when Disneyland was being built. The only people who really worked for Disneyland, Inc. were the Administration group, the ride and attraction people, and the maintenance people. All the restaurants, all the retail locations and everything else were manned and staffed by what they called lessees and what we at Walt Disney World later called participants.

The lessee that had the newspaper shop (Castle News) on Main Street was Ray Amendt. He asked me if I wanted to sell newspapers for the opening of Disneyland. I told him, "Sure." I was very interested. He said, "You can find me outside of the gate every morning. We'll get you set up with newspapers."

On July 19, I started selling the *Disneyland News* when I was twelve. I would wear cut-off Levi jeans and a gingham shirt. That was my costume. I went early and found Ray in the morning. The deal was that if I sold 100 papers outside the gate, I could go inside and sell the papers inside on Main Street. I did that all of the summer of 1955. I got to go in the park every day I sold papers. Only two or three of us did that.

I used to rent myself out to push people around in wheelchairs, too. So I was rather ingenious during that time.

Claude Coats

Ken Anderson had been working on some of the black-light rides. I got to do the model for the Mr. Toad attraction. I painted it from Ken's sketches and I painted in black light. It was the first time I had any experience working with those fluorescent colors. Walt thought it would enhance the experience. In the past, it had been used in amusement park rides for scary effects like skeletons, but Walt wanted to use it to look like the cartoons.

Later, he came around to tell us that the scenic company [Grosh Studios] painting the actual rides for the park weren't able to do all the work and we were going to finish it. I had just painted backgrounds for animation, so I went from a 12" format to sets that were eighteen-feet high and these plywood flats that weighed 500 pounds or so, it seemed. It was just bigger backgrounds as far as I was concerned. We played with forced perspective to give a better illusion. We tried to keep the same mood as the animated films.

We did a mock-up at the studio and then took it to Disneyland to be installed and the stuff we did for Mr. Toad didn't fit. It was too big, so they knocked out a wall. Ken and I did the big murals for the entrances as well. Walt just thought we could do it since we had worked on the films.

Jack Lindquist

I started in September 1955, but I was there opening day as a guest. We took my oldest son, David, who at the time was five, and we finally got him on one attraction. It was the Canal Boats. The boat took off and was supposed to be back in five minutes, but it never came back. About 55 minutes later, his boat came back being pulled by ropes with six people wearing waders in the water. He asked if we could go home now. We got in the car and went to Knott's Berry Farm for a chicken dinner. That was the only attraction he got on that day, but it was still a tremendous thrill to be at Disneyland.

That first Christmas Eve at the park, I was walking down Main Street just before closing, behind a family. They were neatly dressed, but you could tell they were not well off. When they reached the Emporium and were looking in the windows, the little girl looked up at her mother and said, "You're right, Mommy. This is better than having Santa Claus visit tomorrow." I knew then that the girl and her brother and probably the parents weren't getting any presents that Christmas. That moment showed me what Disneyland means to people.

Steve Martin

In 1955, when I was ten, our family moved to Garden Grove, California, only two miles from the nascent Disneyland, a place that seemed to me like a distant Shangri-la. I had seen films of it on TV being built and I had seen photos in the newspapers of Walt Disney shoveling up the first bucketful of dirt. I had heard that Disneyland was hiring kids to sell the *Disneyland News*, and I sped on my bicycle two miles up Katella street to sign on. Somehow I was hired—I'm sure today's labor laws would prevent my benefit-less employment conditions—and given a Gay Nineties outfit complete with striped shirt, bow tie and arm garters, and told to stand in front of the magic castle in Fantasyland where I hawked the in-house newspaper for several months—and never sold one. I did this job diligently, earning nothing, while my parents financed my lunches and Coca-Cola purchases.

Fess Parker

Opening day was really my first live television appearance. I was an actor who had started with one line three years earlier and here I was expected to sing and dance. And dance on dirt! I felt a lot of tension, but it all went well. Later, after everything, Buddy [Ebsen] and I went up to [Walt's] apartment over the firehouse and had a drink. You know, you often see a certain look on athletes' faces after they have won some sort of championship. That was the look on Walt's face that day. A couple of months earlier, Buddy and I had gone to the park for publicity photos of us walking around the fort and splitting a log or two. Walt even encouraged us to slide down the fire pole in his apartment.

Dick Nunis

I'll never forget my first day of work. We worked out of an old home from the orange grove that had been moved to West Street. My first day, I showed up all spruced up in a blue-checked jacket, blue pants, blue suede shoes. Van France looked me over and finally said, "Well, get rid of the suede shoes at least...and can you use a broom?" The house was filthy! So I changed my shoes and we cleaned up the place and then it became the training center.

During the summer of 1955 the fate of Disneyland was very questionable. Facilities for guests and personnel were primitive compared to today. Money was in short supply. We received complaints about attraction breakdowns...lack of drinking fountains...long lines..food..high prices...you name it. In August, the temperatures were the hottest they'd ever been... and the humidity! Temperatures were in the 100s with humidity as high as 90%. Attendance went down to next to nothing. You could literally fire a cannon down Main Street on Saturday night—in the summer—and not hit a soul. But Walt believed in it. Walt had hocked everything he had to get it open. He wanted to make sure we gave the guest a good show.

But we had one special asset which compensated for all of our shortcomings during that period. That special asset was our Disneyland PEOPLE. The compliments far overshadowed the complaints...compliments for the friendliness of our people and the cleanliness of the park.

Walt originally approached Hilton and others to build a hotel adjacent to Disneyland, but they felt the venture was too risky. Walt then turned to his friend Jack Wrather, a Texas wildcatter oil man and television pioneer, and after some discussion convinced him to build a hotel near the park. He leased 60 acres along West Street directly across from the Disneyland exit. Wrather wanted the hotel to be located at the entrance to Disneyland, but Walt said, "Jack, our guests aren't going to be thinking about a hotel when they begin their visit to Disneyland. They'll start looking for a room when they leave the park. The best place to build your hotel is near Disneyland's exit." The place opened October 5, 1955.

Bill Cottrell

The professional advice that we had was that you've got to have two things if you want to succeed and make any money. You've got to have a roller coaster. And you've got to have a Ferris wheel. And Walt said, "I don't want to have either one of those."

John Hench

I had dinner with Walt at the park during that first week. He arrived late. When he showed up, he said, "There's a lot of happy people out there. I saw a lot of happy faces." The happiest face I saw was Walt's. He always told us, "You get down to Disneyland at least twice a month and you walk in the front entrance, don't walk in through the back. Eat with the people. Watch how they react to the work you've done down there." This made an enormous difference in how we approached our work.

Milt Albright

Our first administration building was called the Old Farmhouse. It was the Dominguez house and the Callen house put together with a second story "bridge" connecting the two homes. Those cramped quarters were used for years. Air conditioning was non-existent (except for the portable window kinds) and the acoustics were abominable. An upstairs whisper could be heard downstairs. And there was little if any privacy. Desks were butted against each other in tiny corners and file cabinets jammed the halls and closets.

The reception area was a front porch. A colorful but messy mulberry tree in front did very little toward cooling any section of the building and a lot toward changing the color of the entrance carpeting to a permanent deep purple. In those unbelievably hectic twelve months of building Disneyland, Walt was in and out almost daily. Always moving, guiding, questioning... he didn't even have (or want) a desk.

The fire chief maintained an office here with the fire truck parked a few feet away awaiting their daily warm-ups to maintain battery power. Cash Control and Lessee Relations and more were in this building where stairs led nowhere, noisy plumbing, narrow balconies, room temperatures that varied from hot to frigid, crowded conditions, creaky floors, busy termites who left their calling cards on many a desk and window sill, but it had its charms and I was sorry when it was finally gone. Today Space Mountain stands where all that activity once took place.

Somebody had to decide what to do with the houses on the property, whether to tear them down, burn them, or use them. There was an old, big, one-story house that belonged to an orange grove owner named Willard Olding who said he was glad to be getting out. My daily drive from Burbank was taking its toll, so I asked Walt for Mr. Olding's house and he gave it to me. We moved it to a beautiful rural area near the small village of Olive. We had to pay, of course, for the moving, the site, plumbing, electrical, etc. Altogether it was about $12,000. We got a magnificent, warm, livable home where we raised six daughters.

Joe Fowler

When I came on board, it was nothing but blue sky when it came to the plans. As a matter of fact, it's quite interesting to observe that all the time I was building Disneyland, I never had more than we'll say sixty percent of the finished plans.

We had a big excavation we were making for a dry dock. Walt was very upset about the disfigurement of the area with this open pit, as it were. But Walt had a wonderful habit. If he was upset with someone, he would seldom say directly to him, "You umpity-ump." Walt would just turn to a third party as he did to Dick Irvine when he said, "By the time Joe gets through with that ditch, we won't have any money left." Walt kept referring to it as Joe's Ditch, but eventually he saw the necessity for it. He decided if it had to be there, it may as well be dressed up to look like part of the scene, so he named it Fowler's Harbor.

Herb Ryman

When I tell this story, nobody seems to realize that I could see immediately that the design for the castle was obviously the famous Bavarian castle of King Ludwig, Neuschwanstein. I told Marvin [Davis] and Richard [Irvine] that we couldn't do that. People would say that Walt Disney had no imagination and just copied the castle.

They tried to tell me that it really wasn't that well known, but I knew that more and more people would be traveling all around the world and would make the connection. Fred Joerger made a scale model and before a presentation to Walt, I tried to express again my concern and I touched the model for emphasis. I discovered the top center portion was loose, so I picked up the piece and turned it around and said, "This is better. People won't easily recognize it." They urged me to turn it back around before Walt came in, and then we heard, "I like that better." It was Walt and suddenly Richard and Marvin started to like it better that way, too!

Howard Bastrup

I started work with the Anaheim Police Department on July 10, 1955. During the morning hours of opening day, I was assigned to traffic control on West Street. At 9:30am, Walt Disney drove through the streets surrounding Disneyland to see, I suppose, what the impact of the opening had on traffic. Later, he would host all of us who were working on the streets with boxed chicken lunches, which were served to parking lot personnel and police officers. It was a nice gesture, I thought, for Walt to remember those working under the hot July sun.

Shortly after the opening, a number of pickpockets started to work the park, usually in teams, and short-change artists tried to work on employees working in the ticket booths or in the stores. These activities were soon discovered and all employees who handled money were trained to recognize the cheats.

To handle the pickpockets, I soon realized that most of the pickpockets we arrested were from Los Angeles. I went to the Los Angeles Police Department Detective Bureau and talked to members of the pickpocket detail and they offered to come to Disneyland and assist us. When the detail of six L.A. detectives arrives, it was decided to post three at the entrance gates and three at the exit gates.

Most of the pickpockets known to the detectives were spotted as they entered and were quickly escorted to a room out of sight of guests. The few not spotted by the detectives at the entrance were detained as they exited, especially if a pickpocket crime had been reported. It only took a week for word to get around that criminals working the park were sure to be apprehended. The short change and pickpocket crimes stopped and are almost non-existent today.

In addition to my regular detective duties, I was appointed as the police department's liaison officer with Disneyland. The work included procedural needs for traffic, crime investigation, crowd control, providing security for famous people, and disaster. The training of Disneyland's security guards on mutually-agreed procedures also became my responsibility.

Charles Ridgway

After the opening day fiasco, the press had told people to stay away. Walt began a campaign of inviting all the press to come back, a few at a time, to really see the park. Many were taken on personal tours by Walt himself. To control crowds at the rides, Walt came up with roped aisles that weaved back and forth where people could still see the ride based on similar queues Walt said he had seen at London theaters. He even put in live entertainment for people waiting in line.

Lessees formed the Disneyland Merchants Association to complain to Walt when kids went back to school in the fall and attendance dropped to something like just a thousand guests on a weekday. They wanted Walt to close the park during the off season and only open in summer and on holidays. Walt refused.

Ward Kimball

Walt was down there in his boots every day with the bulldozers, going over the plans. "Plant a tree here," he'd say. "Bring this around to the right, because you won't be able to see the ship coming around the bend if you put it there." All those little details. The things that make things work.

Ollie Johnston

What I remember most about opening day is I spent most of it stuck in the cattle car with kids crying and suffocating. Walt had given us all passes to be there and we were told to be in certain locations so the place would look populated. I also remember the press was furious because it seemed like the television people were getting everything they wanted and they weren't, so there was a lot of bad press for a couple of weeks until Walt was able to turn it around. One reporter said it all felt like a giant cash register.

George Mills

As the guests were coming in the *front* door, we were going out the *back* door to the boneyard with *everything* that wasn't nailed down! The boneyard was a gigantic sea of junk. We had problems pumping the Adventureland River…bluegills were in all the water systems. The strainers were all plugged with the little fish.

Broney Ciesluk

When I came to Disneyland, I was still in the Marine Corps. There were so many Marines employed at Disneyland that if the country had an alert, it would have depleted the park! Walt was so down to earth…nothing pretentious…he would always take time to talk. One time, back in '56, I was picking Roy Disney up in one of the park's old station wagons and it wouldn't run. Roy said, "Well, that figures!"

Bob Allen

Before the park opened, I stood in line for several days running to try to get a job, and though I was told there were "no jobs", I kept coming back. Finally, I made it to the front of the line and was hired. At that point, I was curious and asked the interviewer why he finally hired me. He said, "Because you're the only one wearing a tie!"

Earl Wuestneck

That preview day it was people … people … people. We would open the gates for twenty minutes and then close for twenty minutes. There were celebrities everywhere, and miles of film was taken. I remember our costumes distinctly as Main Gate ticket takers, a little military hat on the side of my head, a gold "Ike" jacket, green pants, brown shoes and white gloves.

CHAPTER TWENTY-TWO

In His Own Words: Walt Disney on Disneyland 1955

From the very first Disneyland souvenir book, *The Story of Disneyland*, comes this introduction by Walt. The book was only available for a few months before it was replaced by an updated edition that included photographs and not just concept art.

Welcome to Disneyland. We hope you will have fun here, and that this souvenir will long recall happy, carefree hours in a place dedicated to your enjoyment.

The first edition illustrations on these pages show buildings and exhibits in artist rendering stage. That was so we could have the booklet ready for our early visitors. But Disneyland will always be building and growing and adding new things...new ways of having fun, of learning things and sharing the many exciting adventures which may be experienced here in the company of family and friends.

What you see in Disneyland represents the combined efforts of hundreds of artists, architects, scientists, expert craftsmen and engineers who have helped us carry out a long-cherished dream.

The park-playground fulfills a wish that those of us who like the same things might more closely share the pleasures I have had in exploring the paths of fable and folklore, of nature and science and historical legend on the screen and television.

So, the opening of Disneyland, where visitors of every age and circumstance can learn joyously from fact and live closely with fantasy, has been for me— as I hope it has been for you—a most happy event—a dream come true.

— Walt Disney

Here is Walt's introduction for the very first Disneyland training manual, from 1955, entitled *A Guide for Hosts and Hostesses* (24 pages):

> Welcome to Disneyland
>
> To make the dream of Disneyland come true took the combined skills and talents of hundreds of artisans, carpenters, engineers, scientists and craftsmen.
>
> The dream that they built now becomes your heritage. It is you who will make Disneyland truly a Magic Kingdom and a happy place for the millions of guests who will visit us now and in the future years.
>
> In creating happiness for our guests, we hope that you will find happiness in your work and in being an important part of Disneyland.
>
> — Walt Disney"

Here are a few quotes from Walt about early Disneyland, taken from various magazine articles, interviews, and other sources:

- In Disneyland, clocks and watches will lose all meaning, for there is no present. There are only yesterday, tomorrow and the timeless land of fantasy. Disneyland is based on the dreams and hard facts that have created America.
- I want this to be a place for parents and children to spend pleasant times together, and for teachers and pupils to discover greater ways of understanding and education.
- I had all my drawing things laid out at home, and I'd work on plans for the park, as a hobby, at night. I talked Disneyland, but no one could see it. So I went ahead and spent my own money. I wanted flat land that I could shape. I don't want the public to see the real world they live in while they're in the park. I want them to feel they are in another world.
- It's quite a chore to keep Disneyland going. It's like a big show you've got to keep on the road, you know. You've got to keep it fresh and new and exciting. And when people come back, you always want to have something new they hadn't had a chance to see before. And we feel a keen responsibility to the customer there. They aren't customers. We call them paying guests.
- Disneyland is not just for children. I don't play down. In the winter time you can go out there during the week and you won't see any children. You'll see the oldsters out there riding all these rides and having fun and everything. Summertime, of course, the average would drop down. But the overall, year-round average, it's four adults to one child.

- Disneyland would be a world of Americans, past and present, seen through the eyes of my imagination—a place of warmth and nostalgia, of illusion and color and delight.
- Disneyland is the star. Everything else is in the supporting role.
- Everybody thinks that the park is a gold mine—but we have had our problems. You've got to work it and know how to handle it. Even trying to keep that park clean is a tremendous expense. And those sharp pencil guys tell you, "Walt, if we cut down on maintenance, we'd save a lot of money." But I don't believe in that—it's like any other show on the road; it must be kept clean and fresh.
- The first year I leased out the parking concession, brought in the usual security guards—things like that. But I soon realized my mistake. I couldn't have outside help and still get over my idea of hospitality. So now we recruit and train every one of our employees. I tell the security officers, for instance, that they never are to consider themselves cops. They are there to help people. The visitors are our guests. It's like running a fine restaurant. Once you get the policy going, it grows.
- Disneyland has that thing—the imagination and feeling of happy excitement I knew when I was a kid.
- It's no secret that we were sticking just about every nickel we had on the chance that people would really be interested in something totally new and unique in the field of entertainment.
- Disneyland will always be building and growing and adding new things…new ways of having fun, of learning things and sharing the many exciting adventures which may be experienced here in the company of family and friends.
- Almost everyone warned us that Disneyland would be a Hollywood spectacular—a spectacular failure. But they were thinking about an amusement park, and we believed in our idea—a family park where parents and children could have fun—together.
- The way I see it, Disneyland will never be finished. It's something we can keep developing and adding to. I've always wanted to work on something alive, something that keeps growing. We've got that at Disneyland.
- I think what I want Disneyland to be most of all is a happy place—a place where adults and children can experience together some of the wonder of life, of adventure, and feel better because of it.

CHAPTER TWENTY-THREE

Disneyland 1956

In 1999, Disney Chief Archivist Dave Smith wrote:
> In its second year of operation, Disneyland saw the opening of more than a dozen new attractions—the most to be added in a single year in the park's entire history. When the park opened, Walt famously said, "Disneyland will never be completed. It will continue to grow, to add new things, as long as there is imagination left in the world." And 1956 certainly demonstrates how much Walt meant those words.

In an expansion program that cost over a million and a half dollars, new attractions were opened and existing ones renovated. In 1956, Disneyland employed 2,190 people with a payroll of $7.8 million dollars to serve the millions of guests who flocked to the park.

Joe Fowler told reporter Bob Thomas:
> In January, after we opened, we had a hell of a storm. We [Walt and Fowler] had come down on a Saturday with Dick Irvine. And, of course, the roads were flooded. Walt said to Dick, "Fine, we'll just spend the time right here." I think that weekend cost Roy millions because that was the weekend when Walt planned the Skyway and a lot of other things.
>
> Walt was planning new things right along. His theory was to have new things and keep them fresh and attractive. By that same token, there were certain things that we subsequently took out that never really quite worked. The Phantom Boats was one of them.

A 1956 Disneyland press release stated:
> With the opening of Rainbow Caverns, Walt Disney has brought to a close his Magic Wonderland's first major expansion program only days from the completion of the Park's first year. The program fulfills Walt's promise for this summer season of "More room, more rides for fun!"

Attractions Added in 1956
- Astro Jets (March 24)
- The Crane Company Bathroom of Tomorrow (April 5)

- Red Horseless Carriage (May 12)
- Storybook Land Canal Boats (June 16)
- Tom Sawyer Island Rafts (June 16)
- Skyway to Tomorrowland (June 23)
- Skyway to Fantasyland (June 23)
- Rainbow Ridge Pack Mules (June 26, renamed)
- Rainbow Mountain Stage Coach (June 26, renamed)
- Rainbow Caverns Mine Train (July 2)
- Indian Village (July, new location)
- Indian War Canoes (July 4)
- Junior Autopia (July 23)
- Main Street Omnibus #1 (August)
- Yellow Horseless Carriage (December)

Shops and Food Locations Added in 1956
- Carefree Corner (Main Street)
- Carnation Plaza Gardens (Main Street)
- Silhouette Studio (Main Street)
- Jimmy Starr's Show Business (Main Street)
- Casa de Fritos (Frontierland, new location)
- Mexican Fiesta Village (Frontierland)
- Oaks Tavern (Frontierland)
- Frontier Gun Shop (Frontierland)
- Fort Wilderness Snack Bar (Frontierland)
- Fantasyland Art Corner (Fantasyland)
- Fantasyland Train Station (Fantasyland)
- Professor Keller's Jungle Killers (Fantasyland)
- 3D Jamboree Film (Fantasyland)
- Mad Hatter Shop (Fantasyland)
- Avenue of the Flags (Tomorrowland)
- The Dairy Bar (Tomorrowland)

Other Additions and Firsts
- "D" tickets were added to Disneyland ticket books in June to help pay for the new attractions.

- C.V. Wood, vice-president and general manager, was asked to resign in January and officially left by February 1.
- On Thursday, January 26, Disneyland unexpectedly closed for the first time because of a storm described as the second worst in all of Southern California's history.
- On April 1, Disneyland held its first Easter Parade.
- The Disneyland Hotel formally opened on August 25.
- On October 3, four year old Debra Rutherford of Quincy, Washington, became the five millionth guest to visit Disneyland. She was officially welcomed by Jack Sayers, director of Customer Relations, and given a key and silver pass to the park. Debra accepted a baton and did a credible job of leading the Disneyland Band playing the theme song from *The Mickey Mouse Club* television show. Then she climbed on top of a big ladder with her father to change the Main Street Railroad Station population sign. From there, Debra and the rest of her family (three-year-old sister Patricia and her dad and mom, Mr. and Mrs. W.L. Rutherford) entered for a full day of rides, treats, and eats, as guests of Disneyland management.
- On November 11, Disneyland announced that Liberty Street is in the planning stages, taking the place of the previously announced International Street.
- The Christmas Festival began November 22.
- From December 15–30, there was a special promotion of Meet Spin & Marty and Annette in Person!
- In a study that many considered overly optimistic, Harrison "Buzz" Price had estimated that park visitors would average $3 in spending and predicted annual attendance of 2.5 to 3 million. What some called Disney's Folly instead generated per-capita spending of $5, Price said, and drew 4 million visits its first year.

Closures
- Davy Crockett Frontier Museum
- Phantom Boats
- Disneyland Bandstand (Plaza Gardens)
- Grandma's Baby Shop
- Mickey Mouse Club Circus
- Intimate Apparel Shop

NEWS FROM DISNEYLAND Disneyland Press Release, July 1956, from Public Relations Dept., Disneyland Inc., Anaheim, California Keystone 5-1181:

DISNEYLAND ONE YEAR OLD

Disneyland concludes its first year of operation this week with attendance at the Magic Kingdom in Anaheim nearing the 4 million mark.

At the end of the day on July 17 of this year, 3,642,597 persons had toured Walt Disney's playland, making it the largest single private enterprise attraction in the Western Hemisphere and "a complete success", according to the Park's management.

Disneyland has scored high with tourists visiting the Southland. An estimated 1,493,465, or 41%, of the Park's guests being drawn from outside this state.

Included in the out-of-state guests were visitors from 64 of the earth's nations, including such far-off places as Saudi Arabia, Iceland, Liechtenstein, and even the Soviet Union.

Intermingled with Disneyland's guests have been notables and celebrities from the worlds of government, politics and industry. The roster of celebrities who have been to Disneyland reads like a who's who of entertainment. Guests from the government have included Vice-President Nixon with his family who toured the Park soon after the July 18 opening. A more recent visitor was President Sukarno of Indonesia. Dr. Sukarno, on a state visit to the United States, made Disneyland one of his stopping places in Southern California.

Proof that Disneyland's appeal has been to persons of all ages is furnished by a breakdown of attendance statistics gathered during the first year which revealed that four adults have visited here for every child.

Average expenditure of Disneyland's guests for the first year was $2.37 per person. This figure includes parking, admission, rides, amusements and Disneyland souvenirs.

Attendance during this first full summer season has equaled and surpassed records set during last July and August. For the week ending July 15, 148,729 persons toured the Park. Since June 1, a total of 768,425 guests have passed through the turnstiles.

Certain of the Park's rides have proved especially popular with the visitors. These have included the Peter Pan dark ride in Fantasyland, the Adventureland Jungle River Boat Ride, the Santa Fe and Disneyland trains, and the Autopia Freeway's miniature autos in Tomorrowland.

During the year the Park's operation has undergone a number of improvements aimed at increasing the guests' enjoyment.

Free exhibits at Disneyland now number 21 compared to a total of 11 available last July. And today the Park offers 33 rides and amusements, seven more than when the Park was opened.

Some of these new rides, part of an overall $2 million expansion program recently completed, include the Disneyland Skyway, the Rainbow Caverns Mine Train Ride, the Indian Village and War Canoes, Storybook Land and Tom Sawyer's Island.

In keeping with Walt Disney's policy, the Park will continue to expand and refine its operation to offer unparalleled entertainment to its millions of visitors each year.

Scheduled for opening next Spring will be the "House of Tomorrow" sponsored by the Monsanto Chemical Company, one of the Park's exhibitors. Other new attractions will be revealed early this fall, with construction to be finished in time for the 1957 summer season.

(The 1957 first new additions would be the Midget Autopia and the Sleeping Beauty Walk-Through in April 1957.)

In June and July of 1956, Walt did a series of interviews with journalist Pete Martin for articles that would appear in the *Saturday Evening Post* beginning November 17, 1956 and later be combined and edited into a book, *The Story of Walt Disney* (Henry Holt & Co. 1957).

Here are Walt's unedited thoughts from summer of 1956 about the business behind Disneyland:

Walt Disney: It really takes a person more than a day to see the park without exhausting themselves. And as I get these new things in, it's going to take more time. It's one of those things that people who come in here for the first time and everything's there and they sort of make a hog of themselves, you see? Well, a lot of people come back the third time and just like to sit and listen to the band, see the horses going around. I like to go down and sit by the river and watch the people.

Chewing gum sticks up things so we don't sell it. And peanut shells. We sell the unshelled. But shelled peanuts, they just crumble them and throw them all over the place. And nothing with round sticks. People trip on them. The ice cream bars got flat sticks and I won't sell any of this spun candy because the kids get it and get it all over everything and people get it on their hands.

No liquor, no beer, nothing. Because that brings in a rowdy element. That brings people that we don't want and I feel they don't need it. I feel when I go down to the park I don't need a drink. I work around that place all day and I don't have one. After I come out of a heavy day at the studio sometimes I want a drink to relax.

When it comes to Disneyland, I feel I've given the public everything I can give them. My daughter Diane says that I spend too much time around the house talking about how I can give them more for their money when they come to the park. You've got to build. You've got to keep it clean. You don't want to walk in a dirty toilet. I won't have 'em. My toilets are spic and span.

Pete Martin: One of the things we should cover is to knock off that rumor that Disneyland's expensive to come to.

Walt Disney: Oh, no. Not at all. That's an old hat thing. You hear it from some people because they don't know what else to say.

By the time this article comes out, I'm raising it to two dollars because I'm adding all these new rides. And to extend my ticket book to take care of the rides, I'm putting this to ten rides for two dollars. Figure it out. It averages twenty cents a ride, doesn't it? It would cost an adult three dollars and a junior two dollars and fifty cents to get in and get ten rides.

If they don't want that, they can pay their buck and pay their fifty cents for their kid and they can come in. They can sit on the park benches, take up the space, dirty up my toilets, litter up the street. They can do all of that if they pay their dollar fifty. They can ride as they want to. They can sit around and hear my band; they can visit my free shows. They can do all that and more for their dollar fifty.

You can't go in a state park without paying that. See, you've got to pay something. You pay so much a head or so much a car to go in a state park. We even have to pay government tax on admission. So it's really ninety-one cents to get in. Now that's what it amounts to. You can't go to the circus for that. I tell you the complaint about the prices is malicious.

Los Angeles is made up of a lot of different characters. How do I know they might not be more interested in some other thing like Marineland? Or some other type of amusement that is competitive. We are competitive, too. Who knows? But there's no foundation for some of these complaints about price. When people make that remark to me, it just sounds to me like they heard it somewhere and they don't know what else to say. How can they compare Disneyland prices with anything else, because there is nothing else like it?

Well, you take your children to Disneyland and for a dollar and a half they get in and spend a whole darn 13 hours if they want to. Now, if you want to go in and buy them expensive toys or you want to buy them bathing suits or your wife happened to go along and sees a wonderful woolen skirt that costs $30, well, people come out and spend all that money. But they don't think twice of going down to Bullocks Wilshire and spending that much on a skirt. If you go into a Broadway department store, you can go in and spend $25 or $30. I'm not insisting people buy things, but I want to give them the opportunity.

So I have to keep improving on ideas. On the jungle ride, I want to get more animation in the animals. I want to really fix it. My monkeys have gone to pot. And I want new monkeys. I'm going to take them out Monday because I'd rather not have them in there looking like that.

Afterword

I was only twenty-three years old and working full-time at Channing Wallace Gilson Industrial Design in Hollywood when in mid-1954 I was asked if I was interested in doing some work on the side at night and on Saturdays for a project Walt Disney was building.

I got caught up in the excitement of the Disneyland project and found that my temporary project soon became my new full-time job. Many others from those days have a similar story.

It still seems like yesterday to me, but it has been over sixty years and many of those people I knew and worked with are long gone and forgotten, so I am grateful that some of their stories are being preserved in this book.

It was different six decades ago. You were expected to go beyond your comfort zone, learn quickly how to do new things and solve problems. There were no committees, just Walt, and he was everywhere and checked everything and gave you the support you needed to make his dream come true.

I was trained as a car stylist and came up with the design for the Autopia cars and the parking lot trams in 1955. Walt didn't want to buy things "off the shelf". He wanted things that were better and uniquely Disneyland.

I was not an engineer, but I had to learn quickly because the parts had to be custom-machined and I was the one that had to draw all of those designs.

I made mistakes. Kaiser Aluminum was one of the sponsors at Disneyland, but aluminum makes terrible bumpers for Autopia cars. They deform and do not return to their original position as a steel spring would. They dragged on the curbs, leaving streaks of scrapings. We discovered all of this on opening day because there had been no time to do sufficient testing at the studio as we were rushed to make the deadline.

There were faulty speed governors, unpadded steering wheels that knocked out children's teeth when they smashed into them when the car was bumped, and axle and brake damage, among other things. The cars were breaking faster than I could fix them.

It wasn't just the Autopia that was facing problems of things not working as they should. Nobody had ever done a place like Disneyland before and many things were being attempted for the first time. It was often chaos, but Walt kept the show going with a smile and a calmness that it would all work out somehow. That was reassuring.

It is amazing to me that all these things were fixed within the first six months, some by the end of that first summer. It never occurred to us that it was impossible and it never occurred to us to just give up. By the start of January 1956, we were introducing new things into the park that had new problems and we fixed those as well.

I have always enjoyed the writing of Jim Korkis. In his articles and books, he has done his research to capture the accuracy and spirit of Disney history. One of the things that he focuses on is that history was not just names, events, and dates, but people. Disney history in 1955 was about the hundreds of people and their stories that made magic for Disneyland guests.

Inside these pages, he talks about Thomas "Mitch" Mitchell, the first fire chief of Disneyland and his 1954 Willys Jeep with a front-mounted pump and fire apparatus kept near the white administration building backstage; and Trinidad Ruiz, with his distinctive white mustache, who was attired as a White Wing on Main Street and swept up after the horses; and swaggering, cigar-smoking Nat Lewis who handled the balloon sellers throughout the park; and Emmert Brooks who ran the Candy Palace on Main Street and set such high standards in service and product that Walt preserved their relationship for a decade after other lessees were phased out.

These names are probably unfamiliar to the casual Disney fan, and thank heaven that Jim interviewed some of the members of Club 55 over the decades to obtain that type of information and later share it so that they will be remembered.

There are many books and articles about early Disneyland. I wrote my memories in the now out-of-print *Design: Just For Fun* (2012 APP-Gurr). As always, Jim found stories and information that haven't appeared in print elsewhere so that people can understand that those first few months of Disneyland were like a constant fire-drill and that some of what we accept today as treasured "traditions" were just us making it up as we went along.

Former president of Imagineering Marty Sklar once said that he liked Jim's articles on Disney history in the quarterly *Disney Files* magazine produced for Disney Vacation Club members because "they bring back memories for me".

I am grateful that Jim took the time to compile all this information to bring back memories of one of the happiest times of my life. You will be informed and entertained that the birth of Disneyland was like a three-ring circus. It was Walt's dream and he was the one who guided us all in the same direction and to the same destination, but it took a lot of talented, wonderful people to make it happen.

Bob Gurr
Disney Imagineer (Retired)
Member of Club 55

APPENDIX A

The United States in 1955

The opening of Disneyland should not be separated from what else was happening in the United States at the same time. Memories of World War II were still fresh as a boom of babies were being born.

The Korean conflict had ended uneasily just two years earlier. In some ways, America was a highly materialistic society that embraced owning new cars (seven out of ten American families owned a car) and family traveling, as well as the questionable delights of early black-and-white television sets in all living rooms and every other new shiny device that was being touted as indispensable for the home.

In the background was the specter of the Cold War and the "Red Scare" that Russia would heat it up into a nuclear confrontation and bury us all. It was also an era that marked the seeds of teen revolution, from the sexual gyrations of singer Elvis Presley to the brooding Marlon Brando in *The Wild One* (1954), the troubled James Dean in *Rebel Without a Cause* (1955), and a classroom of teenage hoodlums in *Blackboard Jungle* (1955).

Some commentators of the era claimed that comic books corrupted the young, rock n' roll encouraged rebellion among teenagers, and television dulled everyone's minds with its vapid wasteland of entertainment. The beatniks, characterized as unkempt and lazy, voiced their objections to what they perceived as the sterility and conformity of American society.

In this tumultuous time, Disneyland offered a balance between the safety and comfort of the past and the hope for an exciting, bright future, without having to address the challenges of the present.

Here are some facts and figures about the United States in 1955:

Government and Population

- President: Dwight D. Eisenhower
- Vice President: Richard M. Nixon
- Number of states: 48
- Population: 165,931,2024

Average Costs of Living

- Bread: 18 cents a loaf
- Coffee: 83 cents a pound
- Eggs: 27 cents a dozen
- Milk: 92 cents a gallon
- Hamburger: 56 cents a pound
- Average income: $4,137 a year
- Minimum wage: 75 cents an hour (raised to a dollar on August 12)
- Unemployment: 4.4%
- Average house price: $10,950
- Cost of a three bedroom home in Anaheim: $13,325
- Average rent: $87.00 per month
- Average cost of a new car: $1,910
- Cost of a 1955 Ford $1,759
- Cost of a 1955 Cadillac de Ville $4,895
- Average price of a gallon of gasoline: 23 cents
- Sofa bed and matching chair: $156
- Bedroom set: $70
- Frigidaire refrigerator: $189
- 21-inch Admiral black-and-white television set: $209
- Movie ticket: 75 cents
- Stamp: 3 cents (rate unchanged since 1932; it would go up a penny in 1958)

Award Winners

- Miss America: Lee Ann Meriwether (19 years old; later a popular actress)
- *Time* Magazine Man of the Year: GM President Harlow Curtice

- World Series Champions: Brooklyn Dodgers
- NFL Champions: Cleveland Browns
- No Nobel Peace Prize was awarded in 1955
- Pulitzer Prize Winner: William Faulkner for *A Fable*

The Top Ten Most Watched Television Programs

1. The $64,000 Question (CBS)
2. I Love Lucy (CBS)
3. The Ed Sullivan Show (CBS)
4. Disneyland (ABC)
5. The Jack Benny Show (CBS)
6. December Bride (CBS)
7. You Bet Your Life (NBC)
8. Dragnet (NBC)
9. The Millionaire (CBS)
10. I've Got a Secret (CBS)

Sixty-four percent of all homes in America had a television. The first commercial television remote was developed by Eugene Polley in 1955.

On October 3, 1955, *Captain Kangaroo* and *The Mickey Mouse Club* both premiered on television. Other television shows that debuted in 1955 were *Gunsmoke*, *Alfred Hitchcock Presents*, *The Honeymooners*, and *The Lawrence Welk Show*. In the U.K., *The Benny Hill Show* debuted.

Jim Henson's *Sam and Friends* television series, with the first appearance of Kermit the Frog (who appeared as a lizard creature), premiered May 9, 1955, on Washington, D.C. station WRC-TV. On December 10, 1955, *Mighty Mouse Playhouse* debuted on CBS Saturday morning; its success sparked the famous Saturday morning cartoon shows.

Emmy Awards

- Best Dramatic Series: *Producers' Showcase*
- Best Actor, Continuing Performance: Phil Silvers, *Phil Silvers Show*
- Best Actress, Continuing Performance: Lucille Ball, *I Love Lucy*
- Best Actor in a Supporting Role: Art Carney, *The Honeymooners*
- Best Actress in a Supporting Role: Nanette Fabray, *Caesar's Hour*
- Best Single Program of the Year: *Producers' Showcase: Peter Pan* (NBC)
- Best Comedy Series: *Phil Silvers Show* (originally titled *You'll Never Get Rich*)

- Best Comedian: Phil Silvers
- Best Comedienne: Nanette Fabray
- Best Variety Series: *Ed Sullivan Show*
- Best Music Series: *Your Hit Parade*
- Best Action or Adventure Series: *Disneyland*
- Best Documentary Program, Religious, Informational, Educational or Interview: *Omnibus*
- Best News Commentator or Reporter: Edward R. Murrow
- Best Children's Series: *Lassie*
- Best Audience Participation Series: *$64,000 Question*

Billboard Top 10 Songs

1. "Cherry Pink and Apple Blossom White" (Perez Prado)
2. "Rock Around the Clock" (Bill Haley & His Comets)
3. "Yellow Rose of Texas" (Mitch Miller)
4. "Autumn Leaves" (Roger Williams)
5. "Unchained Melody" (Les Baxter)
6. "The Ballad of Davy Crockett" (Bill Hayes)
7. "Love Is a Many Splendored Thing" (Four Aces)
8. "Sincerely" (McGuire Sisters)
9. "Ain't That a Shame" (Pat Boone)
10. "Dance with Me, Henry" (Georgia Gibbs)

Tony Awards

- Best Musical: *The Pajama Game*
- Best Play: *The Desperate Hours*
- Best Actor in a Play: Alfred Lunt, *Quadrille*
- Best Actress in a Play: Nancy Kelly, *The Bad Seed*
- Best Musical Actor: Walter Slezak, *Fanny*
- Best Musical Actress: Mary Martin, *Peter Pan*
- Best Supporting Actor in a Play: Francis L. Sullivan, *Witness for the Prosecution*
- Best Supporting Actress in a Play: Patricia Jessel, *Witness for the Prosecution*
- Best Supporting Musical Actor: Cyril Ritchard, *Peter Pan*

- Best Supporting Musical Actress: Carol Haney, *The Pajama Game*
- Best Director of a Play: Robert Montgomery, *Witness for the Prosecution*
- Outstanding Choreographer: Bob Fosse, *The Pajama Game*

Top Ten Movies

1. Lady and the Tramp
2. Mister Roberts
3. Guys and Dolls
4. Rebel Without a Cause
5. Picnic
6. The Seven Year Itch
7. Oklahoma!
8. Love Me or Leave Me
9. The Sea Chase
10. East of Eden

Academy Awards

- Picture: *Marty*
- Actor: Ernest Borgnine, *Marty*
- Actress: Anna Magnani, *The Rose Tattoo*
- Supporting Actor: Jack Lemmon, *Mister Roberts*
- Supporting Actress: Jo Van Fleet, *East of Eden*
- Director: Delbert Mann, *Marty*

Popular Books Released in 1955

- *The October Country* (Ray Bradbury)
- *Hickory Dickory Dock* (Agatha Christie)
- *Earthlight* (Arthur C. Clarke)
- *Auntie Mame* (Patrick Dennis)
- *Moonraker* (Ian Fleming)
- *The Talented Mr. Ripley* (Patricia Highsmith)
- *Andersonville* (MacKinlay Kantor)
- *The Magician's Nephew* (C.S. Lewis)
- *Before Midnight* (Rex Stout)
- *The Lord of the Rings : The Return of the King* (J.R.R. Tolkien)

- *The Mouse That Roared* (Leonard Wibberley)
- *The Man in the Gray Flannel Suit* (Sloan Wilson)
- *Marjorie Morningstar* (Herman Wouk)
- *No Time for Sergeants* (Mac Hyman)

The first edition of *The Guinness Book of Records* (selling an unexpected 70,000 copies in its first printing) was published by the Guinness Brewing Company following a debate in a pub over the fastest species of European game bird. (It is the wood pigeon.)

Other non-fiction books included *Birdman of Alcatraz* by Thomas E. Gaddis and *A Night to Remember* by Walter Lord (about the sinking of the *Titanic*).

Of News and Note

- Founder Ray Kroc's first McDonald's, designed by architect Stanley Meston, opens on April 15, 1955, at 400 Lee Street in Des Plaines, Illinois, inside a red-and-white tile building and the now recognizable large golden arches. It offers lots of parking (no inside service) and a limited menu of hamburgers (fifteen cents), cheeseburgers (nineteen cents), fries (ten cents), shakes (twenty cents), and soft drinks (ten cents). Ray Kroc wanted quality with quick service, and so the first McDonald's character mascot is Speedee, a cute little guy with a hamburger for a head, who was replaced by Ronald McDonald in the 1960s.

  Young Walt Disney was assigned to an American Red Cross Ambulance Corps unit in Sound Beach, Connecticut. When the Armistice was declared on November 11, 1918, there was still the need for drivers not only for ambulances but supply trucks, and Walt went overseas to France. Ray Kroc was also in that same unit, but chose not to go overseas. In 1954, Walt received a letter from Kroc:

  > Dear Walt, I feel somewhat presumptuous addressing you in this way yet I feel sure you would not want me to address you any other way. My name is Ray A. Kroc.... I look over the Company A picture we had taken at Sound Beach, Conn., many times and recall a lot of pleasant memories.... I have very recently taken over the national franchise of the McDonald's system. I would like to inquire if there may be an opportunity for a McDonald's in your Disneyland Development.

  Walt responded with a warm letter informing Kroc that his request had been sent to C.V. Wood Jr. because Walt was currently racing to complete Disneyland. Wood never responded to Kroc.

- On September 30, 1955, actor James Dean, 24, is driving his new Porsche 550 Spyder to an auto rally in Salinas, California, when he is involved in a head-on collision with a 1950 Ford Tutor and killed.

Appendix A: The United States in 1955

- On December 1, 1955, Rosa Parks, 42, a black seamstress, refuses to give up her seat to a white man while riding on a city bus in Montgomery, Alabama, and is arrested and fined. This incident sparks the Montgomery Bus Boycott and is considered the beginning of the modern Civil Rights Movement.
- Two labor unions, the AFL and the CIO, unite to become the AFL-CIO, with George Meany its first president. The new organization begins with fifteen million members.
- The Warsaw Pact is created to oppose NATO, with eight "Iron Curtain" signatories: the Soviet Union, Albania, Bulgaria, Czechoslovakia, East Germany, Hungary, Poland, and Romania
- Polio shots are given in schools for the first time.
- The iconic "Don't Walk" signs make their first appearance in New York City.
- Ann Landers starts her famous advice column in the *Chicago Sun-Times*.
- Albert Einstein dies from heart failure at the age of 76.
- Winston Churchill resigns as British prime minister.
- Argentina's president Juan Peron is overthrown by a military coup and flees to Spain.
- Instant oatmeal is introduced by Quaker Oats Company. Crest toothpaste is introduced as well.
- Harland "Colonel" Sanders goes on the road selling his fried chicken recipe.
- The first *American Bandstand* is broadcast in Philadelphia on WFIL-TV. Substitute host Dick Clark became the regular host in 1956.
- Mound Metalcraft Company of Mound, Minnesota, is renamed the Tonka Trucks named after the nearby Lake Minnetonka.
- Congress passes legislation requiring the phrase "IN GOD WE TRUST" on both U.S. coinage and currency.
- H&R Block is founded in Kansas City.

APPENDIX B

Walt Disney Productions in 1955

The primary focus in 1955 for Walt Disney Productions was to get Disneyland up and running and then maintain it through those early challenging months.

As a result, the soundstages were converted into workshops. While the *Mark Twain's* hull was constructed at Todd Shipyards in San Pedro, California, the superstructure of the 105-foot long, 150-ton stern wheeler was built on the Disney Studio lot, and was trucked down one deck at a time to Anaheim where it was assembled. The other soundstages were filled with the stagecoaches, trains, and jungle animals then under construction.

However, despite the concentration on Disneyland, Walt and his team did manage to produce some TV shows, films, and records.

Television

The television show *Disneyland* premiered on ABC on Wednesday night, October 27, 1954, and by 1955 it was the only ABC television show in the Top 25 most-watched programs of that year.

The following episodes aired during 1955:

- January 5: *Treasure Island* (part one of the theatrical movie)
- January 12: *Treasure Island* (part two of the theatrical movie)
- January 19: "Monsters of the Deep"
- January 26: "Davy Crockett Goes to Congress"
- February 2: "The Wind in the Willows" (cartoon)
- February 9: Progress Report on Disneyland / "Nature's Half Acre"
- February 16: "Cavalcade of Songs"
- February 23: "Davy Crockett at the Alamo"

- March 2: "From Aesop to Hans Christian Andersen"
- March 9: "Man in Space" (first of the Tomorrowland trilogy by Ward Kimball)
- July 13: Pre-Opening Report from Disneyland

After a summer hiatus and reruns, the second season began:
- September 14: "Dumbo"
- September 21: "Behind the True-Life Cameras"
- September 28: "Jiminy Cricket Presents Bongo"
- October 5: "People and Places—Tiburon, Sardinia, Morocco/Icebreakers"
- October 12: "The Adventures of Mickey Mouse"
- October 19: "The Story of the Silly Symphony"
- October 26: "The Legend of Sleepy Hollow" (cartoon)
- November 2: *The Story of Robin Hood* (part one of the live-action film)
- November 9: *The Story of Robin Hood* (part two of the live-action film)
- November 16: "Davy Crockett's Keelboat Race"
- November 30: "The Story of the Animated Drawing"
- December 7: "The Goofy Success Story"
- December 14: "Davy Crockett and the River Pirates"
- December 28: "Man and the Moon"

Theatrical Releases

- May 25: *Davy Crockett, King of the Wild Frontier* (an edited compilation of the first three *Davy Crockett* television episodes that became a surprise hit with audiences paying to see it on a big screen and in color rather than on a small black-and-white television screen. It was accompanied in theaters by the live-action Disney short *Arizona Sheepdog*.)
- June 16: *Switzerland* (the third *People and Places* film)
- June 22: *Lady and the Tramp* (released in both regular format and wide-screen CinemaScope)
- September 14: *The African Lion* (a *True-Life Adventures* film)
- October 5: *Music Land* (the final Disney animated feature to be released by RKO to fulfill the contract before Disney's own Buena Vista distribution took over. This was a hastily cobbled together compilation feature with individual cartoons from *Make Mine Music* and *Melody Time*. It usually isn't noted on lists of Disney animated

features, and was subsequently aired only once more, at a tribute to Walt Disney in 1970, before disappearing forever.)
- October 13: *The Emperor Penguins* (a live-action short film)
- December 21: *Men Against the Arctic* (the fourth *People and Places* film)
- December 22: *The Littlest Outlaw*

Animated Shorts

In addition to four new Donald Duck animated shorts, Disney released short animated segments from earlier compilation features, primarily *Saludos Amigos*, that have not been seen by the public in over a decade.
- January 14: *No Hunting* (a new Donald Duck short)
- February 18: *Lake Titicaca* (originally a Donald Duck segment in *Saludos Amigos*)
- March 11: *Contrasts in Rhythm* (combines the shorts "Bumble Boogie" and "Trees" from the film *Melody Time*)
- April 1: *Blame It on the Samba* (first released as part of *Melody Time*)
- May 13: *Pedro* (first released as part of *Saludos Amigos*)
- June 10: *El Gaucho Goofy* (first released as part of *Saludos Amigos*)
- June 24: *Aquarela do Brasil* (first released as part of *Saludos Amigos*)
- July 15: *Flying Gauchito* (first released as part of the film *The Three Caballeros*)
- August 19: *Bearly Asleep* (Humphrey the Bear)
- September 2: *Beezy Bear* (Humphrey the Bear)
- September 14: *Peter and the Wolf* (first released as part of the film *Make Mine Music*)
- September 23: *Up a Tree* (Chip 'n' Dale)
- December 25: *Johnny Appleseed* (first released as part of *Melody Time*)

Pecos Bill was also released to theaters as a stand-alone short. It was previously released as part of *Melody Time*. There are conflicting reports on its exact release date in 1955.

March 7 Emmy Awards
- Best Individual Show: *Operation Undersea*
- Best Television Film Editing: *Operation Undersea*
- Best Variety Series: *Disneyland* television series

March 30 Academy Awards Oscars
- Art Direction/Set Direction Color: *20,000 Leagues Under the Sea*
- Special Effects: *20,000 Leagues Under the Sea*
- Documentary, Features: *The Vanishing Prairie*

Comic Strips
- *Mickey Mouse* (daily): art by Floyd Gottfredson, story by Bill Walsh.
- *Donald Duck* (daily): art by Al Taliaferro, story by Bob Karp.
- *Uncle Remus and His Tales of Br'er Rabbit* (Sunday only): art by Dick Moores.
- *Merry Menagerie*: daily single panel but with no Disney characters; art by Bob Grant, story by Bob Karp.
- *Treasury of Classic Tales* (Sunday only). An adaptation of *Lady and the Tramp* ran from January 2, 1955, through July 10, 1955, with art by Dick Moores. An adaptation of *The Legends of Davy Crockett* ran from July 17, 1955, through January 8, 1956, with art by Jesse Marsh.
- *True-Life Adventures* (daily with a debut on March 14): art by George Wheeler, story by Dick Huemer.
- *Scamp* (daily, with a debut on October 31): The first eight months of continuity was written by Ward Greene, the King Features editor whose short story and novelization contributed to the development of the storyline of the animated feature *Lady and the Tramp*. Dick Moores was the original artist. In January 1956, a Sunday installment was added. (Scamp was the son of Lady and the Tramp.)

Comic Books
The following listings are the Disney Dell comic books available at newsstands, drugstores, and Disneyland from July 1955 through January 1956:

Regular Dell Comic Books
These comics cost ten cents each and were thirty-two pages long.
- *Mickey Mouse* #42, 43, 44, 45
- *Walt Disney's Comics and Stories* #179, 180, 181, 182, 183, 184, 185
- *Walt Disney's Donald Duck* #43, 44, 45
- *Walt Disney's Uncle Scrooge* #11, 12
- *Walt Disney's Chip 'n' Dale* #44
- *Dell Junior Treasury* #1 (Walt Disney's *Alice in Wonderland*; fifteen cents and 48 pages long)

Dell Giants
These comics cost twenty-five cents and were ninety-six pages long. The content included not just comic panels but also games, cutouts, and puzzles.
- *Walt Disney's Donald Duck in Disneyland* #1
- *Mickey Mouse Club Parade* #1
- *Walt Disney's Christmas Parade* #7
- *Walt Disney's Silly Symphonies* #6
- *Lady and the Tramp* #1

Four Color (FC)
Dell had a series called Four Color (FC) in which each issue featured a different one-shot. If sales warranted, the characters in the one-shots were later given their own continuing series. This series was also used for comic books that did adaptations of television shows and feature film movies. The comics cost a dime and were thirty-six pages long.
- *Walt Disney's Davy Crockett King of the Wild Frontier* #1
- *Walt Disney's Lady and the Tramp with Jock* #629
- *Walt Disney's Lady and the Tramp Album* #634
- *Walt Disney's Duck Album* #649
- *Walt Disney's Pluto* #654
- *Walt Disney's Goofy* #658
- *Walt Disney's Daisy Duck Diary* #659
- *Walt Disney's Davy Crockett in the Great Keelboat Race* #664
- *Walt Disney's Dumbo* #668
- *Walt Disney's Robin Hood* #669 (live action feature film)
- *Walt Disney's When Knighthood Was in Flower* #682 (an adaptation of the 1953 Disney live action film *The Sword and the Rose* which would air in 1956 on the weekly television show)

Records
Musical rights to Disney material were spread out over a number of different companies, with Capitol, Decca, RCA, and Columbia each releasing records with Disney music.

In 1955, Disney leased masters of some of their recordings for one year to ABC-Paramount. The label produced six 45-rpm singles primarily featuring Jimmie Dodd and songs from *The Mickey Mouse Club*.

Various other record companies licensed "The Ballad of Davy Crockett" theme song for 45- rpm singles. There were over 200 cover versions of the song issued around the world. The most popular recording was on Cadence and sung by Bill Hayes. It sold over a million-and-a-half records. The Fess Parker version released later by Disney sold almost a million.

Mickey Mouse Club records were on store shelves the same week that the TV show premiered in October, thanks to the marketing skill of Disney executive Jimmy Johnson who had recently been hired to handle Disney music.

The success of the Mickey Mouse Club and Davy Crockett records convinced Roy O. Disney that the company should produce and distribute its own records. In 1956, Disneyland Records was founded as a division of the Walt Disney Music Company, a wholly owned subsidiary of Walt Disney Productions, with Jimmy Johnson as its head.

Here are some of the Disney records issued in 1955:

DBR (Disney Big Record) 45/78 RPM

- DBR-50 *Mickey Mouse Club* (Jimmie Dodd/The Mouseketeers)
- DBR-51 *Fun With Music, Vol I* (Jimmie Dodd/The Mouseketeers)
- DBR-52 *Fun With Music, Vol II* (Jimmie Dodd/The Mouseketeers)
- DBR-53 *Fun with Music from Many Lands* (Jimmie Dodd/The Mouseketeers)
- DBR-54 *Mousekedances: 6 Dances and How to Do Them* (Jimmie Dodd/The Mouseketeers)
- DBR-55 *Mouseketunes* (Jimmie Dodd/The Mouseketeers)
- DBR-56 *Jiminy Cricket Sings 5 Mickey Mouse Club Songs* (Cliff Edwards)
- DBR-57 *Jiminy Cricket Presents Bongo* (Cliff Edwards)

78 RPM

- *Davy Crockett: Indian Fighter* (Columbia)
- *Davy Crockett: Goes to Congress* (Columbia)
- *Davy Crockett: At the Alamo* (Columbia)

33 1/3 RPM LPs

- *Davy Crockett-King of the Wild Frontier* (Fess Parker; Columbia/Harmony)
- *Songs from Walt Disney's Magic Kingdom* (Dottie Evans, Johnny Anderson and The Merry Makers; Columbia/Harmony)
- *Lady and the Tramp* (Peggy Lee Victor Young Orchestra; Decca)
- *Music from Disneyland* (Jack Pleis & Orchestra; Decca)

In addition that year, Mattel released *The Legend of Davy Crockett on Records* as an accordion-style fold-out book with five one-sided cardboard cartoon picture-disc 78-rpm records to be cut out and played on a record player. Mattel did a similar set entitled *Your Trip to Disneyland on Records* with five cardboard discs and a map of the park, and also *Your Own Mickey Mouse Club on Records*.

Walt Disney Takes You to Disneyland

Although officially released in early 1956, the first non-soundtrack record produced and distributed by Disney's new in-house studio was *Walt Disney Takes You to Disneyland*, a gatefold album cover that opens up to show a collection of Disneyland park photos with a map of Disneyland on the back cover.

The record has five sections of instrumental music and sound effects that match the five lands of the park. Main Street was written by Oliver Wallace, Tomorrowland and Frontierland by George Bruns, and Adventureland and Fantasyland by Tutti Camarata. Some of the music was completely original and some were interpretations of familiar Disney songs like "The Ballad of Davy Crockett".

Jimmy Johnson had Walt do a short introductory narration for each land, making it the only time that Walt (other than doing the voice of Mickey Mouse) appeared on a phonograph record.

Under its alternate title *A Musical Tour of Disneyland*, it was also released on five 45-rpm records for each land in 1956. Then, in 1957, it was re-released again, as *A Day at Disneyland*, with new material featuring narration by Cliff Edwards as Jiminy Cricket. It came with an illustrated book.

Little Golden Books

- *Disneyland on the Air,* Annie North Bedford (writer) Samuel Armstrong (illustrator)
- *Donald Duck in Disneyland,* Annie North Bedford (writer), Walt Disney Studios (illustrator; updated and redrawn by Grant Campbell in 1960)
- *Robin Hood* (live action), Annie North Bedford (writer), Walt Disney Studios (illustrator)
- *Davy Crockett,* Irwin Shapiro (writer), Mel Crawford (illustrator)
- *Little Man of Disneyland,* Annie North Bedford (writer), Dick Kelsey (illustrator)
- *Davy Crockett's Keelboat Race,* Irwin Shapiro (writer), Mel Crawford (illustrator)

Annie North Bedford was a pseudonym used by Jane Werner Watson who was one of the original editors of Little Golden Books and was highly prolific in writing various children's books. The name is a reference to her employer's street address on the West Coast.

Selected Bibliography

In addition to my thirty-five years of personal interviews with original Disneylanders, multiple articles, and books, I drew upon these sources for the material in this book:

Books

Ballard, Donald. *The Disneyland Hotel: The Early Years 1954–1988* (Ape Pen Publishing 2005).

Bright, Randy. *Disneyland Inside Story* (Crown 1987).

Broggie, Michael. *Walt Disney's Railroad Story* (Pentrex 1997).

Boag, Wally and Gene Sands. *Wally Boag: Clown Prince of Disneyland* (Disney Editions 2009).

Disneyland: the First Quarter Century (Disneyland 1979).

Dunkelberger, Robert. *Keller's Jungle Killers* (Columbia County Historical and Genealogical Society 2013).

Dunlop, Beth. *Building a Dream: The Art of Disney Architecture* (Hyperion 1996).

Evans, Bill. *Disney World of Flowers* (Disneyland 1965).

France, Van Arsdale. *Window on Main Street* (Theme Park Press 2015).

Gennawey, Sam. *The Disneyland Story* (Unofficial Guides 2013).

Gordon, Bruce and Tim O'Day. *Disneyland: Then, Now and Forever* (Disney Editions 2005).

Gordon, Bruce and David Mumford. *Disneyland: The Nickel Tour* (Camphor Tree Publishers 1995).

Gurr, Bob. *Design: Just for Fun* (App Gurr Design 2012).

Kurtti, Jeff. *Disneyland Through the Decades* (Disney Editions 2010).

Kurtti, Jeff and Bruce Gordon. *The Art of Disneyland* (Disney Editions 2006).

Lindquist, Jack. *In Service to the Mouse* (Chapman University Press 2010).

Marling, Karal Ann (editor). *Designing Disney's Theme Parks: the Architecture of Reassurance* (Flammarion 1997).

Marling, Karal Ann with Donna Braden. *Behind the Magic: 50 Years of Disneyland* (Henry Ford Museum 2005).

Nelson, Miriam. *My Life Dancing with the Stars* (Bear Manor Media 2009).

Pierce, Todd James. *Three Years in Wonderland* (University of Mississippi Press 2016).

Price, Harrison "Buzz". *Walt's Revolution! By the Numbers* (Ripley Entertainment 2004).

Rafferty, Kevin and Bruce Gordon. *Walt Disney Imagineering* (1996).

Reynolds, Bob. *Roller Coasters, Flumes & Flying Saucers: The Story of Ed Morgan and Karl Bacon* (N.L. Publishing 1999).

Ridgway, Charles. *Spinning Disney's World* (Intrepid Traveler 2007).

Schultz, Jason and Kevin Yee. *Jason's Disneyland Almanac* (Zauberreich Press 2011).

Shannon, Leonard. *Disneyland: Dreams, Traditions and Transitions* (Disney Kingdom Editions 1994).

Sklar, Martin. *Walt Disney's Disneyland* (Disneyland 1964).

Smith, Dave. *Disney A–Z The Official Encyclopedia* (Disney Editions 2006).

Strodder, Chris. *The Disneyland Encyclopedia* (Santa Monica Press 2012).

Thie, Carlene. *Homecoming Destination Disneyland* (Ape Pen Publishing 2005).

Thomas, Bob. *Walt Disney: An American Original* (Fireside 1976).

Thomas, Bob. *Building a Company: Roy O. Disney and the Creation of an Entertainment Empire* (Disney Editions 1998).

Trahan, Kendra. *Disneyland Detective 50th Anniversary Update* (PermaGrin Publishing 2005).

Van Eaton Galleries. *Collecting Disneyland: An Exhibition and Auction* (Van Eaton Galleries 2015).

Publications

- *The E Ticket*
- *Disney News*
- *Disney Magazine*
- *Disneyland Line*
- *Disneyland News*
- *Tomart's Disneyana*
- *Los Angeles Times*
- Disneyland anniversary press kits
- Disneyland training manuals

Acknowledgments

As always, I would like to acknowledge not only the people who directly helped me with this specific book, but those who have inspired or supported me over the years. There are indeed angels in this world, and I have been blessed to know so many of them.

I would like to thank all the people who have bought my Disney history books because their support has allowed *this* book to be published.

This book would not have been possible without the skills and encouragement of publisher Bob McLain and his Theme Park Press.

Thanks to my brothers, Michael and Chris, and their families, including their children Amber, Keith, Autumn, and Story. Also, my grand-nieces Skylar, Shea, and Sidnee (Fairbanks) and grand nephew Alex (Johansen).

Thanks to all the original Disneylanders who were so gracious and generous in sharing their memories with a wet-behind-his-ears eager kid who had endless questions.

Thanks to all the historians who have written about Walt's original Disneyland: Jeff Kurtti, Todd James Pierce, David R. Smith, Donald Ballard, Randy Bright, Michael Broggie, Bruce Gordon, Kevin Kidney, Howard Lowery, Paula Sigman Lowery, David Mumford, Cecil Munsey, Dave Mason, Tim O'Day, Jason Schultz, Chris Strodder, Robert Tieman, Jeff Pepper, Tom Tumbusch, and others who took the time to do the research and share it with the rest of us.

For this book in particular, I am grateful to the following historians whose outstanding work and entertaining blog posts made me fall in love with Walt's original Disneyland all over again:

- Werner Weiss (yesterland.com)
- Dave De Caro (davelandweb.com)
- David Eppen (gorillasdontblog.blogspot.com)
- Patrick Jenkins (matterhorn1959.blogspot.com)
- Vintage Disneyland Tickets (vintagedisneylandtickets.blogspot.com)

Finally, thanks to Walt Disney for having a vision and the persistence to make a dream come true for all of us.

About the Author

Jim Korkis is an internationally respected Disney historian who has written hundreds of articles and a dozen books about all things Disney over the last thirty-five years.

Jim grew up in Glendale, California, where he was able to meet and interview Walt's original team of animators and Imagineers.

In 1995, he relocated to Orlando, Florida, where he worked for Walt Disney World in a variety of capacities, including Entertainment, Animation, Disney Institute, Disney University, College and International Programs, Disney Cruise Line, Disney Design Group, and Marketing.

His original research on Disney history has been used often by the Disney Company as well as other organizations like the Disney Family Museum.

Several websites currently feature Jim's articles about Disney history:

- MousePlanet.com
- AllEars.net
- Yesterland.com
- CartoonResearch.com
- YourFirstVisit.net

In addition, Jim is a frequent guest on multiple podcasts as well as a consultant and keynote speaker to various businesses and groups.

Beginning in 1959, Jim was able to experience Disneyland as an elementary school student with his parents and brothers and gathered a lifetime of fond memories and several priceless souvenirs that have been lost over the years. Many things from 1955 remained unchanged in the park while others had been greatly enhanced.

Jim is not currently an employee of the Disney company.

To read more stories by Jim Korkis about Disney history, please check out his other books, all available from ThemeParkPress.com.

More Books from Theme Park Press

Theme Park Press is the largest independent publisher of Disney, Disney-related, and general interest theme park books in the world, with dozens of new releases each year.

Our authors include Disney historians like Jim Korkis and Didier Ghez, Disney animators and artists like Mel Shaw and Eric Larson, and such Disney notables as Van France, Tom Nabbe, and Bill "Sully" Sullivan, as well as many promising first-time authors.

We're always looking for new talent.

In March 2016, we published our 100th title. For a complete catalog, including book descriptions and excerpts, please visit:

ThemeParkPress.com

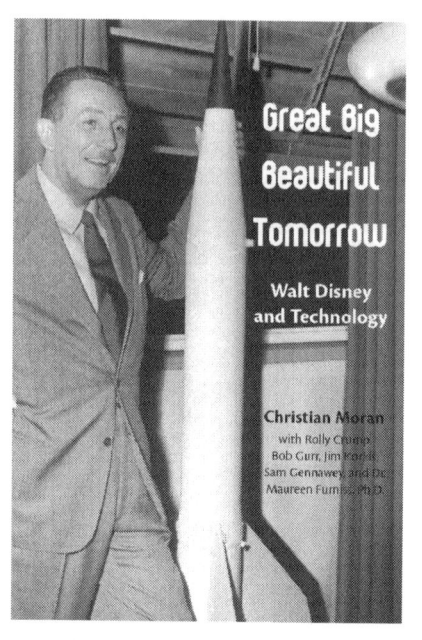

Walt Disney and the Pursuit of Progress

Walt Disney is well-known for animation, theme parks, and Mickey Mouse. But his real passion was technology, and how he could use it to shape a better, prosperous, peaceful future for everyone.

themeparkpress.com/books/great-big-beautiful-tomorrow.htm

Walt's Disney's Final Imagineer

Walt hired George McGinnis in 1966, and right away George found himself in design meetings with his new boss. For the next three decades, George contributed to such high-profile projects as the new monorails, Epcot's Horizons, and two Space Mountains. This is his life as a Disney Imagineer.

themeparkpress.com/books/horizons-space-mountain.htm

Disney History—Written by You

Who writes the Disney history you love to read? A select group, immersed in the history and culture of Disney, from films to theme parks. Now these authors reveal their inspirations, their methods, and their secrets. Why just read Disney history when you can write it yourself!

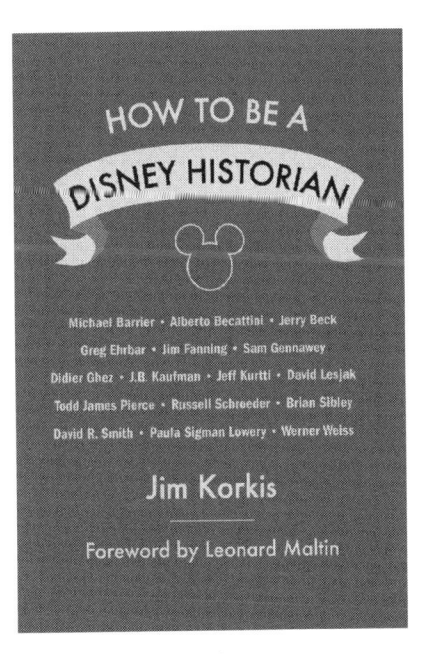

themeparkpress.com/books/disney-historian.htm

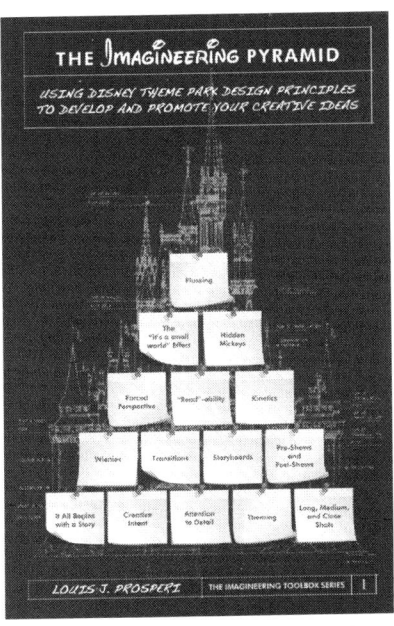

Learn from the Disney Imagineers

Creativity. Innovation. Success. That's Disney Imagineering. It was the Imagineers who brought Walt Disney's dreams to life. Now *you* can tap into the principles of Imagineering to make *your* personal and professional dreams come true.

themeparkpress.com/books/imagineering-pyramid.htm

Four Decades with Disney

Disney Legend William "Sully" Sullivan got his start in 1955 with Walt Disney and Disneyland, taking tickets for the Jungle Cruise. Forty years later he retired as vice-president of Magic Kingdom. This is his never-before-told story.

themeparkpress.com/books/sullivan-jungle-cruise-legend.htm

Walt Hired Me

In 1955, twelve-year-old Tom Nabbe was selling newspapers at Disneyland when he heard that Walt needed someone to play the role of Tom Sawyer. Tom pestered Walt until he got the job. Nearly fifty years later Tom retired, a Disney Legend. These are the adventures of Tom Nabbe.

themeparkpress.com/books/adventures-tom-nabbe.htm

Made in the USA
Lexington, KY
07 January 2017